T0339449

JOB INSECURITY, UNION INVOLVEMENT AND UNION ACTIVISM

Job Insecurity, Union Involvement and Union Activism

Edited by
HANS DE WITTE
Department of Psychology – K.U.Leuven

Routledge
Taylor & Francis Group

LONDON AND NEW YORK

First published 2005 by Ashgate Publishing

Reissued 2018 by Routledge
2 Park Square, Milton Park, Abingdon, Oxon OX14 4RN
605 Third Avenue, New York, NY 10017

First issued in paperback 2021

Routledge is an imprint of the Taylor & Francis Group, an informa business

A Library of Congress record exists under LC control number: 2005001844

ISBN 13: 978-0-815-38997-2 (hbk)
ISBN 13: 978-1-351-15492-5 (ebk)
ISBN 13: 978-1-138-35824-9 (pbk)

DOI: 10.4324/9781351154925

Contents

List of Contributors

Hans De Witte (PhD) is professor, and teaches work psychology at the Department of Psychology (K.U.Leuven) in Belgium. His research fields include the psychological consequences job insecurity, unemployment, temporary employment and downsizing, attitudes towards work, participation in trade unions, and the impact of job characteristics on well-being and attitudes.
Address: K.U.Leuven, Department of Psychology, Tiensestraat 102, BE-3000 Leuven, Belgium. E-mail: *hans.dewitte@psy.kuleuven.ac.be*

Sjoerd Goslinga (PhD) was researcher at the Department of Social Psychology and coordinator of the CNV/VU Research Program at the Free University Amsterdam when he wrote the chapter of this book. Currently, he is researcher at the Dutch Criminal Investigation Service of the Tax and Customs Administration (FIOD-ECD). His research fields are union participation, organisational commitment, collective action, law enforcement and persuasion.
Address: PO Box 546, NL-2003 RM Haarlem, The Netherlands. E-mail: *sgoslinga@hotmail.com*

Mika Happonen (Licentiate of Social Sciences) is a labour market analyst at the Personnel Department of Ministry of Finance. His research field is job insecurity.
Address: PO Box 28, FI-00023 Government, Finland. E-mail: *mika.happonen@vm.fi*

Johnny Hellgren (PhD) is a researcher and part-time lecturer at the Department of Psychology of the Stockholm University. His main research interests include organisational change, downsizing, job insecurity, employability, work climate and new employment contracts in relation to employee attitudes and well-being, as well as the role of the union in today's working life.
Address: Stockholm University, Department of Psychology, SE-106 91 Stockholm, Sweden. E-mail: *jhn@psychology.su.se*

Kerstin Isaksson (PhD) is an associate professor and has a position as a researcher in the National Institute for Working Life in Stockholm, Sweden. Main research areas: downsizing, precarious employment and psychological contracts.
Address: National Institute for Working Life, SE-113 91 Stockholm, Sweden. E-mail: *kerstin.isaksson@niwl.se*

Peter Kerkhof (PhD) is researcher and lecturer at the Department of Communication Science of the Free University Amsterdam. His research fields are organisational communication, works councils and communicating through the Internet.

Address: Free University Amsterdam, Department of Communication Science, De Boelelaan 1081, NL-1081 HV Amsterdam, The Netherlands. E-mail: *p.kerkhof@fsw.vu.nl*

Ulla Kinnunen (PhD) works as senior researcher at the Family Research Centre in the University of Jyväskylä. Her main research areas are well being at work, work-family interface, and job and financial insecurity in families.
Address: University of Jyväskylä, Family Research Centre, PO Box 35, FI-40014 University of Jyväskylä, Finland. E-mail: *ulla.kinnunen@psyka.jyu.fi*

Bert Klandermans (PhD) is professor of social psychology at the Free University Amsterdam, The Netherlands. He is the dean of the Faculty of Social Sciences. The emphasis in his work is on the social psychological consequences of social, economical and political change. He has published extensively on the social psychology of participation in social movements and labour unions. His 'The Social Psychology of Protest' appeared with Blackwell in 1997.
Address: Free University Amsterdam, Faculty of Social Sciences, De Boelelaan 1081, NL-1081 HV Amsterdam, The Netherlands. E-mail: *pg.klandermans@fsw.vu.nl*

Anthony Masi (PhD) is professor of sociology as well as deputy provost and chief information officer of McGill University. His research interests include the sociology of the labour force, industrial policy, the relationship between institutions and economic development in Italy and population studies.
Address: McGill University, Office of the Deputy Provost and Chief Information Officer, James Administration Building, 845 Sherbrooke Street West, CA-Montreal H3A 2T5, Quebec, Canada. E-mail: *anthony.masi@mcgill.ca*

Saija Mauno (PhD) is special researcher at the Department of Psychology of the University of Jyväskylä. Her research fields are job stress, well-being at work, work-family interface and organisational culture.
Address: University of Jyväskylä, Department of Psychology, PO Box 35, FI-40014 Finland. E-mail: *saija.mauno@psyka.jyu.fi*

Katharina Näswall (PhD) is working as researcher at the Department of Psychology, Stockholm University. Her main research interests concern job insecurity, stress, and employee well-being.
Address: Stockholm University, Department of Psychology, SE-106 91 Stockholm, Sweden. E-mail: *knl@psychology.su.se*

Jouko Nätti (PhD) is senior researcher and lecturer at the Department of Social Sciences and Philosophy of the University of Jyväskylä. His research fields are new forms of employment, working time, unemployment, job insecurity, knowledge work and time use.
Address: University of Jyväskylä, Department of Social Sciences and Philosophy, PO Box 35, FI-40014 Finland. E-mail: *natti@yfi.jyu.fi*

Pär Pettersson (PhD) is researcher at the Department of Psychology, Stockholm University and also works as a consultant. His main areas of research are management and leadership and organisational change and development.
Address: Fil dr Pär Pettersson, Lönhult 1:25, SE-277 55 Brösarp, Sweden. E-mail: *pere_pettersson@yahoo.se*

Bram Steijn (PhD) is professor at the Department of Public Administration, Faculty of Social Sciences of the Erasmus University Rotterdam. His research fields are sociology of labour and social inequality.
Address: Erasmus University Rotterdam, Faculty of Social Sciences, Department of Public Administration, PO Box 1738, NL-3000 DR Rotterdam, The Netherlands. E-mail: *steijn@fsw.eur.nl*

Caroline Stjernström is a PhD student at the Department of Psychology, Stockholm University. Her research fields are organisational change, employability, and health. Besides being a PhD student, she works as a union consultant.
Address: ATK Arbetstagarkonsultation AB, Högbergsgatan 62, SE-118 91 Stockholm, Sweden. E-mail: *caroline.stjernstrom@atk.se*

Magnus Sverke (PhD) is professor of work and organisational psychology at the Department of Psychology of the Stockholm University. His research interests include organisational change and its effects on employees, downsizing and job insecurity, labour market flexibility and new employment contracts, employee attitudes and well-being, and union member attitudes and behaviour.
Address: Stockholm University, Department of Psychology, SE-106 91 Stockholm, Sweden. E-mail: *mse@psychology.su.se*

Axel van den Berg (PhD) is professor of sociology at McGill University. His research fields are industrial sociology, the sociology of labour markets and sociological theory.
Address: McGill University, Department of Sociology, Sherbrooke Street West 855, CA-Montreal H3A 2T7, Quebec, Canada. E-mail: *axel.vandenberg@mcgill.ca*

Annemieke Winder was researcher at the Department of Social Psychology at the Free University Amsterdam and conducted part of the study on works councils. She collaborated in various reports on the works council project.

Chapter 1

Does Job Insecurity Affect the Union Attitudes of Workers and Their Participation in Unions? Introduction to this Volume

Hans De Witte

During the last decennia, the economy of Europe has dramatically changed. Many organisations have been involved in large-scale restructuring processes, mergers, downsizing, plant closures and privatisations, in the hope to reduce costs and increase efficiency (Hitt, Keats, Harback and Nixon, 1994). Interventions of this kind are usually accompanied by massive staff dismissals (Kozlowski, Chao, Smith and Hedlung, 1993). The number of temporary employees also shows a significant increase, in order to meet the need for more (internal) flexibility (Purcell and Purcell, 1998). One can assume that these trends resulted in the rise of feelings of job insecurity among many workers in Europe and abroad. This is illustrated by the results of an OECD study in 1996, suggesting that about 38 percent of the employees in one of the European OECD member states found that their company offered less job security than most other companies in the same sector (OECD, 1997). When the wording of the question is narrowed down to the individual job, percentages tend to decline as a rule. The results of a recent survey in eight European countries show that 9.4 percent of the respondents perceived the probability to become unemployed within one year to be rather or very large (De Weerdt, De Witte, Catellani and Milesi, 2004). Converted to absolute numbers, however, this seemingly low percentage refers to several millions of workers all over Europe.

The psychological concept 'job insecurity' can be defined in various ways. Jacobson (1991) defines it as 'a concern about the future of one's job'. Heaney, Israel and House (1994) refer to the 'perception of a potential threat to the continuity of the current job', and Sverke, Hellgren and Näswall (2002) define it as the 'subjectively perceived likelihood of involuntary job loss'. Despite these differences, most authors distinguish a more or less similar set of core characteristics to the concept of job insecurity (see e.g. Hartley, Jacobson, Klandermans and van Vuuren, 1991; Sverke and Hellgren, 2002). Job insecurity is first of all a subjective perception: the same 'objective' situation can be perceived in very different ways by different workers, depending on e.g. their position in the organisation, previous experiences with unemployment, and personality traits. Next, job insecurity concerns feelings of insecurity about the future. The workers concerned do not know whether they will keep their actual job or be dismissed. The consequence of this lack of clarity about their future is that they do not clearly know how to respond to this situation. This contrasts with the certainty of dismissal. In the latter situation, it is clear that one will become unemployed, allowing employees to take concrete action (e.g. to look for another job). Two aspects are generally added to the previous characteristics: job insecurity generally includes feelings of helplessness in retaining desired job continuity (e.g. Greenhalgh and Rosenblatt, 1984), and the nature of insecurity is involuntary (Sverke, Hellgren and Näswall, 2002). Authors do diverge, however, regarding the content of job insecurity. Some refer to the job 'as such', whereas others focus on the quality of the job. This distinction is known as quantitative versus qualitative job insecurity (Hellgren, Sverke and Isaksson, 1999). Quantitative, or global job insecurity, refers to concerns about the future existence of the present job (versus becoming unemployed). Qualitative job insecurity refers to the possible loss of valued job features (such as e.g. income, career opportunities and colleagues). Both conceptualisations will be used in this volume, even though a global (or quantitative) operationalisation will be dominant in most chapters.

The increase in job insecurity gave rise to an extensive research tradition, analyzing its causes and consequences. Research documents the negative consequences of job insecurity for *individual employees* (e.g. Hartley et al., 1991; De Witte, 1999; Klandermans and van Vuuren, 1999; Nolan, Wichert and Burchell, 2000; Sverke and Hellgren, 2002). Job insecurity is first of all consistently associated with lower levels of job related well-being (e.g. job satisfaction), and with higher levels of burnout and job stress. Next, job insecurity is also negatively related with more general indicators of mental well-being, such as life satisfaction, anxiety and depression. Finally, also negative associations with psychosomatic complaints and aspects of physical health are reported. A recent meta-analysis documents stronger correlations with work related well-being (e.g. job satisfaction), compared to mental health and aspects of physical health (Sverke, Hellgren and Näswall, 2002). The negative associations with physical health are still substantial, however, as well as statistically significant. Longitudinal research, finally, confirmed the causal impact of job insecurity on these indicators, suggesting that job insecurity impairs well-being instead of the other way round (e.g. Burchell, 1994; Hellgren and Sverke, 2003).

Job insecurity also influences various organisational attitudes and behaviours, thus also affecting the organisation (see e.g. Ashford, Lee and Bobko, 1989; Hartley et al., 1991; Klandermans and van Vuuren, 1999; Sverke and Hellgren, 2002; for meta-analytic evidence, see: Sverke, Hellgren and Näswall, 2002). The perception of job insecurity is frequently linked to reduced organisational commitment, mistrust in the organisation and in management and to lower performance. Job insecurity also strengthens intentions to leave the company ('turnover intentions').

These effects of job insecurity threaten the organisation's survival, since they reduce the work efforts of the employees concerned, whereas the best qualified workers try to leave the company as soon as possible, resulting in the need for renewed and expensive recruiting efforts.

Consequences for Unions

It is striking to note that research on the effects of job insecurity focussed almost exclusively on its consequences on the individual employee (e.g. health and well-being) and the company (e.g. organisational commitment and turnover). Surprisingly little attention has been paid to the possible influence of job insecurity on *trade unions* and on (aspects of) *union participation*.[1] This is striking for at least two reasons. First, trade unions are crucial partners in the collective bargaining systems in Europe in general (e.g. Waddington and Hoffmann, 2000). Their position in this system exceeds the level of plants and sectors, extending to collective bargaining at the national and international level. As a consequence, one could easily state that unions are cornerstones of European industrial democracy. Since trade unions are a crucial social partner, job insecurity faces unions with specific threats and challenges. Job insecurity may have made recruitment and participation in actions more difficult, which may pose a threat to the existence and survival of unions in our societies, endangering the continuity of contemporary industrial democracy. Dealing with these threats thus poses an important challenge for European unions.

Second, unions aim to promote the interests of workers, and to protect them from arbitrary treatment (e.g. Barling, Fullagar and Kelloway, 1992). Since job insecurity negatively affects workers' health and well-being, reducing job insecurity and its harmful consequences became an important task for unions. Interest promotion also relates to the position of unions during organisational restructuring itself. Unions often play an important role in the negotiations between employers and employees during the restructuring process. As a consequence, they have a role to play both in attempting to reduce insecurity as such (e.g. by trying to reduce the amount of redundancies), and in the reduction of the negative effects of insecurity on workers (e.g. in trying to influence the conditions of dismissals, and by offering help and support to workers). Since unions have a crucial position in defending the interests of workers, it is remarkable that so little research has been devoted to analyse whether unions can reduce job insecurity or mitigate its negative consequences for individuals (and organisations).

The volume '*Job insecurity, union involvement and union activism*' presents contributions from European psychologists and sociologists, who report empirical analyses designed to explore aspects of this broad topic. The focus of their research is on reactions of individual workers towards trade unions. The key questions of the research relate to the impact of job insecurity on union participation and union attitudes, and to the consequences of the participation of unions in downsizing processes on the attitudes of workers towards unions. Do workers more easily join (or quit) unions because of insecurity? Do feelings of job insecurity prevent workers to take part in industrial action (e.g. because one fears to be dismissed when participating), or do they stimulate them to participate (e.g. because they hope to gain stable employment)? Are insecure workers less satisfied with their unions and less committed to them? And does the involvement of the union in the process of restructuring effect union satisfaction and commitment?

The chapters addressing these research questions can be divided in two parts. Both include four chapters each. The first part of this volume discusses research related to the impact of job insecurity on aspects of individual workers' *union participation*. The second part addresses the consequences of participation of unions in downsizing processes on the *attitudes* of workers *towards these unions*. We will further elaborate these two topics, and locate the different contributions in this dual frame.

Job Insecurity and Trade Union Participation

In the first four chapters, we analyse whether job insecurity affects the participation of workers in unions. The term *'union participation'* is used in a broad sense. Following Klandermans (1996), union participation can be categorised according to two dimensions: efforts and time needed. Participation can be limited in time or indefinite, and can involve little or considerable effort. The combination of these two dimensions results in four types of union participation, which can be influenced by feelings of job insecurity. Becoming a union member ('joining a union') is a form of union participation that combines low demands with a (mostly) indefinite time frame. Voting in union elections (e.g. work's council elections) also requires little effort, but its duration is limited in time (e.g. once every four or five years). Participating in a strike (or in a similar kind of industrial action) is also limited in time, but involves considerable efforts and costs. Becoming a union activist (e.g. a shop steward or a 'militant') combines high efforts with a commitment of longer duration. All four types are important for (the survival of) trade unions and for the achievement of their goals. Mobilisation is impossible without activists, and membership figures constitute an important base for the union movement's power. As a consequence, this volume contains contributions that analyse the (possible) consequences of job insecurity on all four types of union participation.

Chapter 2 (*'Job insecurity, temporary work and trade union membership in Finland 1977-2003'*) contains the results of a thorough trend analysis of the Finnish researchers Jouko Nätti, Mika Happonen, Ulla Kinnunen and Saija Mauno. They analyse the relationship between perceived job insecurity and trade *union membership* during the period 1977 and 2003, using no less than five representative datasets of Finnish employees. They also analyse the associations of job insecurity with background variables and with the evolution of unemployment during this period. Their analysis is not limited to perceptions of job insecurity, however. Additionally, they analyse the evolution of trade union membership and temporary work during this period, and the association of temporary work with both job insecurity and union membership. Finally, they examine whether union membership is affected by the interaction between perceived job insecurity and temporary work, and by the voluntary versus involuntary nature of temporary work.

In Chapter 3 (*'The insecure middle class and unionisation: an empirical investigation of class, job insecurity and union membership'*), Bram Steijn also focuses on the relationship between job insecurity and union membership. He too uses five representative data sets of employees, this time gathered between 1990 and 1998 in the Netherlands. His main research topic relates to the question whether workers are more likely to become a union member when they experience job insecurity. Next to this issue, he also Analyses the relationship of job insecurity with the occupational position of the respondents (their 'social class'), assuming that this relationship may have changed over time (e.g. assuming that the middle class became more insecure). Finally, he examines whether the association between job insecurity and union membership is different within different social classes: do white-collar workers react in a different way to job insecurity than blue-collar workers, when union membership is concerned?

In Chapter 4 (*'Job insecurity and works council participation'*), Peter Kerkhof, Annemieke Winder and Bert Klandermans shift the focus to *voting* in *union elections* (e.g. work's council elections) and to the *intention* to become a *candidate* in such elections. This means that they focus on two strongly opposed aspects of union participation: one of limited duration and requiring little effort (voting), whereas the other implies an unlimited time frame combined with high effort (the intention to become an activist). They Analyse a cross-sectional dataset gathered among a specific sample of the public sector: civil servants in municipalities in the Netherlands. Using Hirschman's theory (1970) about exit, voice and loyalty, they examine whether participation in the works council in reaction to job insecurity is a kind of voice: an active and constructive response to a dissatisfying situation (e.g. job insecurity).

Finally, also participation in *union actions* and *union activities* are addressed by Sjoerd Goslinga in Chapter 5 (*'Job insecurity, union participation and the need for (new) union services'*). On the basis of two cross-sectional datasets among (Christian) trade union members in the Netherlands, Goslinga examines various aspects of this issue. First of all, he analyses whether job insecurity is associated with participation in industrial action, in attending union meetings and in contacting union representatives. Next, he analyses whether job insecurity is related to holding the position of union representative, an aspect of union activism. Finally, in a second study, he investigates the relationships between job insecurity and the need for information about job opportunities and the labour market, and the need for career guidance and advice. The latter aspects are not related to militancy, but rather to the (instrumental) need to get individual services from the union, when one faces problems on the labour market.

Job Insecurity and Attitudes Towards Unions

The next four chapters of this volume do not focus on union participation, but examine the relationship of job insecurity with the *attitudes* of workers (or union members) towards unions. These attitudes can have important consequences for trade union participation, since they may trigger (or reduce) the willingness to participate. The attitudes of union members and non-members can also influence union politics. As a rule, unions respond to the demands and evaluations of members and non-members, since their aim is to promote the interests of workers. The reported studies specifically examine the impact of unions and their activities during *organisational restructuring* or *downsizing*. Most studies collected data in a single organisation (case study design), in which the union was actively involved in the restructuring process (e.g. by negotiation a favourable agreement for the workers affected). One of the important questions then, is whether unions will be blamed for their involvement, when the results of the restructuring process are less positive than expected or hoped for. Also relevant is the question whether union membership can mitigate the negative consequences of downsizing for workers.

Kerstin Isaksson, Johnny Hellgren and Pär Pettersson address these issues in Chapter 6 (*'Union involvement during downsizing and its relation to attitudes and distress among workers'*). They analyse the effects of union participation (framed as a collective coping strategy) on satisfaction with union involvement and with (union) assistance offered, in a Swedish union-friendly company after a downsizing operation. Their cross-sectional study allows them to compare the attitudes of four subgroups, two years after the downsizing took place: the survivors, those who were dismissed but found a new job, those who became unemployed and retirees. The union had taken an active role in the structural changes, and negotiated as favourable agreements as possible for the affected workers. They were, however, unsuccessful in reducing the number of redundancies. Additional to analysing the consequences of union involvement in the restructuring process, these researchers also examine differences in health and well-being, and analyse whether the predictors of attitudes and distress symptoms are different for those who survived the downsizing, and those who lost their job.

In Chapter 7 (*'The union side of downsizing: investigating members' union attitudes'*), Johnny Hellgren, Magnus Sverke and Caroline Stjernström analyse data from the staff of a Swedish emergency hospital undergoing organisational change. As in Chapter 6, the unions were actively involved in the change process. The authors focus on the effect of the restructuring operation on three union attitudes of union members: their satisfaction with the union, union commitment and union justice. Additionally, they analyse the impact of stressors associated with downsizing (role stressors and job insecurity) on these attitudes, and examine whether three aspects of global process control (organisational justice, participation in the change process and workplace control) reduce the negative consequences of downsizing.

Magnus Sverke, Johnny Hellgren and Katharina Näswall use the same Swedish dataset in Chapter 8 (*'We get by with a little help from our unions: psychological contract violations and downsizing'*). Following Hirschman's theory regarding reactions to unsatisfactory events (cf. Chapter 4), they analyse the effects of job insecurity and union membership on exit (withdrawal), voice (protest and disengagement) and loyalty reactions (commitment and performance) of workers during downsizing. Their main interest, however, is to evaluate if union membership has direct effects on these coping strategies, and to examine whether membership moderates the effects of job insecurity. Stated otherwise, these authors Analyse whether union members react differently to job insecurity during downsizing than non-members. A different reaction would suggest that unions can buffer the negative consequences of job insecurity for individuals during organisational restructuring.

Chapter 9 (*'Responses to downsizing under different adjustment regimes: a two-country comparison'*) also relates to Sweden. In this chapter, however, Axel van den Berg and Anthony Masi compare the responses of a representative sample of Swedish blue-collar manufacturing workers with those of a similar sample of workers from Canada. Their focus is on the socio-institutional context of downsizing, and the effects this context might have for perceptions of individuals. They analyse the effect of downsizing on the degree to which survivors worry about their employment situation (an aspect of job insecurity). These authors hypothesise that this effect depends on the quality of the relations between labour and management at the organisational level, on the degree of external security for workers (e.g. whether they can easily find another job outside their actual organisation) and on the industrial relations climate and structure in the country. Regarding the latter, the co-operative position of unions in Sweden is contrasted with the adversarial position of unions in Canada.

In Chapter 10, conclusions are drawn regarding the core research questions raised in this volume, and some recommendations for research and practice are discussed.

Finishing a volume like this obviously demands a lot of work and energy from many people. As a consequence, it can become stressful. First of all, there was the insecurity of whether to publish this volume. Fortunately, our publisher could be persuaded that publishing this volume was worthwhile. We sincerely hope that the chapters in this volume can add to our understanding of the harmful effects of job insecurity for unions (and for society at large), and can even play a role in reducing the future negative consequences of job insecurity for workers in Europe and abroad. Second, the authors of the various chapters in this book probably felt insecure and powerless at times, when they did not hear from me. This stressful situation sometimes lasted for a considerable time. I'm grateful for their patience, and can only hope that they will be able to regain their faith and optimism when they hold this book in their hand. Finally, the contributions of Sandra Volders, Evy Van Dael and in a 'slightly distant' past, also Jeannine Hooge of my former institution, the Higher Institute for Labour Studies, need to be mentioned. Without their efforts, this book would not have been possible at all. If making this book was stressful, then they carried the largest part of the burden. I am eternally in debt to their professionalism and kindness.

References

Ashford, S., Lee, C. and Bobko, P. (1989), 'Content, Causes, and Consequences of Job Insecurity: A Theory-based Measure and Substantive Test', *Academy of Management Journal*, Vol. 32(4), pp. 803-29.

Barling, J., Fullagar, C. and Kelloway, E. (1992), *The Union and Its Members: A Psychological Approach*, Oxford University Press, New York.

Burchell, B. (1994), 'The Effects of Labour Market Position, Job Insecurity and Unemployment on Psychological Health' in D. Gallie, C. Marsh and C. Vogler (eds), *Social Change and the Experience of Unemployment*, University Press, Oxford, pp. 188-212.

De Weerdt, Y., De Witte, H., Catellani, P. and Milesi, P. (2004), *Turning Right? Socioeconomic Change and the Receptiveness of European Workers to the Extreme Right. Report on the Survey Analysis and results.* Deliverable 4 for the project 'Socio-Economic Change, Individual Reactions and the Appeal of the Extreme Right' (SIREN), HIVA–K.U.Leuven, Leuven.

De Witte, H. (1999), 'Job Insecurity and Psychological Well-being: Review of the Literature and Exploration of some Unresolved Issues', *European Journal of Work and Organizational Psychology*, Vol. 8(2), pp. 155-77.

Greenhalgh, L. and Rosenblatt, Z. (1984), 'Job Insecurity: Toward Conceptual Clarity', *Academy of Management Review*, Vol. 9(3), pp. 438-48.

Hartley, J., Jacobson, D., Klandermans, B. and van Vuuren, T. (1991), *Job Insecurity. Coping with Jobs at Risk*, Sage Publications, London.

Heaney, C., Israel, B. and House, J. (1994), Chronic Job Insecurity Among Automobile Workers: Effects on Job Satisfaction and Health, *Social Science and Medicine*, Vol. 38(10), pp. 1431-37.

Hellgren, J. and Sverke, M. (2003), 'Does Job Insecurity Lead to Impaired Well-being or Vice versa? Estimation of Cross-lagged Effects Using Latent Variable Modeling', *Journal of Organizational Behavior*, Vol. 24, pp. 215-36.

Hellgren, J., Sverke, M. and Isaksson, K. (1999), 'A Two-dimensional Approach to Job Insecurity: Consequences for Employee Attitudes and Well-being.' *European Journal of Work and Organizational Psychology*, Vol. 8, pp. 179-95.

Hirschman, A. (1970), *Exit, Voice and Loyalty: Responses to Decline in Firms, Organizations and States*, Harvard University Press, Cambridge, M.A.

Hitt, M., Keats, B., Harback, H. and Nixon, R. (1994), 'Rightsizing-building and Maintaining Strategic Leaderschip: A Long-term Competitiveness', *Organizational Dynamics*, Vol. 23, pp. 18-32.

Jacobson, D. (1991), 'The Conceptual Approach to Job Insecurity' in J. Hartley, D. Jacobson, B. Klandermans and T. van Vuuren, *Job Iinsecurity. Coping wit Jobs at Risk,* Sage Publications, London, pp. 23-39.

Klandermans, B. (1996), 'Ideology and the Social Psychology of Union Participation' in P. Pasture, J. Verberckmoes and H. De Witte, (eds), *The Lost Perspective? Trade Unions Between Ideology and Social Action in the New Europe. Significance of Ideology in European Trade Unionism,* Avebury, Aldershot, Vol. 2, pp. 259-74.

Klandermans, B. and van Vuuren, T. (1999), 'Job Insecurity', Special Issue of the *European Journal of Work and Organizational Psychology,* Vol. 8(2), pp. 145-314.

Kozlowski, S., Chao, G., Smith, E. and Hedlung, J. (1993), 'Organizational Downsizing: Strategies, Interventions and Research Implications', *International Review of Industrial and Organizational Psychology,* Vol. 8, pp. 263-332.

Nolan, J., Wichert, I. and Burchell, B. (2000), 'Job Insecurity, Psychological Well-being and Family Life' in E. Heery and J. Salmon (eds), *The Insecure Workforce,* Routledge, London, pp. 181-209.

OECD (1997), 'Is Job Insecurity on the Increase in OECD Countries?', *OECD Employment Outlook,* July, pp. 129-59.

Purcell, K. and Purcell, J. (1998), 'In-sourcing, Out-sourcing, and the Growth of Contingent Labour as Evidence of Flexible Employment Strategies', *European Journal of Work and Organizational Psychology,* Vol. 7, pp. 39-59.

Sverke, M. and Hellgren, J. (2001), 'Exit, Voice, and Loyalty Reactions to Job Insecurity: Do Unionized and Non-unionized Employees Differ?', *British Journal of Industrial Relations,* Vol. 39(2), pp. 167-82.

Sverke, M. and Hellgren, J. (2002), 'The Nature of Job Insecurity: Understanding Employment Uncertainty on the Brink of a New Millennium', *Applied Psychology: An International Review,* Vol. 51(1), pp. 23-42.

Sverke, M., Hellgren, J. and Näswall, K. (2002), 'No Security: A Meta-analysis and Review of Job Insecurity and Its Consequences', *Journal of Occupational Health Psychology,* Vol. 7(3), pp. 242-64.

Waddington, J. and Hoffmann, R. (2000), 'Trade Unions in Europe: Reform, Organization and Restructuring' in J. Waddington and R. Hoffmann (eds), *Trade unions in Europe. Facing Challenges and Searching for Solutions,* European Trade Union Institute, Brussels, pp. 27-79.

Note

[1] With the exception of e.g. Hartley et al. (1991), and Sverke and Hellgren (2001).

Chapter 2

Job Insecurity, Temporary Work and Trade Union Membership in Finland 1977-2003

Jouko Nätti, Mika Happonen, Ulla Kinnunen and Saija Mauno

Introduction

During the last decades, many of the changes taking place in the economies and labour markets of industrialised countries may have increased job insecurity. The most obvious changes have been the increased economic instability and unemployment in most European countries and the rapid restructuring of global and national economies (shifting industrial structure, mergers and take-overs). In addition, the government policies of many European countries have supported a drive towards flexibility and market-driven economy (deregulation of labour markets and privatisation of the public sector).

At the organisational level, the need to adapt to leaner times and cut back costs has often meant a more flexible use of labour (shorter tenures, temporary and part-time work and subcontracting). These changes are often assumed to increase precarious, atypical (Delsen, 1995) or peripheral (Kalleberg, 2000) forms of employment. In social sciences, the increase in 'flexible work' is referred to as an indicator of risk society (Beck, 2000) or corrosion of character (Sennet, 1998).

At the individual level, economic instability and employer-driven flexibility have been experienced, on the one hand, in the form of changes in working conditions, and on the other hand, as unemployment. For example, in the European Union member states, unemployment rose from 4 per cent to 8 per cent between 1975 and 2002. At the same time, flexible forms of work - especially part-time and temporary work - have become more common. Temporary employment contracts and unemployment can be interpreted as forms of structural job insecurity, or as objective components of insecurity (see De Witte and Näswall, 2003). Among the employees who have managed to keep their jobs, changes in the workplace may have increased their subjective feelings of insecurity concerning the nature and continuity of their work. A new feature in the labour market is that these changes have also concerned educated professionals (Roskies and Louis-Guerin, 1990). According to an OECD report (1997), perceived job insecurity had become widespread in the OECD countries, especially in the 1990s. In Finland, perceived job insecurity was above the average.

The aim of this chapter is to analyse the relations between perceived job insecurity, temporary work and trade union membership with representative data on Finnish employees in 1977, 1984, 1990, 1997 and 2003. Temporary work can be viewed as an objective dimension of job insecurity and the perceived threat of job loss as a subjective dimension of job insecurity (De Witte and Näswall, 2003). Earlier literature has regarded job security issues as a primary motive for joining a trade union (Brown Johnson, Bobko and Hartenian, 1992). On the other hand, studies have mentioned increased temporary employment as one explanation for the declining unionisation rate (Delsen, 1995). In this chapter, we are especially interested in the relationship between these forms of job insecurity and trade union membership.

Perceived Job Insecurity

Concept and antecedents of perceived job insecurity In the most general sense, job insecurity can be seen as a discrepancy between the level of security a person experiences and the level he or she might prefer (Jacobson and Hartley, 1991). The starting point is usually that job insecurity is a subjective estimate of one's chances to lose one's job, which is based on the objective circumstances, e.g. downsizing or temporary job contracts in organisations (e.g. Klandermans and van Vuuren, 1999). According to the definition, it is natural to expect the two sides of job insecurity - objective and subjective - to associate with each other. However, there is also evidence that subjective experience of job insecurity is possible in contexts where no objective threat of unemployment exists (Rosenblatt and Ruvio, 1996). According to the subjective definition of job insecurity, the most important issue is how individual employees perceive their work situation (e.g. De Witte, 1999; Kinnunen, Mauno, Nätti and Happonen, 1999; Klandermans and van Vuuren, 1999; Sverke, Hellgren and Näswall, 2002). Hence, an individual's appraisal plays a remarkable role, and some employees may feel a higher level of job insecurity than others - even though they might share similar 'objective' organisational circumstances.

Subjective job insecurity has most often been defined as a threat of involuntary job loss (e.g. De Witte and Näswall, 2003; Mauno and Kinnunen, 2002; Sverke and Hellgren, 2002), signifying that employees are uncertain of whether they may keep their jobs in the future. Specifically, this conceptualisation has been regarded as 'quantitative' (Hellgren, Sverke and Isaksson, 1999) or 'global' job insecurity, which focuses on the threat of job discontinuity. From this point of view, researchers have looked at job insecurity as an anticipatory phase, characterised by the threat of impending unemployment (Joelson and Wahlquist, 1987), which does not mean, however, that unemployment necessarily follows.

The questions in the studies that utilise a global view to job insecurity (e.g. Kinnunen and Nätti, 1994; Roskies and Louis-Guerin, 1990) can be divided into two groups: there are, on the one hand, questions implementing a cognitive appraisal of the likelihood of losing one's job, and on the other hand, questions reflecting an affective concern about job-related changes (Jacobson, 1991). In this article, we will approach perceived job insecurity through the probability of job loss.

In earlier studies (Ashford, Lee and Bobko, 1989; Greenhalgh and Rosenblatt, 1984; Klandermans, van Vuuren and Jacobson, 1991; Roskies and Louis-Guerin, 1990; van Vuuren, Klandermans, Jacobson and Hartley, 1991), the factors that influence perceived job insecurity exist on three levels: (1) environmental and organisational conditions (e.g. organisational change and organisational climate); (2) individual and positional characteristics of employees (e.g. age, gender, socio-economic status, type of job contract); and (3) employees' personality characteristics (e.g. optimism-pessimism, sense of coherence). In addition, the feelings of job insecurity might be connected to the estimated consequences of losing one's job, such as standard of living, possibility of getting a new job and quality of available jobs. From this point of view, the surrounding society and labour markets, job security, rate of unemployment and available jobs are relevant to perceived job insecurity (OECD, 1997).

In previous studies, the best predictors have usually been positional factors, such as earlier unemployment experiences or temporary job contracts (Kinnunen and Nätti, 1994), personality factors (Roskies and Louis-Guerin, 1990) and signals of potential threats (e.g. rumours of reorganisation or changes in management; Ashford, Lee and Bobko, 1989; Kinnunen, Mauno, Nätti and Happonen, 2000). The best predictors may also depend on the indicator of job insecurity. Objective or positional circumstances might be more likely to determine cognitive job insecurity, whereas personality factors might be more closely associated with emotional job insecurity (Nätti, Kinnunen, Happonen, Mauno and Sallinen, 2001).

Perceived job insecurity and trade unions Most existing research on job insecurity has focussed on its negative consequences for employee well-being, as well as for organisations (Sverke, Hellgren and Näswall, 2002). In contrast, the relationship between job insecurity and trade union membership has received only scarce attention in the literature (Sverke and Hellgren, 2001). However, the few studies have shown that individual emphasis on job security represents an important determinant of union membership (Brown Johnson, Bobko and Hartenian, 1992; Crockett and Hall, 1987; Guest and Dewe, 1988), and the members of trade unions rank job security as an important issue (Allvin and Sverke, 2000). In addition, Bender and Sloane's (1999) econometric study partially supports the view that job insecurity encourages workers to join trade unions. A more complex question is whether trade unions decrease or increase job insecurity. On the one hand, Freeman and Medoff (1984) have found that the presence of unions significantly reduces labour turnover. Furthermore, Bender and Sloane (1999) have reported that there is some evidence that the overall impact of trade unions is to reduce the proportion of workers who are insecure in their jobs. On the other hand, Brown Johnson, Bobko and

Hartenian (1992) have found that unions do not have a significant impact on job insecurity. Näswall and De Witte (2003) reported similar results from Sweden and Italy. In Belgium, however, union members experienced more job insecurity than non-members did.

The relationship between job insecurity and trade unions has also been studied from the point of view of coping strategies and social support. Sverke and Hellgren (2001) have studied to what extent unionised and non-unionised employees make use of divergent strategies to cope with job insecurity by using Hirschman's (1970) exit, voice and loyalty framework. Previous studies have argued, on the one hand, that without the collective support of union membership, employees may have greater difficulties in coping with job insecurity (Dekker and Schaufeli, 1995). On the other hand, non-members may trust their own capacity to redress insecurity (Rosenblatt and Ruvio, 1996). According to Hirschman (1970), discontent employees may respond to unsatisfactory conditions in three ways: they may exit from the organisation, use their voice (e.g. protest against organisational change) or express their loyalty to the organisation. Exit is a major alternative in downsizing organisations, and job insecurity has been found to be associated with turnover intentions (Dekker and Schaufeli, 1995). Exit is a problem for the organisation because qualified workers will find new jobs more easily, and thus, are more likely to quit. Like exit, voice is an active response when compared to loyalty. Voice is characteristic of employees who have substantial involvement in the organisation. Voice can be seen as interest articulation and it can become operationalised, for example as union membership (Freeman and Medoff, 1984). In the Nordic countries, however, this assumption may be problematic because of the high unionisation rate. Loyalty is a product of various factors that bind the employees to the organisation, thus making exit costly and voice troublesome. Loyalty can manifest itself, for instance, in high levels of commitment to the organisation. However, previous studies have shown that job insecurity is usually associated with impaired organisational commitment (see De Witte and Näswall, 2003).

The results on Swedish health care employees in the context of major organisational changes in the 1990s indicated that job insecurity was primarily related to coping strategies in the exit and voice domains (Sverke and Hellgren, 2001). Union members were less inclined to make use of the exit and voice options when compared to their non-unionised co-workers, and more typically expressed loyalty to the organisation. The results were in accordance with previous research (Bender and Sloane, 1999), indicating that unionised workers are more inclined to remain in the organisation than their non-unionised counterparts are. One potential explanation is that a cooperative industrial relations climate facilitates dual commitment to the company and to the union. Thus, the collective support from union membership may make individual voice expressions less important. However, this may be different in countries with lower unionisation rates.

Sverke and Goslinga (2003) have studied whether unionised employees' coping strategies with job insecurity - exit, voice and loyalty - affect primarily the employer or the union. The results from four EU countries (Belgium, Italy, the

Netherlands and Sweden) confirm previous findings of the adverse effects of job insecurity on organisational loyalty and the turnover propensity of employees. The findings were less consistent across countries with respect to union-related outcomes. The study suggests, however, that job insecurity may lead to reduced union loyalty and withdrawal from union membership.

Hellgren and Chirumbolo (2003) have studied if - and how - social support from the union can alleviate the negative effects of job insecurity on well-being. The results from three countries (Italy, the Netherlands and Sweden) indicated that union support did not reduce the effect of job insecurity on mental health complaints. This finding is in line with the results of previous studies (Dekker and Schaufeli, 1995; Sverke and Hellgren, 2001).

Temporary Work

Concept, extent and outcomes of temporary work Temporary work can be viewed as a more objective dimension of job insecurity when compared to subjective perceptions of job insecurity. The literature often defines temporary employment as precarious, non-standard, atypical or contingent work (see Delsen, 1995; Kalleberg, 2000). The growing interest in temporary employment has arisen from a concern for 'marginal' groups in the labour market, on the one hand, and labour market flexibility on the other. Temporary forms of work are regarded as 'precarious' because they involve special risks in respect of workers' legal protection and social security. Therefore, the growth of temporary employment is often expected to increase labour market segmentation and social inequality (Kalleberg, 2000). Still, the promotion of temporary employment is often seen as a way to increase labour market flexibility and/or individual alternatives to standard paid employment (Beck, 2000). From the employer's perspective, temporary work is a form of numerical external flexibility, since it is a way to fluctuate the number of employees who are not among the organisation's core employees (Atkinson, 1987; Bradley, Erickson, Stephenson and Williams, 2000).

In Europe, the most common forms of temporary work are direct fixed-term contracts and temporary employment through specialised agencies (agency labour). In case of a fixed-term contract, the contract period is defined by certain objective conditions (e.g. expiry date or the completion of a particular task). The employer recruits the involved worker directly, on a temporary basis, which distinguishes this form of employment from agency labour, where a third party is involved. Agency labour is based on a contract whereby an agency recruits employees and then places them at the disposal of a user company - to perform a task (Bronstein, 1991). In practice, the proportion of agency labour of total employment has remained small in most Nordic and EU countries (ranging from 0.2 per cent in Italy to 4.0 per cent in the Netherlands; OECD, 1991), although there has been considerable growth since the 1980s (Storrie, 2002).

In Finland, employment on an open-ended contract is the normal form of employment, and fixed-term contracts are restricted to particular situations. On the contrary, in many other EU countries (Belgium, Denmark, Ireland, the Netherlands, UK), fixed-term contracts require no particular justification. According to the Finnish Employment Contracts Act, an employment contract may be drafted for a fixed period only if the nature of the task, a need to replace absent personnel, apprenticeship or a comparable factor requires this. In Sweden and Norway, but not in Denmark, there are similar restrictions to fixed-term contracts (see Nätti, 1993).

The figures on the extent of temporary work are usually based on labour force surveys. In the European labour force surveys, the term 'temporary employee' refers to employees who do not have a permanent (open-ended) contract, including participants in special employment programmes. The attribution of a temporary status in the surveys depends on the individuals' own perception of their employment position. In 2002, about 13 per cent of EU employees held fixed-term contracts, ranging from 31 per cent in Spain to 5 per cent in Ireland. In Finland, the corresponding figure was 16 per cent, which was the third highest among EU countries. In the 1990s, the proportion of fixed-term contracts in EU countries increased from 11 per cent (1992) to 13.6 per cent in 2000 (European Commission, 2003). Since then, the proportion has declined slightly.

Earlier studies on the consequences of temporary work on employee well-being have reported contradictory results. On the one hand, many studies show that temporary employment is associated with higher levels of mental stress and physical symptoms (Aronsson, Gustafsson and Dallner, 2002; Klein Hesselink and van Vuuren, 1999) and lower levels of job satisfaction and job involvement (Kinnunen and Nätti, 1994). On the other hand, there are also studies showing that temporary employees have better self-rated health (Virtanen, 2003) than permanent staff. Consistent with this, De Witte and Näswall (2003) found that temporary work was not associated with reduced job satisfaction and organisational commitment. Accordingly, Parker, Griffin, Sprigg and Wall (2002) have recently concluded that temporary job contracts may have both positive and negative outcomes, and one important factor determining this direction is whether the temporary employment is voluntary or involuntary. The latter form of contingent work usually results in negative health outcomes (Ellingston, Gruys and Sackett, 1998; cf. Saloniemi, Virtanen and Vahtera, 2004).

It is plausible that the relationship between temporary work and health is associated with the psychosocial characteristics of work and working environment (Virtanen, 2003). General psychosocial risk factors at work originate from stress that results, for example, from job insecurity, job loss, demotion, low job control, work overload, time pressure and inequality in advancement opportunities and rewards at work, such as pay and prestige. In most studies, temporary work has been associated with higher job insecurity (Kinnunen and Nätti, 1994; Näswall and De Witte, 2003), lower levels of occupational training (Aronsson, Gustafsson and Dallner, 2002), and less pay and other rewards (Delsen, 1995; Kalleberg, 2000; Parker et al., 2002; Kauhanen, 2002; Nätti, 1997). On the other hand, some studies have found that temporary employees reported fewer problems in social support, high demand and low control when compared to permanent employees (Saloniemi, Virtanen and Vahtera, 2004).

There has also been discussion on whether temporary work is a trap or a bridge in the labour market (Aronsson, 2001; Korpi and Levin, 2001; Nätti, 1993). We can define temporary work as a trap when it relates closely to unemployment, when it is involuntary and when there are few opportunities to get a more permanent job (Nätti, 1993). In Finland, temporary work seems to be a bridge to permanent posts among well-educated employees, but a trap for those whose employment status is unstable, as indicated by changes between temporary job, subsidised job and unemployment (Kauhanen, 2002).

Temporary work and trade unions Research on union participation and union attitudes has usually focused on traditional employees with full-time and permanent contracts, neglecting atypical employees in part-time and temporary contracts (Goslinga and Sverke, 2003) - partly due to the lower union density rates of part-time and temporary employees. One explanation for the lower unionisation rate could be that it is more difficult to organise part-time and temporary employees into unions, partly because they seem to be more reluctant to join unions. In addition, part-time and temporary employees can be difficult to trace, particularly if they frequently move in and out of employment or between jobs (Bradley et al., 2000). Another reason may be that many unions have been reluctant to accept part-time and temporary jobs because these jobs supposedly offer less security and rewards (see Delsen, 1995). Part-time and temporary employees may also quit their union membership more often than traditional employees. By using data from three EU countries (Sweden, Italy and the Netherlands), Goslinga and Sverke (2003) compared the union attitudes and union turnover intentions of full-timers and part-timers, as well as employed, permanent and temporary trade union members. However, they found only few attitude differences between the groups, and no differences in union turnover intentions.

Labour Relations, Trade Unions and Unionism in Finland

Labour relations and trade unions in Finland Finland is a latecomer in Nordic industrial relations, having converged to the Scandinavian style of centralised corporatism since the 1960s. In this model, both labour and capital are well organised, and the labour market is subject to extensive legal regulation. The other institutional features of the Nordic model of industrial relations include relatively centralised national organisational structures; a strong presence of trade union organisation at the workplace level; a national hierarchical system of collective bargaining; and tripartite cooperation between trade unions, employer organisations and the government (Julkunen and Nätti, 1999, 2002; Kettunen, 1998). These labour relations can also be referred to as social corporatism (Kauppinen, 1994). Corporatism is, in turn, the outcome of wage bargaining at a centralised level.

Trade unions depend largely upon their ability to attract and nurture a loyal membership (Ilmonen and Jokivuori, 1999). In Finland, employees are organised nation-wide by industry. There are almost hundred different national unions, which are members of three central confederations: Central Organisation of Finnish Trade Unions (SAK; blue-collar workers), Finnish Confederation of Salaried Employees (STTK; lower white-collar) and Confederation of Unions of Academic Professionals in Finland (AKAVA; upper white-collar). In addition to this, the workplace level has branch unions and shop stewards.

Theoretical approaches to unionisation   Union density rates and trends vary considerably in EU countries. In the Nordic countries, the unionisation rate is high and has been quite stable since the 1980s and 1990s. In most other EU countries, the unionisation rate is much lower and it has been declining, which has led to renewed interest in the factors that influence the decisions of employees to join unions (Visser, 2002).

Labour economists have analysed the determinants of unionisation with a conventional demand and supply framework (see Schnabel and Wagner, 2003). The demand function expresses workers' demand for union representation and services, while the supply function reflects the supply of union services. The demand for union membership depends negatively on its costs (membership fees) and positively on wage gains and other benefits from a unionised work environment, such as better working conditions and grievance procedures. The lower the costs of substitute services (such as social welfare benefits), the lower the demand for union services should be. Furthermore, the individuals' taste for unionism can affect the demand for union membership. The supply of union services depends positively on revenues (membership fees), whereas the costs of union organisation and servicing affect the supply negatively. The employers' attitude toward unions, collective bargaining and the legal structure within which the unions can operate affects the cost of organisation and servicing. Since most of these factors are not directly measurable, they are often substituted by proxy variables, such as firm size and personal characteristics.

In social sciences, the explanations for union membership have stressed the importance of class-consciousness, values, modes of production, composition of workforce, political climate, and the role of government income policies and centralisation of the labour movement. Klandermans (1986) distinguishes three theoretical and partly overlapping approaches to trade union membership. Firstly, the frustration-aggression approach explains union membership by employees' frustration or dissatisfaction with their work situation. Secondly, the rational-choice approach interprets unionisation as the outcome of a process of weighing the costs and benefits of participation. This approach underlies the economic theories of unionisation, but social scientists also include collective, social and ideological motives. Thirdly, the interaction approach stresses the role of group culture and that the social context, such as living and working environment, strongly influences an individual's decision to join a union. In certain living conditions, for example old industrial areas, and in certain working environments, for example large establishments, unionisation may be a dominant social norm and custom.

Empirical studies on unionisation Empirical studies on unionisation usually take an eclectic approach and combine economic as well as socio-political explanations. Most empirical analyses of unionisation fall within one of three approaches. The first strand of literature stresses cyclical and macro level factors (e.g. business cycle, changes in the composition of labour force and industrial structure, employer policy and government action) by means of time-series studies (Riley, 1997). In examining the unionisation rate in Finland, Pehkonen and Tanninen (1997) stress the importance of the reunification of the trade union movement in the late 1960s. The reunification process increased the legitimacy of trade unions, as well as their attractiveness among employees.

The second strand favours institutional explanations and analyses cross-national variations in institutional settings, such as legislation, centralisation of collective bargaining and union-affiliated unemployment insurance (Blaschke, 2000; Ebbinghaus and Visser, 1999; Schnabel, 2002). Delsen (1995) offers three explanations for the high unionisation rate in Sweden, which also apply to Finland: the union-administered unemployment insurance system; the solidarity principle applied by the unions, attractive for the unskilled workers and those with weak labour market positions; and the fact that the employer automatically reduces trade union contributions from the wages and salaries. In Finland, union membership fees have also been tax deductible since 1969 (Pehkonen and Tanninen, 1997).

The third strand of literature provides a structural explanation for union membership and concentrates on the individual characteristics of union and non-union employees. These individual-level, cross-sectional studies have identified a number of micro determinants - such as personal, occupational and firm characteristics, attitudes and social variables - that are associated with the unionisation decision.

In Riley's review (1997), the evidence is conflicting regarding personal factors, such as gender, age, marital status, race and the level of education. In Schnabel's review (2002), however, men have a greater propensity - according to most studies - to be union members than women, and there is a positive or concave relationship between age and union membership. In Riley's review (1997), significant negative relationships exist with various occupational characteristics, such as part-time work, self-employment and white-collar status. The lower unionisation rate of part-time employees may reflect their lower labour force attachment and irregular working hours. The lower unionisation rate of white-collar workers may be due to the relative scarcity of appropriate skills. Consequently, the professionals may not perceive a need for unionisation. Studies have also found that the relative closeness of white-collar workers to management leads to feelings of cultural homogeneity and shared values.

Various industry- and company-specific variables are related to unionisation. Certain industries, such as mining, construction, manufacturing and wholesale trade, are often positively related to trade union membership (Riley, 1997). These industries exhibit a high level of work standardisation and a clear distinction between managerial and operative tasks, which facilitates unionisation. The historical roots of collective bargaining in sectors such as manufacturing further strengthen the unionisation trend. The public sector is also associated with a high unionisation rate in most countries. The most important company-specific characteristic is the size of the establishment: unionisation rate increases with establishment size. Large establishments are likely to treat employees impersonally, but the employees may feel a greater need for protection. Furthermore, the employees' reference groups at work may exercise peer pressure to conform to a social custom of union membership. In addition to establishment size, many studies have found that regional characteristics and urbanisation have a significant effect on unionisation.

According to many studies, the political and social attitudes of employees, as well as the images of unions are significant determinants of unionisation. Left-wing views, feelings of job dissatisfaction and trust in the union increase the probability of unionisation in most studies. Studies have also investigated the influence of reference groups and key individuals, such as parents and spouses, on the decision maker. If the relatives and spouse are unionised and have a positive attitude towards unions, the employee is more likely to be a union member. In addition, the presence and strength of the union at the workplace seems to be important for joining and staying in the union. These findings are consistent with a social custom interpretation of union membership (see Visser, 2002).

Perceived Job Insecurity, Temporary Work and Trade Union Membership

One aim of this chapter is to examine whether perceived job insecurity and temporary work increase or decrease trade union membership, and what possible interaction effect they have on unionisation. Earlier studies indicate that perceived job insecurity increases (Bender and Sloane, 1999) and temporary work decreases unionisation (Delsen, 1995). Thus, their effects on unionisation are contradictory. Because of the conflicting effects, it is interesting to examine their combined effect on unionisation. In examining this interaction, we will apply two different hypotheses, which De Witte and Näswall (2003) have introduced, concerning the simultaneous effects of subjective and objective job insecurity on well-being.

The first, *intensification hypothesis*, is based on the stress theory (Lazarus and Folkman, 1984). This hypothesis suggests that when two (or more) stressful experiences occur simultaneously, they strengthen each other, which results in impaired well-being. Nevertheless, well-being outcomes are likely to be less severe if the two (or more) stressors are experienced separately (e.g. at different time points). Adapting the intensification hypothesis to our study, we would argue that a high level of objective job insecurity (temporary job) together with a high level of perceived job insecurity yields the most negative well-being effects. Dissatisfaction, in Klandermans' (1986) frustration-aggression approach, may in turn increase unionisation.

The second, *violation hypothesis*, derives from psychological contract theory (see Guest, 1998; Rousseau, 1995, 1998), emphasising the perceived - often implicitly negotiated - balance between employee input and employer reciprocity. Moreover, viewed in a larger context, the psychological contract model also relates to social exchange theory, according to which individuals strive for balance in their exchange relationships (Coyle-Shapiro, 2002). Applying this model on employment relationships, the following cognitive process usually occurs: an employee expects that when his or her work efforts benefit the organisation (employer), the organisation reciprocally offers him or her rewards in terms of job security (Guest, 1998; Rousseau, 1998). If this is not the case, it violates the psychological contract or social exchange process. A violation of the psychological contract is likely to result in many negative consequences. Studies have typically concentrated on attitudinal outcomes by showing that reduced organisational commitment, job satisfaction and increased turnover intentions are common results of such contract violations (e.g. Guest, 1998; Turnley and Feldman, 2000).

Furthermore, De Witte and Näswall (2003) argue that the type of employment relationship (permanent/temporary) affects this reciprocal process. According to them, permanent and temporary employees may have different *expectations* regarding the job security that their employer provides. When faced with subjective job insecurity, particularly permanent employees experience a violation of the psychological contract (or social exchange), and their well-being may decrease because of this. With temporary employees, in turn, the level of subjective job insecurity does not affect their well-being outcomes because they do not expect job security from their employer. Consequently, consistent with the violation hypothesis, high subjective insecurity associated with a permanent job contract (low objective insecurity) may produce the most negative well-being effects - and increase unionisation as a result.

Besides examining the effects of subjective and objective job insecurity on unionisation among employees, we are also interested in the differences in the unionisation rates of temporary employees. On the basis of the intensification approach and earlier studies (Parker et al., 2002), we suppose that involuntary temporary employees are more likely to join the trade unions than voluntary temporary employees.

Aims

The *first* aim of the study is to examine the extent of job insecurity between 1977 and 2003 by using representative samples of the working age population. The research questions are as follows:
1. How has perceived job insecurity changed between 1977 and 2003 at the macro (societal) level?
2. How much does perceived job insecurity vary with the background factors of employees?

The *second* aim of the study is to examine the extent of temporary work and its relation to job insecurity. The questions are:

3. How has temporary work changed between 1977 and 2003?
4. How much does temporary work predict perceived job insecurity? Consistent with previous studies, we proposed that temporary employees experience more job insecurity than their permanent counterparts.

The *third* aim of the study is to examine the extent and antecedents of trade union membership.

5. How has trade union membership changed between 1977 and 2003?
6. What kind of interaction is there between temporary work, job insecurity and trade union membership? This interaction is examined by asking whether high subjective job insecurity together with a temporary job (intensification hypothesis) or a permanent job (violation hypothesis) would lead to increased unionisation. In addition to the interaction, we will examine the direct effects of perceived job insecurity and temporary jobs on trade union membership. Based on earlier studies, we suppose that perceived job insecurity increases and temporary work decreases unionisation.
7. What is the role of the nature of temporary work: does involuntary temporary work increase unionisation more than voluntary temporary work?

Methods

Samples

We studied the features of job insecurity, temporary work and trade union membership through five Working Conditions surveys consisting of representative samples of the working age population (15-64 years) in 1977, 1984, 1990, 1997 and 2003. For each survey, some 3,000-6,000 employees were interviewed. Statistics Finland conducted the surveys as a face to face interview study using a standard questionnaire. The samples were gathered from those employed persons who participated in the regular monthly labour force surveys for the first time (Lehto and Sutela, 1999). The response rate was between 78 per cent and 91 per cent. The questionnaires comprised a comprehensive set of questions dealing with various features of working life. This article will analyse the questions that are especially relevant to job insecurity, temporary work and trade union membership. The study is restricted to employees. Table 2.1 summarises the main characteristics of the surveys.

Measures and Methods

Perception of job insecurity Perceived job insecurity was studied as the threat of losing one's job (global view) by three items in the working conditions surveys:

Table 2.1　Working conditions surveys 1977, 1984, 1990, 1997 and 2003

Year	1977	1984	1990	1997	2003
Data collection	September-December 1977	October-November 1984	August-November 1990	September-October 1997	October-November 2003
Frame population	15-64-year-old population	15-64-year-old employees	15-64-year-old employed persons	15-64-year-old employees	15-64-year-old employees
Sample size/ response rate	10,575 91%	5,070 89%	4,850 85%	3,795 79%	5,262 78%
Respondents (employees)	5,778	4,502	3,503	2,978	4,104

'Does your work carry any of the following uncertainties: threat of temporary lay-off; threat of dismissal; threat of unemployment?' on a dichotomy scale (0=no; 1=yes). A score for the three threats was computed by summing up the ratings of the three variables, divided by the number of items. The reliability (Cronbach's alpha coefficient α) of the 3-item sum-variable varied between 0.77 and 0.82, depending on the year. This scale emphasises the cognitive appraisal of the likelihood of losing one's job and does not implement affective concern about the prospect (cf. Jacobson, 1991).

Temporary work and motives for temporary work　The respondents were divided into temporary (1) or permanent employees (0) based on their own classification. The temporary employees were also questioned on their main reason for working temporarily (unable to find a permanent job; no desire for a permanent job; work is combined with studies).

Trade union membership　The working conditions surveys asked the respondents if they were members of a trade union, white-collar association or similar organisation (0=no, 1=yes).

Antecedents of job insecurity and trade union membership　In the empirical analysis, we used - besides cross tabulation - logistic regression analysis to predict perceived job insecurity and trade union membership. The independent variables included demographic, positional and organisational factors.
1. Demographic characteristics
　The four background variables were gender (0=man; 1=woman), age (1=15-29; 2=30-44; 3=45-54; 4=5-64), family situation (0=living alone; 1=living with a spouse); children (0=no; 1=at least one child under 18 years living at home).

2. Positional characteristics

   The following four indicators were examined as factors describing the employee's position in the workplace: socioeconomic status (0=white-collar employee; 1=manual worker); unemployment experience during the last five years (0=no; 1=yes); working hours per week (0=full-time; 1=part-time) and access to information, assessed by asking when the respondents were usually informed about job-related changes (0=at the planning level or just before the change; 1=during the change).

3. Environmental and organisational conditions

   We considered two general environmental conditions and two organisational conditions. The environmental conditions included the type of industry (0=services; 1=manufacture and construction) and type of employer (0=private; 1=public). The organisational conditions included establishment size (1=1-9 employees; 2=10-49 employees; 3=50 or more employees) and staff changes during the past three years (0=remained unchanged or increased; 1=decreased).

Participants

Table 2.2 shows the main characteristics of the respondents. In Finland, about half of the employees (53 per cent in 2003) were women. When compared to the situation in 1977 (49 per cent), the proportion of women has increased. A majority of the respondents were between 30 and 54 years old (66 per cent). Since 1977, the proportion of younger employees (aged 15 to 29 years) has decreased, whereas the proportion of older employees (aged 55 to 64 years) has increased since 1997. Consequently, the mean age of employees has increased from 37.2 years in 1977 to 41.6 years in 2003. Most respondents were living with a spouse (73 per cent) and this figure has remained quite stable. In 2003, 40 per cent of the employees had children at home, most commonly one or two. Since 1977, this figure has decreased. Thus, the changes in demographic characteristics indicate a feminisation and ageing of employees, with fewer children at home.

Most respondents were white-collar employees (65 per cent in 2003), but in the late 1970s, most of the employees were blue-collar workers. In Finland, the proportion of part-time employment has traditionally been low (6 per cent in 1977). However, in the 1990s, part-time work became more common (12 per cent in 2003). On the other hand, unemployment experiences have been quite common. In 2003, 23 per cent of the employees reported that they had been unemployed during the previous five years. Thus, the changes in positional characteristics indicate a trend towards white-collar employment with a continuity of full-time work and common unemployment experiences.

In environmental and organisational conditions, the most obvious change is the increasing role of services and declining role of manufacturing. Between 1977 and 2003, the proportion of the service sector increased from 59 per cent to 74 per cent. At the same time, changes in the type of employer and establishment size have been modest. The proportions of the public sector (36 per cent in 2003) and small (1-9

Table 2.2   Characteristics of the respondents, in per cent

	1977	1984	1990	1997	2003
Demographic characteristics					
Gender					
Male	51	51	49	47	47
Female	49	48	51	53	53
Age					
15-29 years	35	29	28	20	19
30-44 years	39	45	47	44	37
45-54 years	18	18	18	28	29
55-64 years	8	8	7	8	15
Family situation					
Living alone	--	29	28	27	27
Living with a spouse	--	71	72	73	73
Children					
No	49	52	56	55	60
Yes	51	48	44	45	40
Positional characteristics					
Socio-economic status					
White-collar	48	52	58	62	65
Blue-collar	52	48	42	38	35
Weekly working time					
Full-time	94	93	94	90	88
Part-time	6	7	6	10	12
Has been unemployed (last 5 years)					
No	--	78	83	67	77
Yes	--	22	17	33	23
Organisational conditions					
Type of industry					
Services	59	63	67	71	74
Manufacture and construction	41	37	33	29	26
Type of employer					
Private	--	66	65	66	64
Public	--	34	35	34	36?
Establishment size					
1-9 employees	--	--	24	28	24
10-49 employees	--	--	37	36	38
≥50 employees	--	--	39	36	39
N	5,778	4,502	3,503	2,978	4,104

-- = data missing

employees) establishments (24 per cent in 2003) have remained quite stable. In addition, there are clear gender differences regarding the industrial division, reflecting the strong horizontal gender segregation of Finnish labour markets (Appendix 1). Men are concentrated in manufacture and the private sector, whereas women are located in services and the public sector.

Results

The Prevalence of Perceived Job Insecurity

Perceived job insecurity at the macro level We examined the extent of perceived job insecurity both at the macro (societal) level and at the micro (individual) level. The prevalence of job insecurity at the macro level in connection with the unemployment rate between 1977 and 2003 is illustrated in Figure 2.1. Perceived job insecurity and the unemployment rate seem to correlate in the Finnish labour market. In the late 1970s, unemployment rose to a post-war record level (6 per cent in 1977 and 8 per cent in 1978), and 16 per cent of the employees (on average) felt the threat of temporary lay-offs, dismissal or unemployment. In 1984, the unemployment rate was lower (5 per cent), and on the average 11 per cent of the employees felt job insecurity. In 1990, the situation seems to be - at first glance - different: the unemployment rate was even lower (3 per cent) than in 1984, while feelings of job insecurity were a bit more common (12 per cent). However, in closer examination, we can notice that the year 1990 was a turning point in the business cycle and unemployment rate. The first signs of recession were obvious in the autumn of 1990, which was also the data collection time of that year.

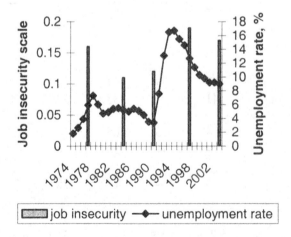

Figure 2.1   **Job insecurity and the unemployment rate**

In the early 1990s, due to the deep economic recession, unemployment rose from 3 per cent (in 1990) to 17 per cent (in 1994). Although the economy grew by 4-5 per cent each year between 1994 and 1997, the unemployment rate was still 13 per cent in 1997. In the same year (1997), 19 per cent of the employees felt job insecurity.

The strong economic growth and declining unemployment continued until 2001. Since then, annual economic growth has been modest and the unemployment rate has stabilised at the level of 9 per cent. In 2003, 17 per cent of the employees felt job insecurity. Thus, despite the strong economic growth, job insecurity seems to have remained at a higher level than in the 1970s and 1980s.

Perceived Job Insecurity at the Individual Level

At the individual level, perceived job insecurity varied each year with the type of insecurity in question and the background characteristics of the respondent (Table 2.3). The threat of temporary lay-offs and unemployment seemed to vary more over time than the threat of dismissal. Thus, the threat of temporary lay-offs and unemployment seemed to be more sensitive to the changes in economy and unemployment rate. In contrast, the threat of dismissal was more stable over time, and it was felt less than the other threats during most years. For example, in 2003, 16 per cent of the respondents felt the threat of dismissal and the threat of temporary lay-offs and 20 per cent the threat of unemployment. Altogether, 27 per cent of the respondents felt at least one dimension of job insecurity, but only 9 per cent felt all three types of insecurity. On the average, 17 per cent of the respondents felt job insecurity. In the following analysis, the job insecurity indicator is a sum-variable of these three items.

Perceived job insecurity varied according to the background characteristics of the individuals. In each year (except 1997), job insecurity was more common among men and in the manufacturing industry than among women and in services. Furthermore, blue-collar workers experienced more insecurity when compared to white-collar employees. One explanation for this pattern is that workers in the male-dominated manufacturing sector had been unemployed more often during the last five years when compared to employees in the female-dominated service sector. In the Finnish economy, the manufacturing industry has been strongly export oriented, and thus more sensitive to the economical cycles than the service sector.

In 1997, we can observe - to a certain extent - new features in perceived job insecurity. In contrast to the earlier years, job insecurity was more common in the public sector than in the private sector in 1997. In addition, the differences between genders and between manufacturing and service industries had disappeared. This could be explainable by the development differentials between economic sectors. In the early 1990s, the economic recession hit the manufacturing industry first and private and public services later. Consequently, economic recovery began earlier in the manufacturing sector than in the other sectors, especially the public sector. Between 1990 and 1994, 29 per cent of the jobs in the manufacturing sector were lost, when compared to 12 per cent in the private and public services. During the period of economic recovery (1994-97), the number of jobs increased by 11 per cent in manufacturing and by 14 per cent in private services, but there was no increase in the public services.

Table 2.3   Perceived threats (per cent) and job insecurity (means) in 1977, 1984, 1990, 1997 and 2003

	1977	1984	1990	1997	2003
Items of job insecurity scale (%)					
Temporary lay-off[a]	19	10	11	18	16
Dismissal[a]	11	8	10	15	16
Unemployment[a]	17	13	13	21	20
Job insecurity scale[b]	0.16	0.11	0.12	0.19	0.17
Gender	***	*	***		
Male	0.19	0.12	0.14	0.18	0.18
Female	0.12	0.10	0.09	0.19	0.17
Age[c]	***			*	***
15-29 years	**0.18**	0.12	0.12	0.21	<u>0.18</u>
30-44 years	<u>0.14</u>	0.10	0.12	0.18	<u>0.19</u>
45-54 years	0.15	0.12	0.11	0.20	<u>0.18</u>
55-64 years	<u>0.11</u>	0.10	0.07	0.15	**0.12**
Socio-economic status	***	***	***	***	*
White-collar	0.10	0.07	0.08	0.17	0.17
Blue-collar	0.21	0.15	0.17	0.21	0.19
Type of industry	***	***	***		***
Services	0.10	0.08	0.09	0.18	0.15
Manufacture and construction	0.22	0.15	0.17	0.19	0.24
Type of employer	***	***	***	***	***
Private	0.19	0.12	0.14	0.17	0.20
Public	0.07	0.08	0.07	0.23	0.13
N	5,778	4,480	3,469	2,964	4,100

[a] Perceived threats, per cent.

[b] Job insecurity scale means. Job insecurity scale is a score of the three threats, computed by summing up the ratings of the three variables and divided by the number of items.

[c] One-way Anova. Bold means differ ($p<0.01$) from underlined means; Scheffe's test.

* <0.05, ** <0.01, *** <0.001 (t/F-test)

In 2003, perceived job insecurity was again more common in manufacturing and the private sector when compared to service industries and the public sector, which seems to reflect different economic development between these sectors. The rapid economic recovery ended in 2000. Between 2001 and 2003, 4 per cent of the jobs in the manufacturing and construction industries were lost, when compared to an increase of 2 per cent in the service industries and 1 per cent in the public sector.

Despite the variation in perceived job insecurity during the recent years, the overall picture is that during the last 20 years, perceived job insecurity has increased especially among women and white-collar employees, and in services and the public sector.

Temporary Work and Job Insecurity

The second aim was to examine the extent of temporary work and its relation to job insecurity: to what extent does perceived job insecurity vary with the type of job contract (temporary or permanent). We will start by examining the extent of temporary work.

Extent of temporary work The proportion of temporary employment in Finland increased from 11 per cent in 1984 to 18 per cent in 1997, but declined to 14 per cent in 2003 (Table 2.4). Temporary work is more common among Finnish female (17 per cent) than male (11 per cent) employees, and correspondingly, most Finnish temporary employees are women (65 per cent in 2003).

It is, however, age rather than gender that typifies employees with temporary contracts: 29 per cent of all 15-29-year-old employees have temporary contracts. Thus, young employees are over-represented in temporary jobs.

Temporary work is more common among white-collar employees (16 per cent in 2003) when compared to blue-collar workers (11 per cent), and temporary jobs are more common in (female-dominated) services than in (male-dominated) manufacture and construction. Furthermore, the proportion of employees in temporary employment is larger in the public sector (state and municipalities; 23 per cent in 2003) than in the private sector (9 per cent). Consequently, temporary employees are concentrated in the public sector (64 per cent).

The reasons for taking up temporary work changed radically in the 1990s. In 1990, before the recession, one out of three temporary employees stated that he or she had been unable to find a permanent job. In 1997, 85 per cent of temporary employees said that they had not been able to find a permanent job. In 2003, the corresponding figure was 81 per cent. Thus, in 1997 and 2003, most temporary employees were classified as involuntary temporary employees.

Temporary work and job insecurity Besides the extent of temporary work, we examined to what extent temporary work predicts feelings of job insecurity by using a logistic regression analysis (Table 2.5). The dependent variable was perceived job insecurity (1=yes; 0=no). Based on the hypothesised factors, the analysis included three groups (demographic, positional and organisational characteristics) of explanatory variables. A value of over 1.00 (Exp B) indicates an increased likelihood for the phenomenon to occur when compared to the reference group.

Table 2.4   Proportion and composition of temporary employment in Finland in 1984, 1990, 1997 and 2003, in per cent

	Proportion				Distribution			
	1984	1990	1997	2003	1984	1990	1997	2003
Total	11	15	18	14	100	100	100	100
Gender	***	***	***	***				
Men	9	12	15	11	43	39	38	35
Women	13	18	21	17	57	61	62	65
Age[a]	***	***	***	***				
15-29 years	**22**	**30**	**38**	**29**	58	55	42	39
30-44 years	<u>8</u>	<u>11</u>	<u>16</u>	<u>14</u>	31	33	38	37
45-54 years	<u>5</u>	<u>5</u>	<u>11</u>	<u>8</u>	8	7	18	17
55-64 years	<u>4</u>	<u>10</u>	<u>6</u>	<u>7</u>	3	5	2	7
Socio-economic status	*			***				
White-collar	12	16	19	16	57	62	65	73
Blue-collar	10	14	17	11	43	38	35	27
Type of industry	***	***	***	***				
Services	13	17	20	16	76	76	80	86
Manufacture	7	11	12	7	24	24	20	14
Type of employer	***	***	***	***				
Private	7	12	14	9	44	51	49	43
Public	18	21	27	23	56	49	51	57
Reasons for temporary work								
Voluntary					..	40	14	19
Involuntary					..	60	86	81
N	4,502	3,503	2,978	4,102	499	372	455	577

[a] One-way Anova. Bold means differ (p<0.01) from underlined means; Scheffe's test.
* <0.05, ** <0.01, *** <0.001 (t/F-test)
Reasons for temporary work: involuntary = unable to find a permanent job; voluntary = does not want a permanent job; work is combined with studies.

The correlations between the different antecedent variables were in most cases low, although earlier unemployment experience showed moderate correlations with temporary work (r=0.35, p<0.001 in 2003); temporary employees had been unemployed more often than permanent employees (Appendix 1).

Perceived job insecurity was related to all three predictor groups. However, the positional and organisational variables best explained the variance in job insecurity in 1990, 1997 and 2003. The best predictors were temporary work and earlier unemployment experience. Temporary employees were 5.6 times more likely to have feelings of job insecurity (in 2003) than permanent employees were. Simi-

Table 2.5 Antecedents of perceived job insecurity in 1984, 1990, 1997 and 2003; logistic regression analysis

Characteristics	1984	1990	1997	2003
Demographic characteristics	Exp(B) (sig.)	Exp(B) (sig.)	Exp(B) (sig.)	Exp(B) (sig.)
Gender (ref.=male)				
Female	1.10	0.86	0.97	1.14
Age (ref.=15-29 years)				
30-44 years	1.48***	1.33*	1.43**	1.63***
45-54 years	1.80***	1.62**	1.76***	1.56***
55-64 years	1.61*	1.10	1.15	1.08
Family situation (ref.=living alone)				
Living with a spouse	1.03	0.92	1.41**	0.94
Children (ref.=No)				
Yes	1.03	1.43**	0.85	0.88
Positional characteristics				
Socio-economic status (ref.=white-collar)				
Blue-collar	1.73***	1.48***	1.20	0.71***
Weekly working time (ref.=full-time)				
Part-time	0.90	0.69	1.00	0.95
Unemployment experience (ref.=no)				
Yes	3.98***	3.34***	2.44***	3.05***
Access to information (ref.=before)				
During the changes	..	1.51***	1.74***	1.68***
Organisational characteristics				
Type of industry (ref.=services)				
Manufacture and construction	1.55***	1.35*	1.24	2.04***
Type of employer (ref.=private)				
Public	0.75*	0.43***	1.90***	0.57***
Establishment size (ref.=1-9)				
10-49 employees	0.82	1.17	0.92	0.99
≥50 employees	0.77	1.11	0.69***	0.98
Staff changes (ref.=no change or incr.)				
Decreased	..	1.63***	1.79***	2.43***
Job contract (ref.=permanent)				
Temporary	8.38***	5.23***	4.70***	5.63***
Constant	0.06***	0.06	0.08	0.11
Chi Square	782.37***	503.53***	552.21***	769.26***
-2LL	3,410.71	2,743.12	3,039.22	3,964.87
N	4,475	3,458	2,937	4,080

* <0.05, ** <0.01, *** <0.001

larly, earlier unemployment experience (3.1) increased the odds of job insecurity when compared to employees without unemployment experience during the previous five years.

In most years, working in the manufacturing sector and in a blue-collar position increased and working in the public sector decreased the likelihood of having feelings of job insecurity. In addition, a decreased number of staff and late access to information also increased the likelihood of having feelings of job insecurity. It is also noteworthy that in most years, job insecurity was statistically unrelated to the demographic variables, except for age (gender, family situation and children).

The main antecedents of job insecurity were the same in 1984 and 2003. However, there were some changes over time, reflecting the different dynamics in economic development between manufacture and services, and between the private and public sector.

Trade Union Membership: Extent and Antecedents

The *third* aim of the study was to examine the extent and antecedents of trade union membership. We accomplished this in three ways. First, we looked at the extent of trade union membership. Second, we examined the role of temporary work and job insecurity with the other antecedents in predicting trade union membership, and third, we looked at how the unionisation rate among temporary employees varied with the nature of temporary work (voluntary or involuntary) and job insecurity.

Extent of trade union membership The proportion of trade union members among employees has been high since the late 1960s in Finland. Between 1977 and 1990, the unionisation rate was quite stable (72-73 per cent) and in the 1990s, the unionisation rate increased in parallel with unemployment. Since 1997 (79 per cent), there has been a minor decline (77 per cent in 2003).

Although the overall unionisation rate in Finland is high, there are clear gender, age and socio-economic differences, as well as differences between economic sectors (Table 2.6). In 2003, the unionisation rate was substantially higher among women (80 per cent) than among men (74 per cent). At the beginning of the 1990s, the difference between women and men was still minor (73 per cent versus 71 per cent). In 2003, the gender gap was largest in the private service sector and among white-collar employees.

In addition to gender, the unionisation rate also varies by age. On the one hand, young employees are less likely to be trade union members than middle-aged and older employees are. Among young employees, the unionisation rate actually decreased in the 1980s. However, between 1990 and 1997, the unionisation rate increased. On the other hand, among older employees (55-64 years of age), there has been a consistently rising trend, especially during the last 20 years.

The unionisation rate has traditionally been higher among blue-collar workers and in manufacturing industries and the public sector when compared to white-collar employees, service industries and the private sector. However, in the late 1990s, the differences between blue-collar and white-collar employees and between manu-facturing and service industries narrowed or disappeared because of the rising unionisation rate among white-collar employees and in the service industries. At the same time, the gap between the private and public sector has remained.

Table 2.6 Unionisation rate of Finnish employees by gender in 1977, 1984, 1990, 1997 and 2003, in per cent

	1977	1984	1990	1997	2003
Unionisation rate	73	73	72	79	77
Gender		*		***	***
Male	74	71	71	75	74
Female	73	74	73	83	80
Age[a]	***	***	***	***	***
15-29 years	**67**	**58**	52	**59**	**58**
30-44 years	77	79	77	83	78
45-54 years	78	80	84	86	84
55-64 years	**69**	73	78	83	85
Socio-economic status	***	***	***		
White-collar	70	70	69	79	77
Blue-collar	76	76	75	80	77
Type of industry	***	***	***	***	*
Services	68	69	69	77	76
Manufacture and construction	80	78	77	84	80
Type of employer	***	***	***	***	***
Private	68	67	65	74	71
Public	89	84	84	90	88
N	5,778	4,502	3,469	2,978	4,104

[a] One-way Anova. Bold means differ (p<0.01) from underlined means; Scheffe's test.
* <0.05, ** <0.01, *** <0.001 (t/F test)

Temporary Work, Job Insecurity and Trade Union Membership

Besides the extent of unionisation, we examined to what extent temporary work and perceived job insecurity predict the unionisation rate with the other antecedents, by using a logistic regression analysis. The dependent variable was trade union mem-bership (1=yes; 0=no). Based on the hypothesised factors, the analysis included three groups (demographic, positional and organisational characteristics) of ex-planatory variables. A value of over 1.00 (Exp B) indicates an increased likelihood for the phenomenon to occur.

Both temporary work and perceived job insecurity had direct, although con-trasting effects on trade union membership. Temporary workers were less likely

(0.5 times in 2003) to be members of trade unions when compared to permanent employees. On the contrary, the employees who felt job insecurity were more likely (1.2 times in 2003) to be union members than the employees without the feelings of job insecurity, although the effect of perceived job insecurity was not statistically significant in 2003, in contrast to the earlier years.

Temporary work and perceived job insecurity also had a combined effect on unionisation in 2003: subjective job insecurity together with a temporary job - but not with a permanent job - increased unionisation. The result is in line with the intensification hypothesis. However, there was no interaction effect at other times.

Besides objective and subjective job insecurity, trade union membership was related to the other predictors as well. Among demographic characteristics, unionisation was related to gender, age and family situation in 2003. Women, older employees and people living with a spouse were more likely to be union members than men, young employees and people living alone. In addition, having children at home increased the likelihood of membership in most years, but not in 2003.

Unionisation was also related to positional characteristics. Working in a blue-collar position increased and working on a part-time basis decreased the likelihood of unionisation when compared to white-collar position and full-time work. In addition, earlier unemployment experience increased the membership likelihood in most years, but not in 2003.

All organisational characteristics were related to unionisation. Working in the manufacturing industries, the public sector, larger establishments and downsizing establishments increased unionisation when compared to the service industries, the private sector and small and stable or expanding establishments.

The direct and interaction effects of temporary work and perceived job insecurity on unionisation are illustrated in Table 2.8. Each year, the employees with feelings of job insecurity were trade unions members more often than the employees without job insecurity feelings. The gap in the unionisation rate has been quite stable (4-7 per cent). On the contrary, temporary employees were union members less often than permanent employees. However, the gap has narrowed from 19 per cent in 1990 to 6 per cent in 2003. This is a result of the increased unionisation rate of temporary employees, from 56 per cent to 72 per cent during the same period.

Temporary work and perceived job insecurity also had a combined effect on unionisation in 2003. Subjective job insecurity markedly increased unionisation among temporary employees, from 61 per cent to 80 per cent, but only slightly among permanent employees, from 78 per cent to 80 per cent. In 1990 and 1997, there was no interaction effect: perceived job insecurity increased unionisation both among temporary and permanent employees, although the increase was more obvious among temporary than among permanent employees.

Table 2.7 Antecedents of trade union membership in 1984, 1990, 1997 and 2003; logistic regression analysis

Antecedents	1984	1990	1997	2003
Demographic characteristics	Exp(B) (sig.)	Exp(B) (sig.)	Exp(B) (sig.)	Exp(B) (sig.)
Gender (ref.=male)				
Female	1.66***	1.36***	1.86***	1.67***
Age (ref.=15-29 years)				
30-44 years	2.07***	2.29***	2.49***	2.05***
45-54 years	2.15**	3.41***	3.16***	2.74***
55-64 years	1.62**	2.60***	3.12***	3.08***
Family situation (ref.=living alone)				
Living with a spouse	1.34**	1.52***	1.22	1.40***
Children (ref.=no)				
Yes	1.29**	1.16	1.42**	0.93
Positional characteristics				
Socio-econ. status (ref.=white-collar)				
Blue-collar	1.66***	1.62***	1.60***	1.43***
Weekly working time (ref.=full-time)				
Part-time	0.22***	0.38***	0.62**	0.56***
Has been unemployed (ref.=no)				
Yes	1.50***	1.91***	1.39**	1.20
Access to information (ref.=earlier)				
During the changes	--	1.26*	1.07	1.12
Organisational characteristics				
Type of industry (ref.=services)				
Manufacture and construction	1.64***	1.68***	1.83***	1.50***
Type of employer (ref.=private)				
Public	4.24***	4.28***	3.50***	3.24***
Establishment size (ref.=1-9)				
10-49 employees	1.55***	1.55***	1.41**	1.29**
≥50 employees	2.62***	2.07***	2.70***	1.70***
Staff changes (ref.=no change or incr.)				
Decreased	--	1.38**	1.34*	1.34**
Job contract (ref.=permanent)				
Temporary	0.29***	0.47***	0.66*	0.51***
Perceived job insecurity (ref.=no)				
Yes	1.40**	1.38*	2.05***	1.15
Job contract* insecurity interaction	1.12	0.76	0.72	1.90***
Constant	0.26***	0.224***	0.264***	0.449***
Chi Square	925.014***	685.274***	486.707***	508.206***
-2LL	7,314.44	3,413.25	2,527.108	3,869.450
N	4,475	3,458	2,936	4,080

Table 2.8 Unionisation rate by perceived job insecurity and type of job contract in 1990, 1997 and 2003, in per cent

	Perceived job insecurity in 1990			Perceived job insecurity in 1997			Perceived job insecurity in 2003		
	No	Yes	Total	No	Yes	Total	No	Yes	Total
All employees	71	75	72	77	85	79	76	80	77
Job contract									
Permanent	74	79	75	78	89	80	78	80	78
Temporary	50	65	56	63	79	74	61	80	72
N (all employees)	2,844	621	3,465	2,070	893	2,963	3,003	1,095	4,098
Reasons for temporary work									
Voluntary	38	52*	41	29*	41*	33	47	71*	54
Involuntary	62*	68	66	72	81	79	69	81	77
N (temporary employees)	199	152	351	149	302	451	220	308	528

* Cases less than 50

Among the temporary employees, the unionisation rate also varied - besides with perceived job insecurity - with the motives to work on a temporary basis. The unionisation rate was higher among involuntary (77 per cent in 2003) than among voluntary (54 per cent) temporary employees. The unionisation gap was largest in 1997 (46 per cent); in 1990 and 2003, the gap was 23-25 per cent. Because of the small size of subsamples, we could not examine possible interaction effects of the motives for temporary work and perceived job insecurity. Especially the group consisting of voluntary temporary employees with subjective insecurity was small (only 5 per cent of all temporary employees in 2003). However, the figures show that the unionisation rate was highest (81 per cent in 2003) among involuntary and insecure temporary employees and lowest among voluntary and secure temporary employees (47 per cent).

Summary and Discussion

In the Finnish labour market during the 1990s, we can observe a simultaneous increase in temporary work, job insecurity and rate of trade union membership. The aim of this chapter was to examine the relations between these three factors.

Firstly, we examined the extent of job insecurity. At the macro level, the prevalence of job insecurity and rate of unemployment seemed to correlate with each other. Especially in the 1990s, both unemployment rate and perceived job insecurity increased, but since 1997, the unemployment rate and perceived job insecurity have decreased. However, perceived job insecurity seems to have remained at a higher level than in the 1970s and 1980s.

Perceived job insecurity varied according to the background characteristics of the individuals. Despite variation in perceived job insecurity during the last few years, the overall picture is that during the last 20 years, perceived job insecurity has increased especially among women and white-collar employees, and in service industries and the public sector (see also Nätti et al., 2001).

Overall, perceived job insecurity became a persistent feature of the Finnish labour market during the economic crisis of the 1990s and it remained at a high level during the economic boom period. This is partly explainable by the structural insecurity of the labour market: high unemployment and continuous changes in the workplaces give rise to perceived insecurity. Furthermore, many industries are undergoing structural changes in the form of corporate mergers and acquisitions, creating uncertainty about organisational and personnel changes. As organisations try to reduce costs, it causes pressure on the employees who remain at work to modify their jobs and accept different employment conditions (Jacobson, 1991). All these changes are likely to fuel job insecurity among the people who remain at work.

Secondly, we investigated the extent of temporary work and its relation to job insecurity. The proportion of temporary employment in Finland increased from 11 per cent in 1984 to 18 per cent in 1997, but declined to 14 per cent in 2003. Temporary work is more common among Finnish female than male employees, although the difference between the genders is not as overwhelming as in part-time work (17 per cent versus 7 per cent). This is mainly because temporary work is also quite common in male-dominated industries (agriculture and forestry, construction, some manufacturing industries). Still, most Finnish temporary employees are women (65 per cent in 2003). The same applies to most EU countries (OECD, 1996).

It is, however, age rather than gender that typifies employees with temporary contracts: young employees are overrepresented in temporary jobs. The situation is similar in other EU countries as well. One explanation for this trend is that many young, temporary employees combine studying and work. Others may consider their current job to be temporary because they are job shopping before settling into a more permanent situation. Furthermore, the creation or expansion of government programmes to help young unemployed people also accounts for the over-representation of young people in temporary jobs (Delsen, 1995).

Temporary work is also more common among white-collar employees and in service industries and the public sector, when compared to blue-collar workers, manufacturing industries and the private sector. The situation is similar in other EU countries as well, except regarding the public sector (Delsen, 1995). In most EU countries, the share of temporary employment has generally been lower in the public than in the private sector.

Besides the extent of temporary work, we examined to what extent temporary work predicts feelings of job insecurity by using a logistic regression analysis. Temporary employees were 5.6 times more likely to have feelings of job insecurity (in 2003) when compared to permanent employees. Also in earlier studies (Kinnunen and Nätti, 1994; Näswall and De Witte, 2003; De Witte and Näswall, 2003), temporary employees have reported feelings of job insecurity more often than permanent employees have. A temporary contract includes a structural element of uncertainty: there is no guarantee of continuity after the contract expires.

In addition, in most years, working in the manufacturing sector and in a blue-collar position increased and working in the public sector decreased the likelihood of having feelings of job insecurity. Blue-collar workers have traditionally been more subjected to reorganisation with reductions in personnel, which may increase their feelings of job insecurity (Näswall and De Witte, 2003). In Finland, another explanation is that the male-dominated manufacturing sector has been strongly export-oriented, and thus more sensitive to economical cycles than service industries and the public sector. Similarly, earlier unemployment experience and a decreased number of staff increased the likelihood of having feelings of job insecurity.

The main antecedents of job insecurity were the same in 1984 and 2003. However, there were some changes over time, reflecting the different dynamics in economic development between manufacture and services, and between the private and public sector.

The role of demographic factors in predicting job insecurity was minor. On the one hand, gender, family status and children showed no significant relationship with perceived insecurity, but on the other hand, insecurity increased slightly with age. The study of Näswall and De Witte (2003) found similar results: gender, family status and presence of children were not related to perceived job insecurity. The result that older employees perceived more job insecurity is also in line with previous research (van Vuuren et al., 1991; Näswall and De Witte, 2003).

The finding that perceived job insecurity was linked to access to information suggests the potential importance of information in reducing job insecurity (see also Ashford, Lee and Bobko, 1989). By disseminating adequate information in advance, organisations can promote a sense of security in people during periods of transition, thereby reducing employee insecurity.

Thirdly, we examined the extent and antecedents of trade union membership. The proportion of trade union members among employees has been high in Finland since the late 1960s (Pehkonen and Tanninen, 1997). In the 1990s, the unionisation rate increased in parallel with unemployment. Since 1997, there has been a minor decline. The overall picture is that during the last 20 years, the unionisation rate has increased especially among women and among older and white-collar employees, and in service industries.

Besides the extent of unionisation, we examined to what extent temporary work and perceived job insecurity predict the unionisation rate with the other antecedents. Both temporary work and perceived job insecurity had direct, although contrasting effects on trade union membership. Temporary workers were less likely to be members of trade unions than permanent employees. Delsen (1995) has reported similar findings. On the contrary, the employees who felt job insecurity were more likely to be union members than the employees without the feelings of job insecurity, although the effect of perceived job insecurity was not statistically significant in 2003 - in contrast to the earlier years. Bender and Sloane (1999) have also reported that job insecurity increases unionisation.

In addition to the direct effects, we examined possible interaction effects by asking whether high subjective job insecurity together with a temporary job (the intensification hypothesis) or a permanent job (the violation hypothesis) would lead to increased unionisation. We found that temporary work and perceived job insecurity had a combined effect on unionisation in 2003: subjective job insecurity together with a temporary job - but not with a permanent job - increased unionisation. The result is in line with the intensification hypothesis. However, there was no interaction effect in the other years.

The results do not support the violation hypothesis, according to which subjective insecurity with a permanent job would increase unionisation. One possible explanation is that the overall unionisation rate is already high among permanent employees, or that other, structural factors are more important predictors of unionisation. On the other hand, recent experiences from the Finnish service industry of information technology indicate that when facing downsizing, and thus perceived job insecurity, the unionisation rate increases among permanent employees.

In addition to objective and subjective job insecurity, trade union membership was also related to other predictors. Among the demographic characteristics, unionisation was related to gender, age and family situation in 2003. Women, older employees and people living with a spouse were more likely to be union members than men, young employees and people living alone. In addition, having children at home increased the likelihood of membership in most years, but not in 2003.

The higher unionisation rate of women when compared to men is a new phenomenon in Finland. In the early 1990s, the difference between women and men was still minor. In other countries, either gender differences have been insignificant (Riley, 1997) or the unionisation rate has been higher among men than women (Schnabel and Wagner, 2003). The results are more consistent with age. Most studies show a positive or concave relationship between age and union membership. It has been suggested that the lower unionisation rate of young employees reflects their different socialisation, resulting in lower identification with unions and a related change in values (Schnabel and Wagner, 2003).

Unionisation was related to positional characteristics as well. Working in a blue-collar position increased and working on a part-time basis decreased the likelihood of unionisation when compared to white-collar position and full-time work. In addition, earlier unemployment experience increased the membership likelihood in most years, but not in 2003. In most other studies, blue-collar status and full-time work have also increased unionisation. Blue-collar workers are supposed to have rather homogeneous preferences and working conditions, which makes it easier to organise them (Schnabel and Wagner, 2003). In addition, the relative closeness of white-collar workers to management could lead to feelings of cultural homogeneity and shared values with the managers. The lower unionisation rate of part-time employees may reflect their lower labour force attachment and irregular working hours (Riley, 1997).

All organisational characteristics were related to unionisation. Working in the manufacturing industries, the public sector, larger establishments and downsizing establishments increased unionisation, as opposed to service industries, the private sector, and small and stable or expanding establishments. Also earlier studies (Riley, 1997) have found higher unionisation rates in manufacturing than in service industries. The manufacturing industries exhibit a high level of work standardisation and a clear distinction between managerial and operative tasks, which facilitates unionisation. The public sector and establishment size are also associated with a high unionisation rate in most countries (Schnabel and Wagner, 2003). In large establishments, employees are more likely to be treated impersonally and may feel a greater need for protection. Furthermore, the employees' reference groups at work may exercise peer pressure to conform to a social custom of union membership.

Among temporary employees, the unionisation rate varied - besides with perceived job insecurity - with the motives to work on a temporary basis. The unionisation rate was higher among involuntary than voluntary temporary employees. Because of the small size of the sub-samples, we could not examine possible interaction effects of the motives for temporary work and perceived job insecurity. However, the figures show that the unionisation rate was highest among involuntary and insecure temporary employees and lowest among voluntary and secure temporary employees. Thus, especially the temporary employees who experienced job insecurity and preferred permanent work were joining trade unions.

Overall, the objective and subjective dimensions of job insecurity have contrasting effects on unionisation. On the one hand, the employees who experience job insecurity are more likely to be union members than the employees who do not experience job insecurity. On the other hand, temporary employees are less likely to be members of trade unions than permanent employees are. Therefore, increased temporary employment is regarded as one explanation for the declining unionisation rate (Delsen, 1995). In Finland, however, the unionisation gap between temporary and permanent employees has gradually narrowed because of the increased unionisation rate of temporary employees. Thus, increased temporary employment does not necessarily imply a declining unionisation rate. A topic for further study would be the motives of trade union membership. Objective and subjective job insecurity are likely to emphasise security issues as motives for becoming a trade union member.

Our study setting contained some limitations that - to be overcome - require new approaches and further research. Due to the cross-sectional nature of our data, we cannot make causal conclusions. The measurement of job insecurity had drawbacks in the response content and form of response (yes/no-dichotomy). The job insecurity measurement of this study concentrated on unemployment risk. Roskies and Louis-Guerin (1990) argue that job insecurity encompasses much more than the fear of losing one's job (see also Greenhalgh and Rosenblatt, 1984). According to their findings, long-term prospect of job loss, prospect of demotion, and especially deterioration in working conditions were also associated with decreased well-being and work commitment. In addition, the concept of job insecurity should include the likelihood and seriousness of losing one's job. The severity aspect was not included in this data.

Although this study included several variables related to perceived insecurity, other insecurity predictors need further research. In previous studies, the tendency of employees to be more or less concerned about the future of their job has been related to various personality characteristics, such as locus of control, self-esteem, pessimism, role conflict and role ambiguity (Ashford, Lee and Bobko, 1989; Roskies and Louis-Guerin, 1990; van Vuuren et al., 1991). Therefore, we need further research into the cognitive and emotional processes that underlie insecurity.

Appendix 1 / Variable intercorrelations in 2003

Variables	1	2	3	4	5	6	7	8	9	10	11	12	13	14
Demographic characteristics														
1. Gender (1=man, 2=woman)														
2. Age	0.043													
3. Living with a spouse	-0.011	0.153												
4. Children	-0.007	-0.135	0.305											
Positional characteristics														
5. Blue-collar work	-0.314	-0.028	-0.058	-0.067										
6. Part-time work	0.151	-0.024	-0.094	-0.098	-0.006									
7. Unemployment experiences	0.020	-0.202	-0.076	0.030	0.123	0.058								
8. Late access to information	-0.037	0.037	-0.033	-0.008	0.191	0.021	0.045							
Organisational characteristics														
9. Manufacturing industry	-0.344	-0.019	0.017	-0.010	0.369	-0.127	0.025	0.102						
10. Public employer	0.269	0.146	0.065	0.058	-0.284	-0.040	-0.055	-0.091	-0.400					
11. Establishment size	-0.066	0.055	0.024	-0.016	-0.026	-0.092	-0.135	0.022	0.204	0.039				
12. Staff decreased	-0.054	0.075	0.014	0.002	0.039	-0.028	-0.044	0.085	0.142	-0.096	0.155			
13. Job contract (temporary)	0.096	-0.203	-0.089	-0.009	-0.062	0.116	0.350	-0.035	-0.116	0.192	-0.075	-0.088		
14. Perceived job insecurity scale	-0.005	-0.049	-0.040	0.001	0.037	0.005	0.254	0.120	0.129	-0.109	0.026	0.177	0.207	
15. Trade union membership (0=no, 1=yes)	0.081	0.201	0.108	0.040	0.002	-0.124	-0.026	0.032	0.035	0.192	0.123	0.071	-0.053	0.045

$r > 0.031$, $P < 0.05$, $r > 0.040$, $P < 0.01$

References

Allvin, M. and Sverke, M. (2000), 'Do New Generations Imply the End of Solidarity? Swedish Unionism in the Era of Individualisation', *Economic and Industrial Democracy*, Vol. 21, pp. 79-95.

Aronsson, G. (2001), 'A New Employment Contract', *Scandinavian Journal of Work, Environment and Health*, Vol. 27, pp. 361-4.

Aronsson, G., Gustafsson, K. and Dallner, M. (2002), 'Work Environment and Health in Different Types of Temporary Jobs', *European Journal of Work and Organizational Psychology*, Vol. 11, pp. 151-75.

Ashford, S., Lee, C. and Bobko, P. (1989), 'Content, Causes and Consequences of Job Insecurity: a Theory-Based Measure and Substantive Test', *Academy of Management Journal*, Vol. 32(4), pp. 803-29.

Atkinson, J. (1987), 'Flexibility or Fragmentation?', *Labour and Society*, Vol. 12(1), pp. 87-105.

Beck, U. (2000), *The Brave New World of Work*, Polity Press, Cambridge.

Bender, K. and Sloane, P. (1999), 'Trade Union Membership, Tenure and the Level of Job Insecurity', *Applied Economics*, Vol. 31, pp. 123-35.

Blaschke, S. (2000), 'Union Density and European Integration', *European Journal of Industrial Relations*, Vol. 6, pp. 217-36.

Bradley, H., Erickson, M., Stephenson, C. and Williams, S. (2000), *Myths at Work*, Polity Press, Cambridge.

Bronstein, A.S. (1991), 'Temporary Work in Western Europe: Threat or Complement to Permanent Employment?', *International Labour Review*, Vol. 130, pp. 291-310.

Brown Johnson, N., Bobko, P. and Hartenian, L.S. (1992), 'Union Influence on Local Union Leaders' Perceptions of Job Insecurity: An Empirical Test', *British Journal of Industrial Relations*, Vol. 30(1), pp. 45-60.

Coyle-Shapiro, J. (2002), 'A Psychological Contract Perspective on Organizational Citizenship Behavior', *Journal of Organizational Behavior*, Vol. 23, pp. 927-46.

Crockett, G. and Hall, K. (1987), 'Salaried Professionals and Union Membership: An Australian Perspective', *Journal of Industrial Relations*, Vol. 29, pp. 49-65.

Dekker, S. and Schaufeli, W. (1995), 'The Effects of Job Insecurity on Psychological Health and Withdrawal: A Longitudinal Study', *Australian Psychologist*, Vol. 30(1), pp. 57-63.

Delsen, L. (1995), *Atypical Employment: An International Perspective*, Wolters-Noordhoff, Groningen.

De Witte, H. (1999), 'Job Insecurity and Psychological Well-being: Review of the Literature and Exploration of Some Unresolved Issues', *European Journal of Work and Organizational Psychology*, Vol. 8, pp. 155-79.

De Witte, H. and Näswall, K. (2003), ''Objective' Versus 'Subjective' Job Insecurity: Consequences of Temporary Work for Job Satisfaction and Organizational Commitment in Four European Countries', *Economic and Industrial Democracy*, Vol. 24, pp. 149-88.

Ebbinghaus, B. and Visser, J. (1999), 'When Institutions Matter - Union Growth and Decline in Western Europe, 1950-95', *European Sociological Review*, Vol. 15, pp. 135-58.

Ellingston, J.E., Gruys, M.L. and Sackett, P.R. (1998), 'Factors Related to the Satisfaction and Performance of Temporary Employees', *Journal of Applied Psychology*, Vol. 83, pp. 913-21.

European Commission (2003), *Employment in Europe*, Luxembourg.

Freeman, R.B. and Medoff, J.L. (1984), *What Do Unions Do?*, Basic Books, New York.

Goslinga, S. and Sverke, M. (2003), 'Atypical Work and Trade Union Membership: Union Attitudes and Union Turnover Among Traditional Versus Atypically Employed Union Members', *Economic and Industrial Democracy*, Vol. 24(2), pp. 290-312.

Greenhalgh, L. and Rosenblatt, Z. (1984), 'Job Insecurity: Toward conceptual clarity', *Academy of Management Review*, Vol. 9(3), pp. 438-48.

Guest, D.E. (1998), 'Is a Psychological Contract Worth Taking Seriously?', *Journal of Organizational Behavior*, Vol. 19, pp. 649-64.

Guest, D. and Dewe, P. (1988), 'Why Do Workers Belong to a Trade Union? A Social Psychological Study in the UK Electronics Industry', *British Journal of Industrial Relations*, Vol. 88(26), pp. 178-92.

Hellgren, J. and Chirumbolo, A. (2003), 'Can Union Support Reduce the Negative Effects of Job Insecurity on Well-Being?', *Economic and Industrial Democracy*, Vol. 24(2), pp. 271-89.

Hellgren, J., Sverke, M. and Isaksson, K. (1999), 'A Two-Dimensional Approach to Job Insecurity: Consequences for Employee Attitudes and Well-Being', *European Journal of Work and Organizational Psychology*, Vol. 8, pp. 179-95.

Hirschman, A.O. (1970), *Exit, Voice, and Loyalty: Responses to Decline in Firms, Organizations, and States*, Harvard University Press, Cambridge, MA.

Ilmonen, K. and Jokivuori, P. (1999), 'A Social Movement of the Mature Stage of Post-Industrial Society? The Internal Division of the Finnish Trade Union Movement in the 1990s', *Work, Employment and Society*, Vol. 14(1), pp. 137-57.

Jacobson, D. (1991), 'The Conceptual Approach to Job Insecurity' in J. Hartley, D. Jacobson, B. Klandermans and T. van Vuuren (eds), *Job Insecurity. Coping with Jobs at Risk*, Sage, London.

Jacobson, D. and Hartley, J. (1991), 'Mapping the Context' in J. Hartley, D. Jacobson, B. Klandermans and T. van Vuuren (eds), *Job Insecurity. Coping with Jobs at Risk*, Sage, London.

Joelson, L. and Wahlquist, L. (1987), 'The Psychological Meaning of Job Insecurity and Job Loss: Results of a Longitudinal Study', *Social Science and Medicine*, Vol. 25(2), pp. 179-82.

Julkunen, R. and Nätti, J. (1999), *The Modernization of Working Times. Flexibility and Work Sharing in Finland*, SoPhi, University of Jyväskylä.

Julkunen, R. and Nätti, J. (2002), 'Reforming Working Times in Finland During the 1990s' in P. Koistinen and W. Sengenberger (eds), *Labour Flexibility - a Factor of Economic and Social Performance of Finland in the 1990s*, Tampere University Press, Tampere.

Kalleberg, A. (2000), 'Non-standard Employment Relations: Part-Time, Temporary and Contract Work', *Annual Review of Sociology*, Vol. 26, pp. 341-65.

Kauhanen, M. (2002), *Määräaikaiset työsuhteet ja toimeentulon riskit*. Kela, Sosiaali- ja terveysturvan tutkimuksia 69, Helsinki.

Kauppinen, T. (1994), *The Transformation of Labour Relations in Finland*, Finnish Labour Relations Association, Publications 8, Helsinki.

Kettunen, P. (1998), 'Globalisation and the Criteria of 'Us' - A Historical Perspective on the Discussion of the Nordic Model and New Challenges', *Global Redefining of Working Life - A New Nordic Agenda for Competence and Participation?*, Nord 1998:12, Copenhagen.

Kinnunen, U, Mauno, S., Nätti, J. and Happonen, M. (1999), 'Perceived Job Insecurity: A Longitudinal Study among Finnish Employees', *European Journal of Work and Organizational Psychology*, Vol. 8, pp. 243-59.

Kinnunen, U., Mauno, S., Nätti, J. and Happonen, M. (2000), 'Organizational Antecedents and Outcomes of Job Insecurity: A Longitudinal Study in Three Organizations in Finland', *Journal of Organizational Behavior*, Vol. 21, pp. 443-59.

Kinnunen, U. and Nätti, J. (1994), 'Job Insecurity in Finland: Antecedents and Consequences', *European Work and Organisational Psychologist*, Vol. 4(3), pp. 297-321.

Klandermans, B. (1986), 'Psychology and Trade Union Participation: Joining, Acting, Quitting', *Journal of Occupational Psychology*, Vol. 59, pp. 189-204.

Klandermans, B. and van Vuuren, T. (1999), 'Job Insecurity: Introduction', *European Journal of Work and Organizational Psychology*, Vol. 8, pp. 145-55.

Klandermans, B., van Vuuren, T. and Jacobson, D. (1991), 'Employees and Job Insecurity' in J. Hartley, D. Jacobson, B. Klandermans and T. van Vuuren (eds), *Job Insecurity. Coping with Jobs at Risk*, Sage, London.

Klein Hesselink, D. and van Vuuren, T. (1999), 'Job Flexibility and Job Insecurity: The Dutch Case', *European Journal of Work and Organizational Psychology*, Vol. 8, pp. 273-93.

Korpi, T. and Levin, H. (2001), 'Precarious Footing: Temporary Employment as a Stepping Stone Out of Unemployment in Sweden', *Work, Employment and Society*, Vol. 15(1), pp. 127-48.

Lazarus, R. and Folkman, S. (1984), *Stress, Appraisal and Coping*, Springer, New York.

Lehto, A.M. and Sutela, H. (1999), *Efficient, More Efficient, Exhausted. Findings of Finnish Quality of Work Life Surveys 1977-97*, Statistics Finland, Labour Market 1999:8, Helsinki.

Mauno, S. and Kinnunen, U. (2002), 'Perceived Job Insecurity Among Dual-Earner Couples: Do its Antecedents Vary According to Gender, Economic Sector and the Measure Used?', *Journal or Occupational and Organizational Psychology*, Vol. 75, pp. 295-314.

Näswall, K. and De Witte, H. (2003), 'Who Feels Insecure in Europe? Predicting Job Insecurity from Background Variables', *Economic and Industrial Democracy*, Vol. 24(2), pp. 189-215.

Nätti, J. (1993), 'Temporary Employment in the Nordic Countries: A 'Trap' or a 'Bridge'?', *Work, Employment and Society*, Vol. 7(3), pp. 451-64.

Nätti, J. (1997), *Atypical Employment and Gender in Finland*, ETLA Discussion papers 602, Helsinki.

Nätti, J., Kinnunen, U., Happonen, M., Mauno, S. and Sallinen, M. (2001), 'Perceived Job Insecurity among Finnish Employees in 1990-2000: Prevalence and Antecedents' in J. Kalela, J. Kiander, U. Kivikuru, H. Loikkanen and J. Simpura (eds), *Down from the Heavens, up from the Ashes*, VATT, Helsinki.

OECD, *Employment Outlook*, Paris (various years).

Parker, S.K., Griffin, M.A., Sprigg, C.A. and Wall, T. (2002). 'Effects of Temporary Contracts on Perceived Work Characteristics and Job Strain: A Longitudinal Study', *Personnel Psychology*, Vol. 55, pp. 689-719.

Pehkonen, J. and Tanninen, H. (1997), 'Institutions, Incentives and Trade Union Membership', *Labour*, Vol. 11(3), pp. 579-97.

Riley, N.M. (1997), 'Determinants of Union Membership: A Review', *Labour*, Vol. 11(2), pp. 265-301.

Rosenblatt, Z. and Ruvio, A. (1996), 'A Test of Multidimensional Model of Job Insecurity: The Case of Israeli Teachers', *Journal of Organisational Behavior*, Vol. 17, pp. 587-605.

Roskies, E. and Louis-Guerin, C. (1990), 'Job Insecurity in Managers: Antecedents and Consequences', *Journal of Organisational Behavior*, Vol. 11, pp. 345-59.

Rousseau, D. (1995), *Psychological Contracts in Organizations: Understanding Written and Unwritten Agreements*, Sage, Thousands Oaks, CA.

Rousseau, D.M. (1998), 'Why Workers still Identify with Organizations?', *Journal of Organizational Behavior*, Vol. 19, pp. 217-33.

Saloniemi, A., Virtanen, P. and Vahtera, J. (2004), 'The Work Environment in Fixed-Term Contracts: Are Poor Psychosocial Conditions Inevitable?', *Work, Employment and Society*, Vol. 18(1), pp.193-208.

Schnabel, C. (2002), *Determinants of Trade Union Membership*, Discussion papers 15, Friedrich-Alexander-Universität Erlangen-Nürnberg.

Schnabel, C. and Wagner, J. (2003), *Determinants of Trade Union Membership in Western Germany: Evidence from Micro Data, 1980-2000*, Discussion paper 708, IZA, Bonn.

Sennet, R. (1998), *The Corrosion of Character. The Personal Consequences of Work in the New Capitalism*, W.W. Norton and Company, New York.

Storrie, D. (2002), *Temporary Agency Work in the European Union*, European Foundation for the Improvement of Living and Working Conditions, Dublin.

Sverke, M. and Goslinga, S. (2003), 'The Consequences of Job Insecurity for Employers and Unions: Exit, Voice and Loyalty', *Economic and Industrial Democracy*, Vol. 24(2), pp. 241-70.

Sverke, M. and Hellgren, J. (2001), 'Exit, Voice and Loyalty Reactions to Job Insecurity in Sweden: Do Unionized and Non-Unionized Employees Differ?', *British Journal of Industrial Relations*, Vol. 39(2), pp. 167-82.

Sverke, M. and Hellgren, J. (2002), 'The Nature of Job Insecurity. Understanding Employment Uncertainty on the Brink of a New Millennium', *Applied Psychology: An International Review*, Vol. 51, pp. 23-42.

Sverke, M., Hellgren, J. and Näswall, K. (2002), 'No Security: A Meta-Analysis and Review of Job Insecurity and its Consequences', *Journal of Occupational Health Psychology*, Vol. 7, pp. 242-64.

Turnley, W.H. and Feldman, D.C. (2000), 'Re-examining the Effects of Psychological Contract Violations: Unmet Expectations and Job Dissatisfaction as Mediators', *Journal of Organizational Behavior*, Vol. 21, pp. 25-42.

van Vuuren, T., Klandermans, B., Jacobson, D. and Hartley, J. (1991), 'Predicting Employees' Perceptions of Job Insecurity' in J. Hartley, D. Jacobson, B. Klandermans and T. van Vuuren (eds), *Job Insecurity. Coping with Jobs at Risk*, Sage, London.

Virtanen, M. (2003), *Temporary Employment and Health*, People and Work Research Reports 61, Finnish Institute of Occupational Health, Helsinki.

Visser, J. (2002), 'Why Fewer Workers Join Unions in Europe: A Social Custom Explanation of Membership Trends', *British Journal of Industrial Relations*, Vol. 40(3), pp. 403-30.

Chapter 3

The Insecure Middle Class and Unionisation: An Empirical Investigation of Class, Job Insecurity and Union Membership

Bram Steijn

Introduction

Despite the prosperous economy in the nineties, academic interest in job insecurity has shown a strong increase over the last decade (OECD, 1997; Gallie, Whyte, Cheng and Tomlinson, 1998; Jacobson and Hartley, 1991; Burchell, Lapido and Wilkinson, 2002). The widespread attention devoted in the late nineties to the study by Sennet (1998) concerning the adverse effects of work flexibilisation on personality is a good example in this respect. This is related to the fact that even then for many companies high profit rates were associated with regular lay-offs in order to further increase the profitability. Moreover, 'downsizing' strategies are seen as an indicator of the short-run performance of organisations and lead to an enhanced reputation on the financial markets (Grimshaw, Ward, Rubery and Beynon, 2001). This was even truer in early 2001 as the 'new economy' soap bubble exploded and many companies reported lower than expected profits or even losses.[1] Since then, the economic slowdown has in many countries resulted in an increasing number of redundancies and growing unemployment. The discussion in several Western European countries in mid 2004 about the need to prolong the working week in order to cut costs is a nice example of the consequences of these developments for industrial relations. An agreement in Germany in late July 2004 between Daimler-Chrysler and the powerful German union IG Metal about a longer working week in exchange for job guaranties illustrates this. The threat DaimlerChrysler would have to displace factories to countries with cheaper labour costs certainly helped making this agreement. It also illustrates how the theme of job security has grown to the fore of public and media attention.

In the past, job insecurity has traditionally been associated with the working class. However, recent mass lay-offs are also hurting members of the middle class. Workers in banking, insurances, ICT, and also in the public sector, are certainly not safe in this respect (compare Lapido and Wilkinson, 2002). As unionisation has been an instrument for the working class to organise itself and seek collective protection, the question arises as to whether increased job insecurity will lead to a higher unionisation of the middle class in the near future.

Job insecurity, however, is certainly not the only possible reason to join a union. In his classic study, van de Vall (1963) discerns three distinct motives for becoming a union member: instrumental (or individual), collective (or ideological), and social (or traditional motives). The instrumental motive refers to the workers' perception that they need to join a union due to the existence of various concrete problems in the work situation (for instance: unions providing support in the case of work-related conflicts). In contrast to this, the collective motive refers to idealistic considerations, i.e. the idea that a strong union will contribute to societal change. Finally, the social motive refers to pressures to join from within the social environment (colleagues, family).

Recent research supports this typology, although the importance of the ideological motive seems limited. According to Klandermans (1986) the instrumental and social motives are the most important, whereas De Witte (1996) has argued that instrumental motives are by far the most important. However, in contrast to the decision to join a union, ideological motives do play an important role in the decision to participate in union activities that demand more time and effort (De Witte, 1996).

Other research by De Witte (1988) has also shown the importance of several motives. This research (focused on young union members and non-union members) revealed that non-members are often more highly skilled and employed in non-manual occupations. Their relatively strong labour market position leads them to believe that union membership is not a necessity. However, social pressures also proved to be important as parents influence the decision of their offspring to become a union member.

The various findings which indicate the importance of the instrumental motive, suggest increased job insecurity will lead to more union members, as it is likely that insecure workers will seek union support. However, specific research towards the effects of job insecurity provides no clear support for this expectation. Although De Witte (1999), on the basis of a large literature-study, reported various negative effects of job insecurity (such as a lower job satisfaction, a lower psychological health, and less organisational commitment), van Vuuren (1990, p.146) found almost no relationship between job insecurity and actual behaviour: her study found no relationship between job (in)security and union membership. More recently a study of Sverke and Goslinga (2003) even suggested that job security may lead to *reduced* union loyalty and a withdrawal from union membership, though this result was not consistent between several countries.

As previously stated, the growing job insecurity of the middle class is an important issue, which is of particular interest because job insecurity has traditionally been associated with the working class (Lockwood, 1989, p.55; Berting, 1998). The traditional image of an insecure proletariat and a secure middle class even lies at the bottom of the well-known EGP class scheme which is widely used in stratification research (Erikson and Goldthorpe, 1992; Crompton, 1998). According to Goldthorpe (1995, p.315) members of the middle class have a service relationship with their employers and he therefore refers to them as the 'service class'. In exchange for their work effort, these workers are supposed to receive not only a salary, but also several immaterial advantages, including a relatively high job security. In contrast, many manual workers have only a simple labour contract that can easily be terminated.

It is questionable whether the assumption of the EGP class scheme that the employment relation of manual workers differs substantially from that of non-manual workers is still tenable. It has been argued that members of the middle class are being increasingly hit by restructuring processes. It has also been argued that the flattening of organisations is a threat to the position of middle managers (compare Steijn, Berting and de Jong, 1998). Moreover, Savage (1998) has pointed out that government cuts have affected the position of the professional middle class working in education and health. Worrall, Cooper and Campbell (2000) have argued that redundancy, delayering and other forms of organisational change have become a common part of managerial working life. According to their study conducted in 1999, 67 per cent of managers reported some form of organisational chance.

A similar suggestion of a deteriorating position of the middle class can also be found in more popular literature. Sennet's previously mentioned study is one such example and another is a book by Hirsch (1987) written for a more general audience. The title says it all: 'Pack your own parachute. How to survive mergers, takeovers and other corporate disasters'. In his first chapter Hirsch even argues that a 'war on managers' is taking place.

In this chapter we are interested in how members of the middle class will respond to increased job insecurity. Will they seek protection and join trade unions? Based on the instrumental motive this would seem to be a likely result. However, there is another possibility.

De Witte (1999) has discerned two separate hypotheses concerning the relationship between occupational status and job insecurity. Some authors (compare Roskies and Louis-Guerin, 1990; see also King, 2000) have suggested that workers with a high occupational status will react strongly towards increased job insecurity. Compared to manual workers, the threat of becoming unemployed is more serious, as they have more to lose. This, in turn, will lead to an increased willingness to become a union member. However, other authors (compare Schaufeli and van Yperen, 1993) have stated that high occupational status workers will be less affected by job insecurity than low occupational status workers, as they have more options for tackling the negative consequences of unemployment. If this is true, middle class workers will still be less inclined than manual workers to join unions, even in a situation of increasing job insecurity.

Focusing on the relationship between job insecurity and psychological health, De Witte (1999) tested both hypotheses in an analysis which was limited with respect to the number of respondents. Contrary to *both* hypotheses, he did not find an interaction effect between occupational status and job insecurity. This suggests that middle class and manual workers respond to job insecurity in a similar manner.

Therefore many unanswered questions seem to remain. In order to shed more light on several important issues, two main questions will be answered in this chapter.

1. What is the relationship between class position and job insecurity in the Nether-lands, and has this relationship changed in the last decade of the twentieth century?
2. What is the effect of job insecurity on the willingness of workers to become union members and does social class moderate this effect?

The first question refers to the discussion in the second part of this introduction. It is important to find out whether job insecurity is associated with social class. In particular it is important to investigate whether the job insecurity of the 'higher' classes has risen. The second question deals with the consequences of growing job insecurity. Are insecure workers more willing to join a union? Is this willingness among middle class workers higher or lower than that of manual workers? Unfortu-nately, we have to limit ourselves to the nineties, as more recent data are not in our possession.

In the second section the data and measurement of the main variables will be treated. Next, in section three, the recent trends in job insecurity in the Netherlands will be dealt with. The main question - the relationship between job insecurity and union membership - will be central to section four. Finally, the main conclusions will be formulated in section five.

Data and Measurement

The Labour Supply Panel of the Organisation for Strategic Labour Market Research (OSA) was used to answer the research questions.[2] This panel was set up in 1985. About 4,000 panel members are interviewed every two years. The surveys from 1990, 1992, 1994, 1996 and 1998 will be used in this chapter.[3] The OSA data are particularly suitable for the analysis needed here as they are based upon a panel, which means that the same respondents are followed over time. Consequently, we can follow the career of respondents or determine whether or not respondents have become unemployed. The OSA tries to keep the panel representative for the Dutch labour force in general and according to its own publications it succeeds in doing so (Kunnen, 1997). The panel also includes the self-employed and various catego-ries of people without a job. However, the analyses will focus on workers in paid employment with a job of more than eleven hours a week (including those who after a period of paid employment have become unemployed). These restrictions mean that our panel included 2,226 employees in 1990, 2,354 in 1992, 2,374 in 1994, 2,384 in 1996 and 2,640 in 1998.[4]

Class, job insecurity, and union membership are the main concepts in the analyses. A shortened version of the EGP class scheme was used to determine the class of the respondents (compare Erikson and Goldthorpe, 1992). All OSA surveys contain elaborate data about the job and job characteristics of a worker. Using a standard procedure this job was recoded into the EGP class scheme. Next this scheme was shortened into a version containing three classes: (1) the service class (EGP classes I and II); (2) lower white-collar workers (EGP class III); (3) the working class (EGP classes VI and VII). The self-employed and workers in the primary sector (farmers and farm workers) were not included in the analysis. Respondents belonging to EGP class V (mainly blue-collar supervisors) were also excluded. The reason for this is twofold: not only does this class contain very few respondents, but their answers to several questions differ substantially from other classes. This meant that recoding in one of the three classes included in the analysis was not a valid option.

The measurement of the important variable job insecurity includes several indicators. With respect to this it is important to mention the conceptualisation of van Vuuren (1990). She discerns three different aspects: (1) job insecurity is in the first place a *subjective* feeling; (2) this insecurity is oriented towards the *future*; (3) it also implies doubts about the continuation of employment; hence doubts about future career chances are not part of job insecurity. The first aspect means that in her view 'objective' job insecurity is not important. According to van Vuuren job insecurity will only affect human behaviour if people are aware of it.

On the other hand several other authors argue that objective conditions of job insecurity are indeed important (Catalano et al., 1986; Roskies, Louis-Guerin and Fournier, 1993; Gallie et al., 1998) as these conditions influence human behaviour. To shed more light on this controversy both objective and subjective indicators of job insecurity will be included in the analysis.

Our first indicator is a subjective one: the perception of the chance that a respondent will become unemployed in the next twelve months.[5] This indicator fits nicely within the conceptualisation of van Vuuren. A dichotomous variable will be used in the analysis: job secure versus job insecure workers. This last category not only includes respondents who replied affirmatively to the question as to whether they were expecting to become unemployed, but also those answering 'do not know'.[6] Unfortunately - at least from the perspective of the study design - the percentage of job insecure workers is quite low (compare section 3). Therefore, the variable that will be used in the analyses is skewed.

The second indicator of job insecurity has an objective character. An important feature of the survey is that people are not only asked about the labour market position they hold at the time of the interview, but also about what happened in the two year period between the previous and the current interview. Starting with the survey of 1990, we determined whether or not a respondent became unemployed in the periods 1990-92, 1992-94, 1994-96, and 1996-98 (irrespective of the duration of the unemployment and whether or not this happened more than once). The resulting variables were dichotomised, contrasting workers who had become unemployed in such a period (score 1) with those who had not. These variables will be used in two different ways. In the analysis focussing on social class, we will examine the percentage of workers belonging to a certain class that had become unemployed in the next two-year period. This is in accordance with our research question, as we want to know whether members of a certain class have divergent chances of *becoming* unemployed. However, in our analysis of the effects of job security on the willingness to join a union, we will examine the effect of the variable indicating that a person had become unemployed in the year period *before* the interview. This is because we are then interested in the effects of *actual* unemployment on union membership.

In the fourth section a logistic analysis will be carried out with union membership as the dependent variable. This analysis will include three other independent variables: age, gender and economic sector (public or private). The inclusion and measurement of the first two is straightforward; these variables are associated with both job insecurity (OECD, 1997) and the willingness to join a union (De Witte, 1988; Gallie et al., 1998). The inclusion of economic sector is probably less clear-cut. However, its inclusion is important as traditionally the job security of workers in the public sector is higher and recent research also shows that union membership in the public sector is relatively high.

Class and Job Insecurity

In this section we will first focus on several trends with respects to job insecurity. Table 3.1 presents the percentage of workers that were job insecure for each of the two indicators in the several survey years.

Table 3.1   Job insecurity in the Netherlands in the period 1990-98

	1990	1992	1994	1996	1998
% unemployed in previous two years	3.2	2.8	5.6	4.2	2.4
% feeling job insecure	4.2	3.9	5.1	5.2	3.1
N	2,226	2,354	2,374	2,384	2,640

The data in this table generate the following conclusions. Firstly it is clear that in all survey years, the proportion of subjective and objective insecure workers is rather small. Both the subjective and objective work insecurity indicators are somewhat higher in the mid nineties, reflecting the economic situation in that period. Even then, however, work insecurity is rather low. In the late nineties (compare the survey year 1998) renewed economic growth leads to the lowest levels of job insecurity.

Our main conclusion has therefore to be that those expecting widespread, growing job insecurity on the Dutch labour market, are wrong. This is remarkable, as an OECD report from the period under study - at least with respect to subjective job insecurity - holds a different view. However, this study used a different measure. According to the OECD (1997, p.130), workers are insecure if they *do not strongly agree* with the following statement 'My job is secure'. Workers stating they 'just' agree with this statement are therefore regarded as insecure. Not surprisingly, this leads to a substantially higher degree of job insecurity. Whether this is a reliable measurement of job insecurity can be disputed, especially as other more objective indicators used in the same study do not support the conclusion that in the Netherlands, job insecurity is widespread and on the increase.

Of course the relatively low degree of job insecurity does not preclude differences in the degree of insecurity between classes. Moreover, if it is true that the middle class in particular has been hit by job insecurity in recent years, one would expect a change in the association between class and job insecurity over the course of time. Therefore, the relationship between class on the one hand, and job insecurity on the other is examined in greater detail in Tables 3.2, 3.3 and 3.4.[7]

Table 3.2   Class and proportion of Dutch workers that became unemployed in two-year periods between 1990 and 1998

	1990-92	1992-94	1994-96	1996-98
Service class	0.028	0.033	0.032	0.017
Lower middle class	0.045	0.060	0.062	0.036
Working class	0.030	0.075	0.037	0.023
Total	0.034	0.056	0.042	0.024
Eta and N	0.04n.s.	0.08**	0.06**	0.05*
	(2,354)	(2,374)	(2,384)	(2,640)

** $p<0.01$, * $p<0.05$, n.s.=not significant

Table 3.2 shows an interesting pattern. In 1992 there is not a statistically significant relationship between class position and the spell of unemployment in the two preceding years. In the three other periods, however, this relationship *does* exist. But, the nature of this relationship appears to be changing. Whereas in 1994, members of the working class experienced most often the spell of unemployment, this 'honour' went in 1996 and 1998 to members of the lower middle class. This seems to be in line with the observations made above that the middle class is no longer safe from economic restructuring processes. The same, however, seems not true for the service class as their levels of objective job insecurity show only a modest increase in the 1990-96 period and remain the lowest in all the years under study.

Table 3.3   Class and proportion of Dutch workers feeling insecure in the period 1992-98

	1992	1994	1996	1998
Service class	0.020	0.036	0.037	0.023
Lower middle class	0.018	0.067	0.048	0.028
Working class	0.049	0.054	0.074	0.043
Total	0.031	0.051	0.052	0.031
Eta and N	0.08**	0.06*	0.07**	0.05*
	(1,427)	(2,172)	(2,214)	(2,456)

** $p < 0.01$; * $p < 0.05$; n.s.=not significant

However, this same pattern is not reflected in the subjective insecurity (compare Table 3.3). Notwithstanding, their relatively higher objective job insecurity, members of the lower middle class feel more secure compared to members of the working class - although 1994 is an exception to this pattern. It therefore appears, members of the lower middle class are not fully aware of the economic and organisational changes threatening their once secure position. At the same time, in all three survey-years members of the service class felt the most secure, which conforms with their objective situation.

Looking at the two indicators of job insecurity combined, it can be concluded that a relationship between class position and job insecurity still exists. The expectation that job insecurity within the middle class is converging with the working class, is only partially confirmed. This only seems to be the case for the lower middle class. Indeed for the period 1994-96 members of this class experienced the highest unemployment rate of all three classes. This, however, does not reflect itself in the subjective feelings of insecurity within this class.

For members of the service class the situation is clearly different. Although their job insecurity has only increased slightly, the differences with both other classes seem to have increased, especially with respect to the lower middle class. Therefore, the hypothesis that the higher middle class in particular is threatened by job insecurity must be discarded, at least in the case of the Netherlands. At the same time, the data partially support the view that a proletarianisation of the lower middle class is taking place.

It is interesting to note that Gallie et al. (1998, pp.143-5) reached a similar conclusion for the higher middle class. They found that subjective job insecurity of the higher middle class in Britain rose slightly during the 1990s and has become comparable to the working class (this conclusion therefore differs from ours). However, at the same time they also conclude that the suggestion that professionals and managers are relatively more often hit by unemployment than in the past, is false. According to them this perception in public opinion, can be attributed to the large increase in the absolute numbers of managers and professionals. This absolute increase is mirrored in a comparable increase in the number of unemployed managers and professionals. However, this is certainly not the same as a *relative* increase in unemployment chances. Nevertheless, the higher absolute number of unemployed members of the higher middle class means that people perceive this to be the case, as the chance of them meeting an unemployed middle class member has increased.

Class, Job Insecurity and Union Membership

What does this mean for the willingness to join a union? Although according to the two indicators we used job insecurity has at best only slightly increased in the mid nineties, this willingness could nevertheless be affected.

Table 3.4 Logistic regression with union membership as the dependent variable in 1996

	1st step Exp(B)	2nd step Exp(B)
Gender (1=women)	n.s.	n.s.
Age	n.s.	n.s.
Class (ref: lower middle class)		
Working class (1=yes)	2.19**	2.16**
Service class (1=yes)	1.54**	1.55**
Been unemployed (1=yes)	n.s.	n.s.
Feeling insecure (1=yes)	1.51*	n.s.
Economic sector (1=public)	2.54**	2.54**
Working class*been unemployed		n.s.
Working class*feeling insecure		n.s.
Service class*been unemployed		n.s.
Service class*feeling insecure		n.s.
Pseudo R^2	0.07	0.07
(N)	(2,188)	(2,188)

* $p<0.05$, ** $p<0.01$

To find out whether or not this has happened, the next table presents the results of a logistic regression analysis. We performed this analysis only with respect to the year 1996. In that year many people will have been affected by the economic downturn of the mid nineties, and it is also a year showing relatively high levels of job insecurity on our two indicators.[8] In this analysis the dichotomous dependent variable union membership (score 1=member) is regressed against several independent variables (compare section 2): age, gender, economic sector, the two indicators of job insecurity, and class. The last variable is included as two 'dummy' variables (with the lower middle class as reference category). The analysis is carried out in two steps. In the first step only the main effects are considered. Next, a second step is performed which also includes four interaction effects between the two indicators of job insecurity and the two class dummies. The purpose of this second step is to find out whether the data supports the hypothesis that members of the middle and working classes respond differently to job insecurity (compare section 1). If such a divergent response exists, significant interactions must be found. The results are presented in Table 3.4.

An important conclusion is that with respect to union membership, workers belonging to different classes seem to respond to job insecurity in a similar manner. The results show that in the second step of the analyses none of the interaction terms were statistically significant. Therefore, like De Witte (1999), we can find no support for the hypotheses put forward by Roskies and Louis-Guerin respectively Schaufeli and van Yperen mentioned earlier. The almost complete absence of significant interaction effects implies that in the remaining part of this section we will focus on the results from the first step in the analyses.

A major conclusion is that objective job insecurity is not associated with the willingness to join a union; the subjective insecurity, however, is associated with this willingness - which means the above-mentioned finding of van Vuuren is not repeated. If workers are insecure about their employment, they are somewhat more inclined to join a union.

We do also see some important effects on the willingness to join a union of class and economic sector. In the first place, workers in the public sector are more often union member. This can most easily be illustrated by the bivariate association: whereas in the private sector only 31 per cent of the workers in the survey is a member, union membership in the public sector is 50 per cent.

The relationship between class and union membership is probably even more interesting. As Table 3.4 illustrates, both working class and service class workers are more often union member, which of course means that members of the lower middle class show a lesser tendency to do so. Again, this can be illustrated by the bivariate figures: union membership for the working, lower middle and service class is respectively 40 per cent, 25 per cent and 37 per cent. Other survey years show a more or less similar pattern.

The non-existence of interaction effects between class and job insecurity points to an interesting point. It shows that middle class workers - given a certain level of job insecurity - react in the same way to increasing job insecurity compared to working class workers. Given the positive effect of subjective job insecurity in the first step of the analysis, this could mean that in the long run increasing subjective job insecurity will lead to a higher willingness of middle class workers to join a union.

Finally, it is interesting to note that the analysis showed no significant effects of gender and age.

Conclusions

Upon drawing the findings together, the following picture emerges. Generally speaking, job insecurity was almost non-existent in the Netherlands during the early 1990s. The low percentage of job insecure workers suggests a high degree of job security, despite the relatively high unemployment rate in that period and the high number of restructuring processes that were going on in organisations. It must be stressed, however, that the conceptualisation of job insecurity plays an important part in this, as the OECD - using a less strict conceptualisation - has reported a higher degree of insecurity.

The two indicators of job insecurity used in this chapter suggest a modest increase of job insecurity in the mid-nineties, followed by a decrease in the 1996-98 period.

Overall, however, the traditional idea that job security of the working class diverges substantially from the middle class, is not confirmed. This undermines a basic assumption of the EGP class scheme. Generally, in the Netherlands members of the working class also have a high degree of job security. This is possibly related to special characteristics of the Dutch labour market, such as the importance of collective agreements, the relative security provided by the social security system, and the importance of internal labour markets that provide security to white and blue-collar workers (compare Visser and Hemerijck, 1997). Further comparative research is needed to find out whether the same is true for other West-European countries.

The hypothesis that the association between class and job security is decreasing, because members of the (higher) middle class in particular are getting less secure jobs, is also not confirmed. The job security of members of the service class in particular remains high. However, the differences in insecurity between the working class and the lower middle class are rather small. Though bounded by the high degree of security, this suggests that the main division in job security lies *not* between the working and middle class, but between the working and lower middle class on the one hand, and the service class on the other.

The findings do not entirely support two main conclusions of van Vuuren (1990). Firstly she also could not find a relationship between job insecurity and the willingness to join a union, and secondly she has argued that only subjective job insecurity will affect the actual behaviour of workers. Our findings that actual unemployment is not related to union membership, and that in 1996 workers who felt insecure more often joined a union, support this second point in general. At the same time it refutes her first conclusion though, as it shows the existence of a relationship between job insecurity and union membership.

Does this mean job insecurity is not a part of the instrumental motives people have to join a union? I do not think so. These instrumental motives are probably very important, but have a more indirect character. I believe workers will use more indirect instrumental motives in their decision to join a union (like: 'although I am not threatened by unemployment at the moment, you never know what will happen in the future') than direct ones (like: 'I am joining a union now because I will most probably be fired within the next few months'). However, further research is needed to test the validity of this hypothesis.

Contrary to important suggestions in the literature, there is no difference in the response of members of the middle and working classes towards job insecurity. This confirms the earlier findings of De Witte (1999). Nevertheless, it is striking that the degree of unionisation within the service class is comparable to the working class. Further research into this and the question as to why union membership within the lower middle class is substantially lower, is certainly important.

References

Berting, J. (1998), 'Rise and Fall of Middle-Class Society? How the Restructuring of Economic and Social Life creates Uncertainty, Vulnerability, and Social Exclusion' in B. Steijn, J. Berting and M.J. de Jong, *Economic Restructuring and the Growing Uncertainty of the Middle Class*, Kluwer, Dordrecht, pp. 7-24.

Burchell, B., Lapido, D. and Wilkinson, F. (2002), *Job Insecurity and Work Intensification*, Routledge, London and New York.

Catalano, R. et al. (1986), 'Labor Markets and Help-seeking: A test of the Employment Security Hypothesis', *Journal of Health and Social Behavior*, Vol. 27, pp. 287-97.

Crompton, R. (1998), *Class and Stratification. An introduction to Current Debates*, Polity Press, Cambridge.

De Witte, H. (1988), 'Waarom worden jongeren lid van een vakbond (Why do young people join a union)?', *Tijdschrift voor Arbeidsvraagstukken*, Vol. 4(3), pp. 18-33.

De Witte, H. (1996), 'Are Trade Union Members (Still) Motivated by Ideology? A Review of the Importance of Ideological Factors as Determinants of Trade Union Participation in (the Flemish Part of) Belgium', in P. Pasture, J. Verberckmoes and H. De Witte (eds), *The Lost Perspective? Trade Unions Between Ideology and Social Action in the New Europe. Volume 2. Significance of Ideology in European Trade Unionism*, Avebury, Aldershot, p. 275-304.

De Witte, H. (1999), 'Job Insecurity and Psychological Well-Being: Review of the Literature and some Unresolved Issues', *European Journal of Work and Organizational Psychology*, Vol. 8(2), pp. 155-77.

Dronkers, J. and Ultee, W.C. (1995), *Verschuivende ongelijkheid. Sociale gelaagdheid en mobiliteit (Shifting Inequality, Social stratification and mobility)*, Van Gorcum, Assen.

Erikson, R. and Goldthorpe, J.H. (1992), *The Constant Flux: A Study of Class Mobility in Industrial Societies*, Clarendon, Oxford.

Gallie, D., Whyte, M., Cheng, Y. and Tomlinson, M. (1998), *Restructuring the Employment Relationship*, Clarendon Press, Oxford.

Gaspersz, J. and Ott, M. (1996), *Management van employability. Nieuwe kansen in arbeidsrelaties (Management of employability. New chances in employment relations)*, Van Gorcum, Assen.

Goldthorpe, J. (1995), 'The Service Class Revisited' in T. Butler and M. Savage (eds), *Social Class and the Middle Class,* UCL Press, London, pp. 313-44.

Grimshaw, D., Ward, K.G., Rubery, J. and Beynon, H. (2001), 'Organisations and the Transformation of the Internal Labour Market', *Work, Employment & Society,* Vol. 15(1), pp. 25-54.

Hirsch, P. (1987), *Pack your Own Parachute. How to Survive Mergers, Takeovers and other Corporate Disasters,* Addison-Wesley, Reading.

Jacobson, D. and Hartley, J. (1991), 'Mapping the Context' in J. Hartley et al., *Job Insecurity. Coping with Jobs at Risk,* Sage, London, pp. 1-22.

King, J.E. (2000), 'White-Collar Reactions to Job Insecurity and the Role of the Psychological Contract: Implications for Human Resource Management', *Human Resource Management,* Vol. 39(1), pp. 79-91.

Klandermans, B. (1986), 'Participatie in de vakbond. Overzicht van theorie en onderzoek (Union participation. Overview of theory and research)', *Tijdschrift voor Arbeidsvraagstukken,* Vol. 2(4), pp. 14-29.

Kunnen, R. (1997), *Trendrapport aanbod van arbeid (Trend report labour supply),* OSA report no 25, SDU, The Hague.

Lapido, D. and Wilkinson, F. (2002), 'More Pressure, Less Protection' in B. Burchell, D. Lapido and F. Wilkinson, *Job Insecurity and Work Intensification,* Routledge, London and New York, pp. 8-38.

Lockwood, D. (1989), *The Black-coated Worker. A Study in Class Consciousness,* Clarendon Press, Oxford (second edition).

OECD (1997), 'Is Job Insecurity on the Increase in OECD countries?', *OECD Employment Outlook,* July, pp. 129-59.

Roskies, E. and Louis-Guerin, C. (1990), 'Job Insecurity in Managers: Antecedents and Consequences', *Journal of Organisational Behavior,* Vol. 11, pp. 345-59.

Roskies, E., Louis-Guerin, C. and Fournier, C. (1993), 'Coping with Job Insecurity: How Does Personality Make a Difference', *Journal of Organisational Behavior,* Vol. 14, pp. 617-30.

Savage, M. (1998), 'Social Exclusion and Inclusion within the British Middle Classes, 1980-95' in B. Steijn, J. Berting and M.J. de Jong (1998), *Economic Restructuring and the Growing Uncertainty of the Middle Class,* Kluwer, Dordrecht, pp. 25-43.

Steijn, B. (1999), 'De arbeidsmarktpositie van flexibele werknemers: bewijs van een gesegmenteerde arbeidsmarkt (The labour market position of flexible employees: proof of a segmented labour market)?', *Sociale Wetenschappen,* Vol. 42(2), pp. 90-105.

Schaufeli, W. and van Yperen, N. (1993), 'Success and Failure on the Labour Market', *Journal of Organisational Behavior,* Vol. 14, pp. 559-72.

Sennet, R. (1998), *The Corrosion of Character. The Personal Consequences of Work in the New Capitalism,* New York.

Steijn, B., Berting, J. and de Jong, M.J. (1998), *Economic Restructuring and the Growing Uncertainty of the Middle Class,* Kluwer, Dordrecht.

Sverke, M. and Goslinga, S. (2003), 'The Consequences of Job Insecurity for Employers and Unions: Exit, Voice and Loyalty', *Economic and Industrial Democracy,* Vol. 24(2), pp. 241-70.

van de Vall, M. (1963), *De vakbeweging in een welvaartstaat (The trade union movement in a welfare state)*, Boom, Meppel.

van Vuuren, T. (1990), *Met ontslag bedreigd. Werknemers in onzekerheid over hun arbeids-plaats bij veranderingen in de organisatie (Threatened with redundancy. Employees' uncertainty about their tenure in the case of changes in the organisation)*, VU, Amsterdam.

Visser, J. and Hemerijck, A. (1997), *'A Dutch Miracle': Job Growth, Welfare Reform and Corporatism in the Netherlands*, Amsterdam University Press, Amsterdam.

Worrall, L., Cooper, C. and Campbell, F. (2000), 'The New Reality for UK Managers. Perpetual Change and Employment Instability', *Work, Employment & Society*, Vol. 14(4), pp. 647-68.

Notes

[1] A brief scan of relevant newspaper headlines from early 2001 illustrates this: Philips announced a worldwide loss of 6,000 to 7,000 jobs; Corus did the same for its division in Britain alone; Volvo axed 3,000 jobs in 2000 and 2001; Dell computers finally axed 1,700 jobs in February 2001 and was expected to axe a further 3,000 later on.

[2] We thank this organisation for providing the data. We used for the analyses a CD-ROM (P1462/OSA) published by them and the Steinmetz archive containing the surveys from 1985 until 1998.

[3] Unfortunately, the survey of 2000 could not be used as the dataset in my possession did not include enough information about the class position of the respondents.

[4] In fact, another restriction was used as well. Only those respondents that could be given a score in the EGP class scheme were included. Therefore, the respondents were excluded from the analysis if insufficient information about the occupation was available.

[5] The exact phrasing of the question is: Do you think you will keep your job, will become unemployed of will voluntarily stop working over the next 12 months? The last answer category (will stop voluntarily) is not included in the analysis.

[6] In our view - in accordance with the conceptualisation of van Vuuren - workers who are not sure about their future chances of keeping their job, are almost by definition job insecure.

[7] As stated earlier we will look at the percentage of workers in a certain class that has become unemployed in a given two-year period following the interview.

[8] It must be noted however, that comparable analyses for the other survey years do not lead to substantial different conclusions.

Chapter 4

Job Insecurity and Works Council Participation[1]

Peter Kerkhof, Annemieke Winder and Bert Klandermans

Introduction

Employees who experience job insecurity may react in many different ways. Most of these reactions can be characterised as negative for the organisation as well as for the individual. For example, in a study among Israeli teachers job insecurity was associated with lower organisational commitment, lower perceived performance, more resistance to change and a greater intention to leave the organisation (Rosenblatt and Ruvio, 1996; 2000). Other studies show similar reactions among German employees of electronics firms (Borg, 1989), Canadian managers (Roskies and Louis-Guerin, 1990) and American employees (Ashford, Lee and Bobko, 1989; see Sverke, Hellgren and Näswall, 2002 for an overview).

In this study, we take a look at a possible positive outcome of job insecurity: participation in the works council, the mandatory body that represents personnel in communicating with management in the Netherlands and in several other European countries. Before doing so, we will discuss the context in which the study was conducted, that is the current reorganisations in Dutch municipalities. Then, we explain the role that works councils can play when a company, or in this case, a state institution goes through a reorganisation. Finally, we will talk about works council elections and hypothesise about the effect that job insecurity may have on the intention to use one's right to vote and on the intention to stand for council membership.

Reorganising the Dutch Municipalities

Whereas in earlier days being a Dutch civil servant meant lifetime employment, this situation has changed rapidly in the last decades. Numerous services offered to the public have been privatised and in governmental organisations that have not been privatised numerous reorganisations have taken place, sometimes resulting in involuntary dismissals.

The Dutch public sector is not unique in this respect. In many European countries reductions in public spending and changing ideologies concerning the role of

state institutions in providing services to the public, forced public service organisations to reorganise (see Lord and Hartley, 1998 for some British examples).

In many ways, organisations in the Dutch public sector come to resemble private companies. Nowadays, citizens are viewed as *clients* with a desire for high
quality *products*. Municipal organisations are supposed to deliver these high quality
products at a reasonable price and, as a consequence, started to pay a lot of
attention to efficiency. Five changes are most notable in the municipal organisation
(Van de Vijver and Leenders, 1997).

1. The introduction of new models of organisation: instead of a strict organisational
   separation of policy makers and the services provided, policy making and service
   providing are now integrated into so called 'sectors'. The aim is to reduce bureau-
   cracy by confronting policymakers with the direct outcomes of their policies.
2. Rethinking the core tasks: the financial problems of many municipalities force
   them to think about what should and what should not be a public service. As a
   result many services were cancelled or privatised.
3. The development of a more external orientation. Many municipal organisations
   aim at ways to make their organisation more responsive to the citizens' needs.
   This can have far stretching consequences for the organisation, for example when
   the aim is to come to one counter for all citizens' questions.
4. The introduction of policy- and control-instruments such as management reports,
   budget proposals and effect measurements.
5. The introduction of human resource management (HRM). Many HRM instruments are being introduced in order to enable personnel to adapt to all the changes
   in the organisation. Moreover, a new kind of civil servant is needed: more flexible
   and better qualified for the new tasks.

Dutch Works Councils and Reorganisations

Not only the way of organising, but also the labour relations in the Dutch public
sector have come to resemble those in private companies. Current governmental
policy is aimed at equalizing labour relations and terms of employment in the public sector with those in the private sector as much as possible. For example, in the
public sector labour relations have been decentralised, resulting in different collective agreements for different sectors instead of one agreement for all civil servants
(Kerkhof and Klandermans, 1994).

In line with the changes in labour relations, the rules for worker participation in
the private sector have been introduced in the public sector. In the private sector,
worker participation is embedded in the Works Council Act since 1950. Until
1995, rules for worker participation in the public sector were not clearly and
unequivocally established. In 1995 the Works Council Act has been introduced in
the public sector, resulting in the establishment of works councils in Dutch municipal organisations. Since 1996 there are works councils in the Dutch municipalities
with the same rights as those in the private sector. Whereas until 1996 the rights of

the former participation committees were described in unclear terms, the works councils have rights which are described in much detail in the Works Council Act.

Works councils are typically embedded in legislation or in an industrial agreement between trade unions and employers. Rogers and Streeck (1995, p.6) define works councils as '... institutionalised bodies for representative communication between a single employer ('management') and the employees ('workforce') of a single plant or enterprise'. Being representative bodies, works councils consist of elected employee representatives who consult with management on behalf of the workforce. In the Netherlands works councils have a strong legal basis. Dutch law dictates a dual role for works councils: They are to represent employee interests and to organise consultation between employer and employees in order to contribute to the optimal functioning of the organisation (Visser, 1995). Dutch councils have four important rights: the right of consultation (or the right to tender advice on certain proposed decisions), of co-determination (which determines that council approval is necessary on certain issues), of monitoring and of information (see Visser, 1995, for an overview). All of these rights are important during reorganisations: According to Article 25 of the Works Council Act of 1998, advice of the works council is required in case of (among many other topics) a significant reduction, expansion or other change in the enterprise's activities, or in case of major changes to the organisation or to the division of powers within the enterprise. Moreover, according to Article 27, approval is necessary when elements of the social policy for employees change. Visser (1995, p.97) mentions several examples of major reorganisations in which the works council, usually in close co-operation with the trade unions, were able to substantially influence the outcome of a reorganisation. Thus, the introduction of works councils in the Dutch municipalities has important consequences for the way reorganisations are dealt with within the municipalities. Not all works councils are that successful however. Although all councils in the Netherlands function under the same law, a persistent finding in research on Dutch works councils is that they differ greatly in the degree that they use their legal rights (see for example, Hövels and Nas, 1976; Teulings, 1981; Van het Kaar and Looise, 1999).

Works Council Elections and Job Insecurity

The members of a works council are elected through council elections. Elections typically take place every three years. In some municipal organisations however, the number of council candidates equals the number of seats available, or is lower than the number of seats available (see Winder, Kerkhof and Klandermans, 2000). In these organisations, the people who stand for candidate are appointed to the works council automatically. Although works councils are not 'company unions' (Rogers and Streeck, 1995), Dutch law gives recognised trade unions a slight advantage with respect to proposing council candidates during elections (Visser, 1995). A 'union list' of council candidates is automatically recognised, whereas non-unionised employees need to collect a minimum of thirty signatures from employees in the organisation to get their list recognised.

Voter turnout in the 1996 and 1999 municipal works council elections were 71 per cent and 61 per cent respectively (Kerkhof et al., 2001). Thus, not everyone who has the right to vote during council elections, does actually vote. The reasons for using or not using one's right to vote have only recently been explored by Klandermans and Visser (1995) and by Winder, Kerkhof and Klandermans (2000). The main reasons that employees mentioned the most for using the right to vote were that the council contributes to the promotion of employee' interests, that using ones' right to vote strengthens the council's position and that one supports a good council candidate with one's vote (Klandermans and Visser, 1995, p.168; Winder, Kerkhof and Klandermans, 2000, p.154-5).

In this chapter we introduce another possible reason for using the right to vote. In the remaining of this chapter, we will look at the possibility that feelings of job insecurity influence the intention to vote for the works council and to stand for council membership. Exercising the right to vote during council elections may strengthen the works councils' position during a reorganisation and thus may help to reduce employees' insecurity about their job. When faced with a strong works council, that is a works council with strong support from the employees, management might want to rethink some of it's more extreme measures. Standing for works council membership may have the same kind of effects. In order to be able to actually organise council elections it is necessary that more people stand for candidate than there are number of seats available. Recent research shows that managers perceive a council to be stronger when the council is actually elected than when the council is not elected (Winder, Kerkhof and Klandermans, 2000, p.85). Also, without actual works council elections, the opportunity to acquire employee support through employee votes disappears. Apart from strengthening the position of the works council, standing for council member may have some individual advantages: Works council members have better information about reorganisations and, more importantly, the law offers extra protection for works council members against dismissal.

Participation in works council through voting or standing for candidate can be considered a form of collective voice in the exit, voice and loyalty tradition (Hirschman, 1970; Rusbult, Farrell, Rogers and Mainous III, 1988; Withey and Cooper, 1989). Exit, voice and loyalty models state that people may react in a number of ways to dissatisfying situations. According to Rusbult et al.'s (1988) exit, voice, loyalty and neglect model, these reactions can be categorised on the dimensions constructive-destructive and active-passive. Voice is characterised as a constructive and active response to dissatisfaction. Voice is active in that one actively tries to work on improving the dissatisfying situation, and constructive in the sense that one wants to improve matters but not at the cost of disrupting one's relationship with the organisation.

Considering voting during council elections a form of voice is useful because it points us to the fact that people may react in different ways to the dissatisfying situation of job insecurity. Instead of the active and constructive reaction of voting, employees may choose to be passive and not to vote during works council elections. This would be in line with the negative kind of reactions that are typically found when employees are faced with job insecurity, such as lower organisational commitment, lower job satisfaction and higher intention to leave the organisation.

An important question is what determines who chooses the voice option, and participates in a works council, and who chooses not to do so. Exit, voice and loyalty models show us some likely moderators of the relationship between job insecurity and works council participation. Withey and Cooper (1989) argue that employees will choose for voice when they are satisfied about their jobs, feel committed to their organisation and have the idea that voice is effective. Rusbult et al. (1988) state similar predictions: voice is more likely when the investments in one's work or in the organisation are high (e.g. because one has worked in the same organisation for a long time), and when job satisfaction is high. Indeed, the studies that Rusbult et al. (1988) report, show that voice is related positively to job satisfaction and investments.

Both studies differ both theoretically and empirically when it comes to the role of the quality of alternatives for the current situation. Rusbult et al. (1988) state that the availability of alternatives motivates employees to respond actively to dissatisfaction (exit or voice). The authors consider alternatives 'a source of power for bringing about change'. On the other hand, Withey and Cooper (1989) propose that having high quality alternatives promotes destructive reactions because the costs of a deteriorating relationship with one's employer are relatively low. Whereas Rusbult et al. find their predictions confirmed in their studies (that is, a positive relation between voice and the quality of alternatives), Withey and Cooper find no relation between the quality of alternatives and destructive reactions.

What matters most here, is that it is clear that reactions to job insecurity will vary between individuals and that part of this variation can be explained by factors like organisational commitment, job satisfaction and the quality of alternatives. In our first three hypotheses we assume that participation in the works council, as a form of voice, is more likely among employees who experience their work and their organisation as attractive. In all hypotheses that follow, by participation in the works council we mean the intention to use the right to vote during council elections and the intention to stand for council membership. Attractive work and organisation is expressed by high job satisfaction (Hypothesis 1), high organisational commitment (Hypothesis 2) or positive career expectations (Hypothesis 3). This leads us to the following hypotheses:

Hypothesis 1: Employees who combine job insecurity with high job satisfaction have a higher intention to participate in the works council.

Hypothesis 2: Employees who combine job insecurity with high organisational commitment have a higher intention to participate in the works council.

Hypothesis 3: Employees who combine job insecurity with positive career expectations have a higher intention to participate in the works council.

The fourth hypothesis is based on Rusbult et al.'s (1988) findings that constructive reactions to dissatisfaction are more likely when investment is high:

Hypothesis 4: Employees who combine job insecurity with high investments have a higher intention to participate in the works council.

The fifth hypothesis deals with the availability of alternatives. Rusbult et al. (1988) find that active reactions (among which voice) are enhanced when alternatives for the present situation are available:

Hypothesis 5: Employees who combine job insecurity with the availability of alternatives have a higher intention to participate in the works council.

Our sixth hypothesis is derived from Withey and Coopers' (1989) finding that voice is more likely when employees think that voice is effective. We used the concept of trust in the works council as an indicator of perceived effectiveness. Mishra (1996) stated that trust involves the willingness to feel vulnerable to another party, based on the conviction that the latter party is competent, concerned and reliable. Thus, employees who trust the works council and it's members, are convinced that the works council is a competent and reliable body. This may make them more willing to participate in the works council. This leads to our final hypothesis:

Hypothesis 6: Employees who combine job insecurity with high trust in the works council have a higher intention to participate in the works council.

Method

Data collection The data used in this study are part of a larger study on works councils. The data presented in this chapter are based on a questionnaire sent to employees in municipal organisations at the end of 1998. The survey consisted of several questions, including the intention to participate in the works council, job insecurity and the moderator variables mentioned in our hypotheses.

Sample and respondents A stratified sample of 108 works councils was selected from the total population of works councils in municipal organisations in the Netherlands. The sample was stratified according to size of the town where the works councils were seated in order to get a sample that included work councils in both small and big towns. Because works councils in small towns dominate the population of councils, a stratified sample procedure was used to make sure that the sample would include councils in both small and big towns.

The selected councils were requested to participate and 75 (69 per cent) agreed to do so. Next, management of the organisations where these 75 councils were seated were approached to ask for their cooperation in taking a sample of employees, which 56 (75 per cent) organisations agreed to do. Those samples were taken in a variety of organisations, ranging from a small museum in a major city to a big civic centre in a rural district. Organisation size ranged from very small (15 or less employees) to very large (for example, more than 1,000 employees).

Depending on the size of the organisation, a random sample was taken of 60, 40, 20 or 15 employees. A total of 2,299 employees were sampled and 1,021 (44 per cent) responded to the questionnaire. The mean age of the respondents who responded to both questionnaires was 42.4 years (*SD*=9.55 years). Dutch municipal organisations use a job ranking system to scale jobs. This scale ranges from 1, the lowest level, to 16, the highest level. The mean scale level of the respondents was 7.9 (*SD*=2.6). Most respondents were male (67.7 per cent) and 44 per cent were trade union members. The respondents were active in a variety of jobs, ranging from public park keeper to accountant or policymaker.

The Questionnaire

Dependent variables We measured *participation in the works council* by asking the respondents how likely it is that they would vote for the works council or stand for works council membership. The *intention to vote* for the works council was measured using a single item: If works council elections were to be held now, how likely is it that you would vote? The question measuring the *intention to become a works council candidate* was phrased as follows: If works council elections were to be held now, how likely is it that you would become a works council candidate? The respondents were asked to place their answers on a scale ranging from 0 per cent to 100 per cent.

Independent variables Job insecurity was assessed with three items: 'How likely is it that in the near future you will become unemployed?'; 'How likely is it that in the near future there will be involuntary dismissals in your organisation?' and 'How likely is it that in the near future your tasks will change as the result of a reorganisation?'. All responses were made on 5-poing scales (1=*very unlikely*, 5=*very likely*) and were averaged to form a composite measure of job insecurity (Cronbach's Alpha is 0.66; *M*=2.21; *SD*=0.71).

Affective organisational commitment was measured using five items originating from the Meyer, Allan and Smith (1993) measure of affective commitment. Affective commitment refers to commitment based on identification with the organisation. Examples are: 'I feel emotionally attached to this organisation' and 'This organisation has a great deal of personal meaning for me'. All responses were made on 5-point scales (1=*completely disagree*, 5=*completely agree*) and were averaged to form a composite measure of organisational commitment (Cronbach's alpha is 0.83; *M*=3.32; *SD*=0.72).

We assessed *Trust in the works council* with seven items originating from the short version of the Organisational Trust Inventory (Cummings and Bromiley, 1996). We reworded the items somewhat to adapt them to the specific context. Examples are, 'I feel that the works council will keep its word' and 'I feel that the works council tries to get out of its commitments'. All responses were made on 5-point scales (1=*completely disagree*, 5=*completely agree*) and were averaged to form a scale of trust (Cronbach's Alpha is 0.86; *M*=3.75; *SD*=0.50).

Career expectations was assessed using a 3-item scale earlier used by Acampo, Kunst and Soeters (1987). The items were: 'What are your chances of obtaining a higher position within your organisation?'; 'How much experience do you still gain in your present job?' and 'How many possibilities does your current job offer you to develop your skills and knowledge?'. Again, responses were made on a 5-point scale (1=*very little*, 5=*very much*) and averaged to form a scale (Cronbach's Alpha is 0.70; *M*=2.92; *SD*=0.73).

The availability of *alternatives* was measured using one item: 'What are your chances of getting a better job outside of the organisation you currently work?' (1=*very small*, 5=*very substantial*; *M*=2.66; *SD*=1.04).

Job satisfaction was assessed using a one item measure: 'How satisfied are you in general about your work?'. Respondents answered on a 5-points scale ranging from (1) *very unsatisfied* to (5) *very satisfied* (*M*=3.94; *SD*=0.71). A meta-analysis of research in which single-item measures of overall job satisfaction are correlated with multi-item measures of job satisfaction, shows that the use of a single-item measure of overall job satisfaction is acceptable in terms of both reliability and validity (Wanous, Reichers and Hudy, 1997).

Investment was assessed using the number of year employees had worked in their organisation (*M*=13.5; *SD*=9.3).

Table 4.1 summarises the measures and reports their intercorrelations.

Results

Table 4.2 shows the level of job insecurity among our respondents. Job insecurity is not high when the total job is concerned: 4.7 per cent of the respondents think that the chances are high or very high that there will be involuntary dismissals in their organisation. No more than 2.1 per cent think that their own job is at stake. There is however a substantial group of respondents (24.8 per cent) that expect their job will change because of a reorganisation.

Table 4.1 Means, standarddeviatons and correlations of the measures used (917<n<1,020)

	1	2	3	4	5	6	7	8	9	10	11	12	13
1. Job insecurity	-												
2. Intention to vote for the works council	-0.02	-											
3. Intention to become a works council candidate	0.01	0.16	-										
4. Age	-0.02	0.11	0.02	-									
5. Sex (F/M)	-0.01	0.08	0.12	0.34	-								
6. Union member (N/Y)	0.05	0.16	0.13	0.26	0.17	-							
7. Job rank	0.01	0.16	-0.01	0.19	0.18	0.19	-						
8. Organisational commitment	-0.05	0.11	0.07	0.19	0.09	0.01	-0.01	-					
9. Trust in works council	-0.05	0.30	0.08	0.06	0.02	0.03	0.07	0.08	-				
10. Investment	-0.02	0.07	-0.03	0.64	0.30	0.22	0.07	0.24	0.06	-			
11. Career expectations	-0.04	0.05	0.00	-0.24	-0.03	-0.06	0.16	0.21	0.07	-0.22	-		
12. Alternatives	0.04	0.06	0.11	-0.46	-0.07	-0.07	0.15	-0.14	-0.00	-0.44	0.33	-	
13. Job satisfaction	-0.14	0.03	0.00	-0.02	-0.01	-0.02	-0.00	0.39	0.11	-0.00	0.38	-0.03	-
M	2.21	87.85	12.30	42.39	0.68	0.44	7.90	3.32	3.75	13.45	2.92	2.66	3.95
SD	0.71	23.69	22.52	9.55	0.47	0.50	2.64	0.72	0.50	9.26	0.73	1.04	0.71

All correlations >0.06 are significant (p<0.05).

Table 4.2   Job insecurity among Dutch municipal employees, in per cent

What are the chances that ...	(Very) unlikely	Neutral	(Very) likely
in the near future there will be involuntary dismissals in your organisation	83.8	14.2	2.1
you will become unemployed	73.8	21.5	4.7
your job will change because of a reorganisation	42.2	33.0	24.8

Job Insecurity and Voting during Works Council Elections

In Table 4.3 we report the results of a hierarchical multiple regression analysis on the intention to vote during works council elections. In the first model we entered demographic variables and in the second model the main effects of job insecurity and all the hypothesised moderator variables were added (these variables were: organisational commitment, trust in the works council, alternatives, job satisfaction, investment and career perspective). In the final model the interactions of job insecurity with the moderator variables were also included.[2]

The final model is significant, $F(17,859)=8.84$; $p<0.001$, and explains 13 per cent of the differences in the intention to vote. Important for our hypotheses, adding the interactions in Model 3 significantly added variance to the model over and above the main effects, R^2 change=0.02; $p<0.05$. In the final model, there is no direct relationship between job insecurity and the intention to vote for the works council (β=-0.03; *n.s.*). There are, and this is in line with our Hypotheses 1, 2 and 6, indirect effects of job insecurity on the intention to vote: Model 3 shows interactions of job insecurity with trust in the works council (β=0.07; $p<0.05$), job satisfaction (β=-0.08; $p<0.05$), and organisational commitment (β=0.11; $p<0.01$). The data do not confirm our hypotheses regarding the interaction of job insecurity with career perspective (Hypothesis 3), investment (Hypothesis 4) and the availability of alternatives (Hypothesis 5).

The strongest predictor of the intention to vote during works council elections is trust in the works council: employees that trust the works council have a higher intention to vote than their colleagues who do not trust the works council (β=0.27; $p<0.001$). The intention to vote during works council elections is also positively associated with organisational commitment: employed who feel committed to their organisation have a higher intention to vote than employees who feel less committed to the organisation (β=0.11; $p<0.01$). Having alternatives for the current situation at work is also associated in a positive way with the intention to vote (β=0.10; $p<0.01$).

Two personal characteristics are associated with the intention to vote during works council elections. Union members and employees with a relatively high job rank are more likely to vote than non-union members or employees with a relatively low rank (respectively β=0.12; p<0.001 and β=0.09; p<0.05).

Table 4.3 **Regression of the intention to vote during works council elections on the predictors (n=877)**

	Model 1 β	Model 2 β	Model 3 β
Demographic variables			
Age	0.04	0.06	0.06
Sex (F/M)	0.04	0.03	0.03
Job rank	0.12**	0.09*	0.09*
Union member (N/Y)	0.12**	0.12***	0.12***
Main effects			
Job insecurity (JI)		-0.02	-0.03
Trust in works council		0.27***	0.27***
Career expectations		-0.03	-0.04
Alternatives		0.10**	0.10**
Job satisfaction		-0.03	-0.03
Organisational commitment		0.11**	0.11**
Investment		-0.01	-0.01
Interactions with job insecurity			
JI x Trust in works council			0.07*
JI x Career expectations			-0.04
JI x Alternatives			0.05
JI x Job satisfaction			-0.08*
JI x Organisational commitment			0.11**
JI x Investment			0.01
R^2 (adj.)	0.04***	0.12***	0.13***
R^2 change	0.04***	0.08***	0.02*
F	9.74***	12.21***	8.84***
D.f.	4,872	11,865	17,859

* p<0.05; ** p<0.01; *** p<0.001

In Table 4.4 we illustrate the nature of the interaction effects established in our regression analysis. In order to interpret the interactions we first used a median split to dichotomise the variables. Then we crossed job insecurity with organisational commitment, trust and job satisfaction. The means of the intention to vote are shown for different combinations of job insecurity and organisational commitment, trust in the works council and job satisfaction.

Table 4.4   Means and standard deviations of the intention to vote during works council elections

Job insecurity		Organisational commitment		Trust in works council		Job satisfaction	
		Low	High	Low	High	Low	High
Low	M	87.5	89.0	83.1	93.4	89.4	88.2
	(SD)	(24.8)	(22.8)	(28.5)	(16.5)	(24.9)	(23.5)
High	M	83.5	90.9	82.5	94.9	84.5	88.3
	(SD)	(28.6)	(17.3)	(27.0)	(13.4)	(25.2)	(22.9)

The intention to vote is lowest when high job insecurity is combined with low organisational commitment ($M=83.5$; $SD=28.6$), low trust in the works council ($M=82.5$; $SD=27.0$) or low job satisfaction ($M=84.5$; $SD=25.2$). Thus, voting during works council election becomes less likely when the feeling of job insecurity is not combined with a positive attitude towards the organisation (organisational commitment), towards work (job satisfaction) or towards the works council (trust in the works council). This pattern is somewhat different from the pattern we expected. If voting during works council elections is a kind of voice, one would expect that the means of the intention to vote are higher when job insecurity is combined with high organisational commitment, high job satisfaction or high trust in the works council than the means of all other cells. However, the results in Table 4.4 show a different pattern: the cells that are different from the rest are the cells where high insecurity is combined with the absence of positive attitudes towards either the job, the organisation or the works council. It appears that the norm is to vote during works council elections, and that refraining from using the right to vote is a kind of exit or neglect: a destructive reaction to a dissatisfying situation. We will deal with this issue in the discussion.

Job Insecurity and the Intention to become a Works Council Candidate

Table 4.5 shows the results of three regression analyses where the intention to become a works council candidate is regressed on the predictors. The results show that there is no direct relationship between job insecurity and the intention to become a works council candidate. We also do not find any support for our hypotheses concerning the interaction effects of job insecurity and the six moderators.

In Model 3 we are able to explain only 5 per cent of the variance in the intention to become a works council candidate. Demographic differences account for 3 per cent of the variance (see Model 1): the highest intention to become a works council candidate is found among men, among employees with a relatively low rank within the organisation and among union members (respectively $\beta=0.09$, $p<0.05$; $\beta=-0.09$, $p<0.05$; $\beta=0.16$, $p<0.001$).

Surprisingly, the strongest predictor of the intention to become a works council candidate is the availability of alternatives for the present situation (β=0.17; p<0.001). Employees with good alternatives have a higher intention to become a works council candidate. The intention to become a works council candidate is also somewhat higher among employees with high organisational commitment (β=0.09; p<0.05), high trust in the works council (β=0.07; p<0.05), and relatively few investments in the organisation (β=-0.09; p<0.05).

Table 4.5 Regression of the intention to become a works council candidate on the predictors (n=880)

	Model 1 $\underline{\beta}$	Model 2 $\underline{\beta}$	Model 3 $\underline{\beta}$
Demographic variables			
Age	-0.02	0.08	0.08
Sex (F/M)	0.10**	0.09*	0.09*
Job rank	-0.06	-0.09*	-0.09*
Union member (N/Y)	0.14***	0.15***	0.16***
Main effects			
Job insecurity (JI)		-0.01	-0.02
Trust in works council		0.08*	0.07*
Career expectations		-0.06	-0.07
Alternatives		0.16***	0.17***
Job satisfaction		-0.03	-0.03
Organisational commitment		0.09*	0.09*
Investment		-0.10*	-0.09*
Interactions with job insecurity			
JI x Trust in works council			0.05
JI x Career expectations			-0.06
JI x Alternatives			0.01
JI x Job satisfaction			0.03
JI x Organisational commitment			-0.04
JI x Investment			0.03
$\underline{R^2}$ (adj.)	0.03***	0.05***	0.05***
$\underline{R^2}$ change	0.03***	0.04***	0.01
$\underline{F}$	6.82	5.47	3.90
$\underline{D.f.}$	4,875	11,868	17,862

* p<0.05; ** p<0.01; p<0.001

Discussion

In this chapter we explored the effect of job insecurity on works council participation. Using exit, voice and loyalty models (Hirschmann, 1970; Rusbult et al., 1988; Withey and Cooper, 1989), we presented works council participation as a kind of voice: a constructive and active way of reacting to a dissatisfying situation. Based on exit, voice and loyalty models, we predicted that job insecurity will only lead to voice when it is experienced in an environment that is attractive to the employee. Whether the environment is attractive, was assessed by asking employees about their job satisfaction, organisational commitment and career perspectives. Moreover, we predicted that works council participation as a reaction to job insecurity is more likely when alternatives for the current situation at work are available, when the works council is perceived as trustworthy and when the investments in the organisation are high.

The results of our study indicate that the intention to vote during works council elections can indeed be predicted by the interaction of job insecurity with job satisfaction, organisational commitment and trust in the works council. However, the pattern of the interactions was somewhat different from our predictions. We expected to find the strongest intention to vote among employees who experienced both job insecurity and high organisational commitment, job satisfaction or trust in the works council. This pattern was not confirmed by our data. The intention to vote during works council elections was lowest among employees combing job insecurity with low organisational commitment, job satisfaction or trust in the works council.

An explanation for these results may be that we considered voting during works council elections a kind of voice. Given the results however, it is the question whether voting should be considered voice or not voting a kind of neglect. During the municipal works council elections in 1996 over 70 per cent of the employees voted. In our study the mean intention to vote was 88 on a 100-point scale. Thus, voting seems to be the norm. Possibly, when one wants to express one's dissatisfaction it may make more sense not to vote than to vote, since the latter is what most employees do anyway. In such a view, not voting is a way of neglect: a passive and destructive reaction to dissatisfaction.

Voting during works council elections can be considered a kind of extra role behaviour: behaviour that is not prescribed in the job description, and that is under personal control of the employee. Extra role behaviour is more likely when employees have positive experiences at work, for example because decision making procedures are perceived as fair, the leadership as supportive and the tasks as intrinsically satisfying (see Podsakoff, MacKenzie, Paine and Bachrach, 2000 for an overview). For most employees, job insecurity is a negative experience. When this negative experience is not counterbalanced by other positive experiences, as expressed in commitment or satisfaction, employees start to refrain from behaviours that they don't consider necessary for performing their required tasks. Our results indicate that for many employees voting during works council elections is such a behaviour.

Whereas we did find support for our predictions concerning voting, none of our hypotheses concerning the intention to become a works council candidate could be confirmed. Job insecurity did not have any direct or indirect effects on the intention to become a works council candidate. Maybe, becoming a works council candidate is to much of an effort when compared to voting, while the benefits of being a works council member for one's job insecurity may not be entirely clear. Cohen (1993) and McLean Parks, Gallagher and Fullagar (1995) show that union participation has several dimensions that should not be treated as one. Our data indicate that works council participation may also consist of several dimensions. For example, in our study the correlation between the intention to vote and the intention to stand for candidate is only 0.16. Future research should focus on disentangling the different dimension of works council participation and their determinants.

The best predictor for becoming a works council candidate in our study was being a union member and the availability of alternatives: employees who think they can easily find a job elsewhere, have a higher intention to become a candidate for the works council than employees who have fewer alternatives for their situation. This is in line with Rusbult et al.'s (1988) finding that the availability of alternatives is associated positively with active reactions (among which voice) to dissatisfaction. Maybe employees consider becoming a works council candidate a risky kind of behaviour that can only be conducted when there are alternatives available in case things go wrong. Given the growing problems of works councils in mobilising employees more research is needed on the reasons of employees to become (or not to become) a works council candidate.

The results of our study should be interpreted with care. We did not measure actual participation. We do not know whether the employees that stated their intention to vote or to become a works council candidate have indeed started to participate in works council activities. We should be careful with assuming that the intention to become works council candidate is strongly associated with the act of actually becoming one. Especially in the case of the intention to become a candidate one should be careful about drawing strong conclusions based on a study about the intention to become a candidate. In a study on union participation, De Witte (1988) showed that being asked to become a works council candidate is the most important predictor of becoming an active union member.

Despite these limitations, we believe our study adds to the knowledge about participation and job insecurity. Our results indicate that employee reactions to job insecurity depend partly on how attractive their organisation or work situation is to them. An attractive work environment may prevent employees from reacting in a negative way to job insecurity. In future research, the attractiveness of several aspects of the work environment should be included as a moderator if we want to understand how employees react to job insecurity.

References

Acampo, J., Kunst, P. and Soeters, J. (1987), 'OR-lidmaatschap en loopbaanperspectief', *Tijdschrift voor Arbeidsvraagstukken,* Vol. 3, pp. 37-49.

Aiken, L.S. and West, S.G. (1991), *Multiple Regression: Testing and Interpreting Interactions,* Sage, Newbury Park, CA.

Allen, N.J. and Meyer, J.P. (1990), 'The Measurement and Antecedents of Affective, Continuance and Normative Commitment to the Organization', *Journal of Occupational Psychology,* Vol. 63, pp. 1-18.

Ashford, S.J., Lee, C. and Bobko, P. (1989), 'Content, Causes, and Consequences of Job Insecurity: A Theory-based Measure and Substantive Test', *Academy of Management Journal,* Vol. 32, pp. 803-29.

Borg, I. (1989), 'Korrelate der subjektiven Sicherheit der Arbeitsstelle', *Zeitschrift der Arbeits- und Organisationspsychologie,* Vol. 33, pp. 117-24.

Cohen, A. (1993), 'An Empirical Assessment of the Multidimensionality of Union Participation', *Journal of Management,* Vol. 19(4), pp. 749-73.

Cummings, L.L. and Bromiley, P. (1996), 'The Organizational Trust Inventory (OTI): Development and Validation' in R.M. Kramer and T.R. Tyler (eds), *Trust in Organizations. Frontiers of Theory and Research,* pp. 302-30, Sage Publications, London.

De Witte, H. (1988), 'Waarom worden jongeren militant in een vakbond? Een onderzoek naar de factoren die bepalen dat jongeren als militant actief worden in de christelijke vakbond in Vlaanderen', *Tijdschrift voor Arbeid en Bewustzijn,* Vol. 12, pp. 221-47.

Hirschmann, A.O. (1970), *Exit. Voice, and Loyalty: Reactions to Decline in Firms, Organizations and States,* Harvard University Press, Cambridge, MA.

Hövels, B.W.M. and Nas, P. (1976), *Ondernemingsraden en medezeggenschap: een vergelijkend onderzoek naar struktuur en werkwijze van ondernemingsraden* [Works Councils and Participation: A Comparative Study into the Stucture and Working Methods of Works Councils], Samson, Alphen aan den Rijn, The Netherlands.

Kerkhof, P. and Klandermans, P.G. (1994), 'Van centraal overleg naar decentraal onderhandelen: vakbondsleden over de principes en uitkomsten van de veranderende arbeidsverhoudingen binnen de Nederlandse gemeenten', *Tijdschrift voor Arbeidsvraagstukken,* Vol. 10, pp. 54-67.

Kerkhof, P. and Klandermans, P.G. (1998a), *Medezeggenschap beter geregeld? Ervaringen,* A+O Fonds Gemeenten, Den Haag.

Kerkhof, P. and Klandermans, P.G. (1998b), *Ondernemingsraden in Nederlandse gemeenten. Nulmeting,* A+O Fonds Gemeenten, Den Haag.

Klandermans, B. and Visser, J. (1995), *De vakbeweging na de welvaartsstaat,* Van Gorcum, Assen.

Lord, A. and Hartley, J. (1998), 'Organizational Commitment and Job Insecurity in a Changing Public Service Organization', *European Journal of Work and Organizational Psychology,* Vol. 7, pp. 341-54.

McLean Parks, J., Gallagher, D.G. and Fullagar, C.J.A. (1995), 'Operationalizing the Outcomes of Union Commitment: The Dimensionality of Participation', *Journal of Organizational Behavior,* Vol. 16, pp. 533-55.

Meyer, J.P., Allen, N. and Smith, C. (1993), 'Commitment to Organizations and Occupations: Extension and Test of a Three-component Conceptualization', *Journal of Applied Psychology*, Vol. 78, pp. 538-51.

Mishra, A. (1996), 'Organizational Responses to Crisis: The Centrality of Trust' in R.M. Kramer and T.R. Kramer (eds), *Trust in Organizations: Frontiers of Theory and Research*, Sage, Thousand Oaks, CA, pp. 16-38.

Podsakoff, P.M, MacKenzie, S.B, Paine, J.B. and Bachrach, D.G. (2000), 'Organizational Citizenship Behaviors: A Critical Review of the Theoretical and Empirical Literature and Suggestions for Future Research', *Journal of Management*, Vol. 26(3), pp. 513-63.

Rogers, J. and Streeck, W. (eds) (1995), 'The Study of Works Councils: Concepts and Problems' in J. Rogers and W. Streeck (eds), *Works Councils: Consultation, Representation and Co-operation in Industrial Relations*, pp. 3-26, University of Chicago Press, Chicago /London.

Rosenblatt, Z. and Ruvio, A. (1996), 'A Test of a Multidimensional Model of Job Insecurity: the Case of Israeli Teachers', *Journal of Organizational Behavior*, Vol. 17, pp. 587-605.

Rosenblatt, Z. and Ruvio, A. (2000), 'Job Insecurity among Secondary Schoolteachers in Israel: A Multidimensional Approach', *Megamot - Behavioral Sciences Quarterly*, pp. 468-511.

Roskies, E. and Louis-Guerin, C. (1990), 'Job Insecurity in Managers: Antecedents and Consequences', *Journal of Organizational Behavior*, Vol. 11, pp. 345-59.

Rusbult, C.E., Farrell, D., Rogers, G. and Mainous III, A.G. (1988), 'Impact of Exchange Variables on Exit, Voice, Loyalty, and Neglect: An Integrative Model of Responses to Declining Job Satisfaction', *Academy of Management Journal*, Vol. 31, pp. 599-627.

Sverke, M., Hellgren, J. and Näswall, K. (2002), 'No Security: A Meta-analysis and Review of Job Insecurity and its Consequences', *Journal of Occupational Health Psychology*, Vol. 7(3), pp. 242-64.

Teulings, A.W.M. (1981), *Ondernemingsraadpolitiek in Nederland*, Van Gennep, Amsterdam.

van de Vijver, O. and Leenders, P. (1997), 'Tien jaar veranderingen bij de gemeenten' in *Twintig jaar gemeenten: reflectie en perspectief*, A+O Fonds Gemeenten, Den Haag.

van het Kaar, R.H. and Looise, F. (1999), *De volwassen OR. Groei en grenzen van de Nederlandse ondernemingsraad. Resultaten van het grote OR-onderzoek*, Samson, Alphen aan den Rijn.

Visser, J. (1995), 'The Netherlands: From Paternalism to Representation' in J. Rogers and W. Streeck (eds), *Works Councils: Consultation, Representation and Co-operation in Industrial Relations*, pp. 79-114, University of Chicago Press, Chicago/London.

Wanous, J.P., Reichers, A.E. and Hudy, M.J. (1997), 'Overall Job Satisfaction: How Good Are Single-item Measures?', *Journal of Applied Psychology*, Vol. 82, pp. 247-52.

Winder, A.B., Kerkhof, P. and Klandermans, B. (2000), *Medezeggenschap in kaart. Een onderzoek naar de positie van de ondernemingsraad binnen de Nederlandse gemeenten*, Stichting Arbeidsmarkt- en Opleidingsfonds Gemeenten, Den Haag.

Withey, M.J. and Cooper, W.H. (1989), 'Predicting Exit, Voice, Loyalty, and Neglect', *Administrative Science Quarterly,* Vol. 34, pp. 521-39.

Notes

1 This research was supported by the Labour market and Education Fund in the municipal sector (A+O Fonds Gemeenten).
2 All the variables were standardised before we calculated the interaction-terms (see Aiken and West, 1991).

Chapter 5

Job Insecurity, Union Participation and the Need for (New) Union Services

Sjoerd Goslinga

Introduction

Job insecurity, or uncertainty about involuntary changes in a job or about the continuity of employment, is generally viewed as a highly stressful experience for employees (Hartley, Jacobson, Klandermans and Van Vuuren, 1991; Sverke, Hellgren and Näswall, 2002). Consequently, most of the research on job insecurity has focussed on the (negative) consequences of job insecurity and on the ways in which employees cope with this stressor in their working life. Largely neglected in the literature, however, are the consequences of job insecurity for trade unions and the importance of trade unions for employees who experience job insecurity. The main purpose of the present study is to examine whether trade unions are functional for employees who experience feelings of job insecurity. First, we will examine to what extent union members who experience job insecurity differ from members who do not feel insecure about (the future of) their job in the way they participate in their union and in union activities. Secondly, we will examine whether secure and insecure union members have different expectations about their union and different needs regarding the information and services their union provides.

In this chapter, we will depart from a stress perspective on job insecurity. In a very general sense, a stressful situation can be defined as a situation in which an individual experiences deprivation of control. Rothbaum, Weisz and Snyder (1982) distinguish between two types of reactions to control deprivation: (1) primary control; an attempt to bring the environment in line with their wishes; and, if primary control is unsuccessful or impossible, (2) secondary control; attempts to bring themselves in line with environmental forces. Averill (1973) makes a similar distinction and labels this second type of re-establishment of control 'cognitive control'. If people fail to restore control in one way or another, this can have detrimental effects on their well-being. In a work-environment, especially the second type of reaction to deprivation of control (bringing oneself in line with the environment) will be important, because most employees' possibilities of changing the work-environment are very limited (Greenberger and Strasser, 1986).

That job insecurity is an important stressor with negative outcomes for employees, has been confirmed in the empirical studies that have been conducted in the past fifteen years (see also Sverke, Hellgren and Näswall, 2002). For example, Ashford, Lee and Bobko (1989) examined the relationships between job insecurity and several outcome variables. They found that job insecurity is associated with lower levels of organisational commitment, lower trust in the organisation, lower job satisfaction and a stronger intention to quit one's job. Similar results were reported by Lim (1996). Her study found significant relationships between job insecurity and job dissatisfaction, proactive job search, noncompliant job behaviours and life dissatisfaction. In addition, a study by Van Vuuren, Van Gastel and Klandermans (1988) found that job insecure employees were less satisfied with their work and felt less happy than those without feelings of insecurity.

Research has also focussed on the ways in which employees cope with job insecurity and on the factors that protect or buffer employees against the negative consequences of job insecurity. Lim (1996) found evidence for moderating effects of work-based social support (support from colleagues and supervisors) and non work-based social support (support from family and friends) on the relationship between job insecurity and several work-related and health-related outcomes variables. Her study suggests that support provided by others at work reduces the effects of job insecurity on job dissatisfaction, proactive job search and noncompliant behaviour at work. Support derived from family and friends can buffer insecure employees against the negative effects of job insecurity for psychological well-being, such as life satisfaction. Thus, support seems to help people to accept the changes in their work-environment and to adapt to the changed situation. We expect that in this process unions can also play a role. By providing support and information to their members, particularly during a period of reorganisation or downsizing, unions or union representatives can act as support providing others and in this way help their members to cope with job insecurity. Hence, a positive relationship between perceived support from the union and lower levels of job insecurity is expected.

A perspective on the consequences of job insecurity offered by Casey, Miller and Johnson (1997), suggests still other ways in which unions might be helpful for employees in coping with job insecurity. Casey et al. examined employees' information-seeking behaviours before and after a permanent reduction in the workforce of an insurance company. Consistent with the remarks made earlier about the process of secondary control (or cognitive control), these authors hypothesised that following a reduction in workforce employees who remained would seek information to reduce their uncertainty. More specifically, they expected and found that more covert information seeking behaviours, such as observation and approaching outsiders or third parties, increased; and that more overt information seeking behaviours, such as asking questions at colleagues or supervisors, decreased. This third party information-seeking strategy will be used when a primary source is unavailable, when the message of the primary source has been unclear or when the interaction would be uncomfortable (cf. Weiss, Ilgen and Sharbaugh, 1982). Casey et al. (1997) also remark that 'The act of engaging in information seeking may in itself be a coping mechanism for these employees by producing a perception of exerting control over one's situation' (p.757). Unions, in this respect, might function as a third party union members can approach when confronted with job insecurity and in need for reliable information. Therefore, union members with feelings of job insecurity are expected to have a higher need for information and will have more appreciation for the union to provide this information than secure members. These hypotheses will be examined in Study 2.

In studies conducted by Van Vuuren and colleagues (Van Vuuren, Van Gastel and Klandermans, 1988; Van Vuuren, Klandermans, Jacobson and Hartley, 1991), attention was explicitly devoted to the role unions play for employees who experience job insecurity. Apart from employees' individual reactions to job insecurity, these studies also addressed collective responses to job insecurity. Van Vuuren et al. (1991) distinguish between three types of reactions to job insecurity: (1) avoidance; (2) individual action; and (3) collective action. They argue that 'While some people react to job insecurity by withdrawing from their work psychologically, other people choose to attempt to restore their job security either by individual or by collective action' (p.82). Avoidance is a passive reaction, whereby an employee takes distance from the job and the situation of the organisation. Individual action means actively looking for (information about) another job. Different types of collective action were included in their studies: voting for the works council, union membership or the attitude toward union membership, union participation (such as the attendance of union meetings), the attitude toward moderate and militant industrial action, and the willingness to participate in moderate and militant industrial action (Van Vuuren, Van Gastel and Klandermans, 1988).

In their studies Van Vuuren et al. found positive associations between job insecurity and avoidance and between job insecurity and individual action of employees. No differences between employees who felt insecure about their job and employees who did not feel insecure emerged in union participation and voting for the works council. In one of their studies they found a relationship between job insecurity and the attitude towards industrial action as well as between job insecurity and the willingness to participate in industrial action (Van Vuuren et al., 1991). In another study, however, these relationships did not emerge (Van Vuuren, Van Gastel and Klandermans, 1988). Whether job insecurity is related to actual participation in industrial action still remains a question, because only the intention to participate was examined in these studies. However, as was mentioned earlier, the reaction to insecurity (or lack of control) that is most likely to occur in a work setting is secondary (or cognitive) control. Collective protest is a form of primary control; an attempt to (collectively) change the environment. Therefore, we expect that collective protest is not an obvious reaction to job insecurity.

The absence of a relationship between job insecurity and union participation that was found in the studies reported by Van Vuuren et al. does not necessarily mean job insecurity does not affect union participation. Van Vuuren et al. used a composite measure to assess union participation that was limited in scope: only a few types of participation were included. In doing so, differences between specific types of participation were neglected. Existing literature suggests that different motives and processes underlie different types of participation (McShane, 1986; Klandermans, 1996). The fact that different types of participation were combined in a composite score might have led to an underestimation of the relationships between job insecurity and distinct types of union participation. Therefore, in the present study we will examine the relationships between job insecurity and several distinct types of union participation. Not only the relationship between job insecurity and union participation will be examined, but also whether job insecurity can explain differences in union participation over and above two important predictors of union participation: union commitment and perceived union support.

Union commitment is an important determinant of (active) participation of union members in their union and in union activities. Higher levels of union commitment are associated with the intent to remain a union member, taking up voluntary work in or on behalf of the union, attending union meetings and participation in industrial action (see Barling, Fullagar and Kelloway, 1992; Goslinga, 2004). Perceived union support and union commitment are interrelated. This link between union commitment and perceived support is usually explained from a social exchange perspective. The idea is that commitment to an organisation is stronger when someone perceives that the organisation's commitment to himself or herself is also stronger (that means when there is a positive exchange relationship). Perceived commitment from the organisation is another way of describing the commitment that is perceived from the organisation by individual members (Eisenberger, Huntington, Hutchinson and Sowa, 1986; Rhoades, Eisenberger and Armeli, 2001). Shore, Tetrick, Sinclair and Newton (1994) applied this idea to the relation between unions and their members and developed a measure for union members' perceived support from their union. Existing research suggests that union commitment and perceived union support characterise the relationship between members and their union and determine the way in which members participate in their union (see also Goslinga, 1996).

To sum up, the two studies that will be presented in this paper address the following two general questions: (1) are feelings of job insecurity related to (specific types of) participation in a trade union and trade union activities?; and (2) does the need for information and advice increase as feelings of job insecurity are stronger, and to what extent do union members expect and/or appreciate this information and advice to be provided by their union?

Study 1: Job Insecurity and Union Participation

Method

Procedure and sample Data for this study were collected in one wave of a longitudinal telephone survey among members of the largest trade unions affiliated with the National Christian Trade Union Federation (CNV). The unions belonging to the CNV-federation together have approximately 350,000 members, which makes the CNV the second largest trade union federation in The Netherlands. Among these unions are six public sector unions and three private sector unions.[1]

Random samples of between 100 and 150 members per union were interviewed by telephone. The interviews on average took about 25 minutes. Before the first interview the selected members received a letter from their union with some explanation about the procedure and goal of the study and the request to participate.

Respondents For the present study we used data from the members who participated in the first survey of 1998. The total sample consisted of 830 union members. In order to analyse the relationships between job insecurity and job satisfaction on the one hand and union participation on the other hand, the sample was limited to union members with a paid job (N=658). All respondents with missing data on one or more of the items in the survey were excluded, which resulted in 566 union members with complete data sets (80 per cent male, 20 per cent female). The mean age of the sample was 42 years, ranging between 19 and 61 years. The average length of union membership was 13 years, ranging between less than a year and 40 years. The majority of the respondents had a full-time job (86 per cent); 14 per cent was employed part-time.

Measures Job insecurity was measured with three items: 'What are the chances you will become unemployed in the near future?'; 'What are the chances there will be lay-offs in your company in the near future?'; 'What are the chances your job will change because of reorganisations in the near future?'. The items were scored on 5-point scales with anchors ranging from (1) very small or non-existent to (5) very big. The Cronbach alpha yielded by the three items was 0.60.

To measure *union commitment* a modified version of Meyer, Allen and Smith's (1993) affective organisational commitment scale was used. The original scale was translated to Dutch and the wording of the items were changed to fit the union context (for example, the word 'organisation' was replaced by 'union'). The scale consisted of four items (for example 'I really feel as if the union's problems are my own', 'I feel a strong sense of belonging to my union') and answers were scored on 5-point scales ranging from (1) *totally disagree* to (5) *totally agree*. Previous research yielded good reliabilities for this scale (Goslinga, 2001; 2004). In the present study the coefficient alpha was 0.82.

Perceived union support was measured with five items. The items were based on the 'perceived union support' scale developed by Shore et al. (1994) and were translated and adapted to the Dutch context (for example 'My union is always there for me whenever I have a question or problem', 'If I have a complaint my union does not give me any attention'). Answers were scored on 5-point scales ranging from (1) *totally disagree* to (5) *totally agree*. The items were combined, resulting is a scale ranging from (1) little perceived support to (5) strong perceived support. Cronbach's alpha is 0.68.

Union participation: Respondents were asked to indicate whether in the previous six months they had *attended a union meeting at work*, had *attended a union local meeting*, whether they had *participated in union activities in their company*, whether they had *participated in industrial action*, whether they had *contacted their union with a question or problem*, and whether they had called upon their union and had received *legal assistance*. In all cases attendance, participation or contact was coded '2' and no attendance, no participation or no contact was coded '1'. We also assessed whether respondents were presently *union activists* (or shop stewards) by asking whether they were holding a position in or on behalf of their union or the CNV-federation (1=no, 2=yes).

In addition to the demographic characteristics mentioned earlier, respondents' level of education (on a 7-point scale) and net monthly income (on a 8-point scale) were assessed.

Results

First, the means, standard deviations and intercorrelations of the independent variables were calculated. The data revealed that only small proportions of the sample reported strong feelings of job insecurity ($M=1.93$, $SD=0.77$). If we look at the separate items included in the job insecurity measure, the data showed that only 2.8 per cent of the sample reported that the chances they will become unemployed in the near future were big or very big, 11.3 per cent indicated that the chances of layoffs in their company were big or very big, and 21.2 per cent stated that the chances that their job will change because of reorganisations in the near future were big or very big.

Consistent with the ideas of Eisenberger et al. (1986) and Shore et al. (1994), perceived union support correlated significantly with union commitment ($r=0.34$, $p<0.001$). Job insecurity was not related to union commitment ($r=0.02$, n.s.), but job insecurity was significantly correlated with perceived union support ($r=-0.09$, $p<0.05$). In line with the expectations we found that when more support was perceived from the union, reported levels of job insecurity were lower.

Explaining differences in union participation In order to examine the extent to which union commitment, perceived union support, and job insecurity explained differences in union participation, logistic regression analyses were performed. Dependent variables were the different types of union participation. Age, level of education, income level, sex and employment status (full time versus part time) were also entered in the analyses, in order to control for differences in participation due to demographic and work characteristics. Results are displayed in Table 5.1.

The regression models explained between 10 per cent and 31 per cent of the differences in union participation. Several of the personal and work characteristics had significant effects on the different types of union participation. Age made a significant contribution to the explanation of differences in the attendance of union local meetings, in whether members held a position in the union and in participation in union activities at work. When members were older, chances that they had participated in these ways were bigger. When the level of education was higher, members more often had been in contact with their union, had participated in union activities at work and in industrial action (when actions were organised). Compared to women, men had participated in industrial action more often and members with higher income levels had received legal assistance less often than did members with lower levels of income.

With the exception of attendance of union meetings at work, participation in union activities at work and participation in industrial action, union commitment was a significant predictor of differences in union participation. When union commitment was stronger, more often members had attended a union local meeting, members held a representative position in the union, members had been in contact with their union because of a question or problem, members had participated in industrial action, and members had received legal assistance from their union. Perceived union support only had predictive value for the explanation of differences in participation in union activities at work. When perceived support was higher, more often members had participated in this way.

Job insecurity made a significant contribution to the explanation in variance of three of the seven types of union participation. Job insecurity was related to the attendance of a union meeting at work, to whether members had been in contact with their union as well as to whether members had received legal assistance. Members who experienced more job insecurity more often had attended a union meeting at work, had more often been in contact with their union and had more often received legal assistance from their union.

Discussion Study 1

The main objective of Study 1 was to examine the relationships between job insecurity and distinct types of union participation. Results from a survey among members of unions affiliated with the CNV-federation, showed that job insecurity was associated with several types of union participation. When more job insecurity was perceived, union members had more often contacted their union with a question or problem, more often had received legal assistance from their union, and more often had attended a union meeting at work. These relationships were significant even when was controlled for several important personal and work characteristics as well as union commitment and perceived union support.

Table 5.1 Results of logistic regression analyses of different types of union participation

	Attended a union meeting at work[a]		Attended a union local meeting		Holds a representative position		Contacted the union with question or problem	
	B	SE	B	SE	B	SE	B	SE
Age (young-old)	0.02	0.03	0.06**	0.02	0.06**	0.02	-0.02	0.01
Education (low-high)	0.10	0.18	0.02	0.12	-0.02	0.12	0.24**	0.09
Income (low-high)	-0.15	0.21	0.15	0.14	0.24	0.14	-0.01	0.10
Sex (male-female)	-0.06	0.90	0.02	0.52	0.44	0.50	-0.43	0.34
Employment (full-time-part-time)	-0.93	0.84	-0.29	0.60	0.26	0.55	0.65	0.38
Union commitment	-0.02	0.27	0.52**	0.20	0.95***	0.20	0.55***	0.15
Perceived union support	-0.12	0.40	0.20	0.34	0.31	0.35	0.24	0.23
Job insecurity	0.61*	0.31	-0.04	0.19	0.08	0.19	0.32*	0.13
Constant	0.02	2.60	-7.85***	1.87	-11.41***	1.97	-4.92***	1.20
-2 log	136.118		309.559		297.324		551.791	
Chi^2	8.057		33.191***		73.588***		38.225***	
R^2	0.10		0.13		0.23		0.10	

[a] Only when a union meeting was organised N=104.

* p<0.05, ** p<0.01, *** p<0.001

Table 5.1   (continued)

	Participated in activities		Participated in industrial action[b]		Received legal assistance	
	B	SE	B	SE	B	SE
Age (young-old)	0.03*	0.02	-0.04	0.04	0.04	0.03
Education (low-high)	0.34**	0.11	1.08**	0.35	0.59**	0.21
Income (low-high)	-0.10	0.12	-0.26	0.28	-0.74**	0.23
Sex (male-female)	-0.87	0.46	-2.98**	1.05	-1.35	0.86
Employment (full-time-part-time)	-0.17	0.50	0.58	0.88	-1.14	0.97
Union commitment	0.16	0.18	1.01*	0.48	0.73*	0.31
Perceived union support	0.70*	0.30	0.06	0.68	-0.58	0.46
Job insecurity	0.21	0.16	0.46	0.40	0.65*	0.26
Constant	-6.77***	1.57	3.38	3.11	-2.29	2.52
-2 log	384.595		77.083		145.071	
Chi²	30.826***		19.199**		27.929***	
R²	0.10		0.31		0.18	

[b] Only when industrial actions had taken place N=76.

* p<0.05, ** p<0.01, *** p<0.001

No effects of job insecurity were observed on the other types of union participation included in the study. Where participation in the union organisation was concerned (attending a union local meeting, holding a representative position), this study shows that job insecurity did not play a role. Neither did job insecurity have an effect on participation in union activities at work and participation in industrial action.

The results confirm that union commitment is a central factor for union participation. Union commitment had a significant positive effect on five of the seven types of union participation. Exceptions were the attendance of union meetings at work and participation in union activities at work. Existing literature suggests that union commitment becomes more important when participation involves more effort and time. Participation in meetings and activities at work takes considerable less effort and time than, for instance, holding a representative position or taking part in industrial action (cf. Klandermans, 1996). This might explain the fact that especially these two types of participation were not affected by levels of union commitment.

Job insecurity was not associated with union commitment, but was related to perceived union support. When more support from the union was perceived, less job insecurity was reported. This suggests that union support might have a buffering effect between job insecurity and its (negative) outcomes, similar to the effect of social support that was found in previous studies (cf. Lim, 1996). Union support did only directly influence participation in union activities at work. The strong correlation between union commitment and perceived union support might have prevented more significant effects of support from surfacing, because in the regression equations the effect of commitment on participation overruled the effect of support. The fact that we did only find an effect of support on a type of participation that was not influenced by commitment, supports this idea.

In this study, job insecurity did not emerge as a strong determinant of a wide range of types of union participation. However, job insecurity appears to be a factor that has a unique and direct influence on specific types of participation. Support and information are two important factors that can help people to cope with job insecurity. Job insecurity seems to result in a search for support from the union (contacting the union for help or legal assistance) and a search for information from the union (attendance of union meetings at work). As far as types of participation are concerned that are not directly instrumental at the individual level for coping with job insecurity, no effects of job insecurity were found.

Study 2: Job Insecurity and the Need for Information and (New) Union Services

Method

Procedure and respondents The data for the second study were collected by means of a telephone survey among members of the CNV Bedrijvenbond, one of the unions affiliated with the CNV-federation. The CNV Bedrijvenbond organises employees in industry, food-industry and transportation. The original sample consisted of 750 members. A little over half of the members in the sample cooperated in the study (response rate is 52 per cent, N=393). Here the sample was also limited to members who were employed (N=372). Of the respondents, 78 per cent were men and 22 per cent women. The mean age was 41 years, ranging between 20 and 64.

Questionnaire and measures   Apart from the demographics mentioned above, respondents' level of education (on a scale from one to seven) and net income (on a scale from one to eight) were assessed. The measures relevant for the present study were assessed in the following way:

To measure *job insecurity* the same items were used as in Study 1. Cronbach's alpha in the second study was 0.69.

Five items tapped the *need for information* about job opportunities and chances of getting other employment (for example 'Would you like to receive more information about the job opportunities in your region?', 'Would you like to receive more information about the possibilities your current knowledge and skills will provide you on the job market?'). Answers were scored on 5-point scales ranging from (1) certainly not to (5) definitely. Cronbach's alpha was 0.80. A scale was constructed based on the unweighted sum scores of the five items.

With 1 item the *need for career guidance* was measured: 'Do you feel you need career guidance?' (1=no, 2=yes). In addition, the question was presented whether respondents thought it would be a good thing if their union would provide a form of career guidance to the members (1=no, 2=yes).

Results

Like Study 1, the results of Study 2 showed that only a small part of the membership reported strong feelings of job insecurity (M=2.02, SD=0.82). In Study 2, 6.5 per cent of the sample reported the chances they will become unemployed in the near future were big or very big, 11.8 per cent reported that the chances of lay-offs in their company were big or very big, and 9.7 per cent indicated that the chances that their job will change because of reorganisations in the near future were big or very big.

In order to analyse the effects of job insecurity on the need for information about job opportunities and on the need for career guidance, regression analyses were conducted. The need for information was analysed by means of a hierarchical multiple regression analyses and the need for career guidance by means of a logistic regression analyses. In both analyses, the independent variables were entered in two steps. First, the demographic variables included in the study (age, level of education, income and sex) were entered in the analyses. In the second step, job insecurity was entered. This allowed us to assess the impact of job insecurity when at the same time differences in the need for information and the need for career guidance due to demographics were controlled. Results of both analyses are displayed in Table 5.2.

Table 5.2   Results of regression analyses of the need for information and career guidance

	Need for information	Need for career guidance	
	Beta	B	SE
Age (young-old)	-0.21***	-0.01	0.02
Education (low-high)	-0.02	0.16	0.11
Income (low-high)	-0.04	-0.06	0.11
Sex (male-female)	-0.06	0.08	0.42
Job insecurity	0.11*	0.37*	0.18
Constant		0.24	1.32
F	4.30***		
d.f.	5.357		
R^2	0.06		
-2 log		282.369	
Chi^2		4.344*	

* $p<0.05$, ** $p<0.01$, *** $p<0.001$

The results revealed that only a small proportion of the differences in the need for information about the job market and job opportunities was explained by the predictor variables ($R^2 \leq 0.06$) (Table 5.2). Age was a significant predictor of the need for information in both regression-models (with and without job insecurity included). The younger the union members were, the bigger their need for information. Job insecurity, when entered in the analysis, has a significant effect on the need for information; when more job insecurity was experienced, the need for information was bigger.

The results of the logistic regression analysis showed no relationships between the demographic variables entered in the model and the need for career guidance. Job insecurity was a significant predictor of the differences in the need for career guidance. When job insecurity increased, a bigger need for career guidance was reported. The majority of the members (93 per cent) indicated they thought it would be a good thing if their union would provide a form of career guidance for the members. In the answers to this question no differences between secure and insecure members emerged.

Discussion Study 2

The goal of Study 2 was to examine whether insecure members had a bigger need for information and advice about their position and possibilities on the labour market when they felt less secure about the future of their job. A second goal of the study was to assess the extent to which union members appreciate their union to provide such information and advice. The results confirmed that when members felt less secure about their job, they more actively searched for information. Moreover, the need for career guidance and advice was bigger when more job insecurity was experienced.

Whether information about the chances and possibilities on the labour market helps to alleviate the stress resulting from job insecurity will also depend on an individual's future expectations and future perspective. The results revealed that the need for information was bigger among younger members than among older members. This might be reflective of different expectations between younger and older members with regard to the future of their working life. However, as was noted by Casey et al. (1997), searching for information can in itself be a way of coping with a stressful or uncertain situation, because this increases feelings of control over the situation.

The union members in Study 2, secure as well as insecure, all indicated that they would appreciate their union to provide guidance and advice about their careers. Unions could consider providing such services for members, and by doing so might be helpful for members to cope with feelings of job insecurity. The literature suggests that insecure employees prefer third party information-seeking strategies, because in an unsettling period at work primary sources (such as management, co-workers and supervisors) may be unavailable, the message of the primary sources may be unclear and the interaction with the primary sources might be uncomfortable. The present data support the idea that unions could serve as a (third party) source of information. It is difficult, however, to determine the (relative) importance of unions in this respect, since preferences for other sources of information and advice were not examined.

General Discussion and Conclusions

The picture that emerges from the two studies that were presented in this chapter, is that feelings of job insecurity among union members fuel specific types of interaction with their union and increase the need for information and advice from the union. Job insecure union members more often attended union meetings at work, more often had contacted their union with a question or problem, and more often had sought and received legal assistance from their union. However, not all types of participation were found to be sensitive to job insecurity. No effects of job insecurity were observed on participation in the union organisation (that means attending a union local meeting, holding a representative position), participation in union activities in the company and participation in industrial action.

Similar to the findings reported by Van Vuuren et al. (1988), the present results showed that individual action is a more common reaction to job insecurity than is collective action. Adaptation to and acceptance of the changed situation as a way of coping with insecurity is more plausible in a work environment than attempts to change the situation itself. Collective action usually is aimed at changing the situation or to prevent changes and will therefore not be instrumental in dealing with insecurity or discontent. Previous research already showed that individual action, such as gathering information about alternative employment and pro-active job search, is functional for employees when dealing with job insecurity (Ashford, Lee and Bobko, 1989; Lim, 1996).

The results of Study 2 are in line with this: union members who felt insecure about the future of their job, reported an increased need for information about their position and possibilities on the job market and for advice and guidance about their career. An important addition to previous research is that unions (can) play a role in the individual action that union members undertake to cope with job insecurity. Union members who experience job insecurity may turn to their union (as a reliable third party) for assistance and information. Unions, it seems, could play an important role in the process of secondary control for members who experience job insecurity. This suggests that offering information and advice about job opportunities and career plans by unions as a new service to the members might be a promising new direction for unions. Several Dutch unions are currently developing such services for their members. It should be noted, however, that only small proportions of union members in the studies presented here experienced strong feelings of job insecurity. Thus, it could be argued that new services in this direction might only interest a small group of the membership. Unfortunately, no data is available that compares union members and non-union members with regard to feelings of job insecurity. It might well be that job insecurity is more common among non-union members than it is among union members. We know for a fact that vulnerable groups on the labour market - newcomers on the labour market, temporary workers, seasonal workers, etc. - are underrepresented in the labour movement (Goslinga and Klandermans, 2001). It seems likely that especially these groups experience feelings of job insecurity from time to time. Providing services that help individual employees to cope with job insecurity could be a means for unions to make union membership more attractive for these groups of employees.

References

Ashford, S.J., Lee, C. and Bobko, P. (1989), 'Content, Causes, and Consequences of Job Insecurity: a Theory-Based Measure and Substantive Test', *Academy of Management Journal*, Vol. 32, pp. 803-29.

Averill, J.R. (1973), 'Personal Control over Aversive Stimuli and its Relationship to Stress', *Psychological Bulletin,* Vol. 80, pp. 286-303.

Barling, J., Fullagar, C. and Kelloway, E.K. (1992), *The Union and its Members: A Psychological Approach,* Oxford University Press, New York.

Casey, M.K., Miller, V.D. and Johnson, J.R. (1997), 'Survivors' Information Seeking Following a Reduction in Workforce', *Communication Research,* Vol. 24, pp. 755-81.

Eisenberger, R., Huntington, R., Hutchinson, S. and Sowa, D. (1986), 'Perceived Organizational Support', *Journal of Applied Psychology,* Vol. 71, pp. 500-7.

Goslinga, S. (1996), 'Voor wat hoort wat: een ruiltheoretische benadering van vakbondsbinding', Paper presented at the *WESWA congress,* Utrecht, The Netherlands.

Goslinga, S. (2001), 'Betrokkenheid bij een belangenorganisatie: de ontwikkeling van een meetinstrument op basis van het 3-componenten model van organisatiebetrokkenheid', *Gedrag & Organisatie,* Vol. 14, pp. 191-200.

Goslinga, S. (2004), *Betrokkenheid, participatie en ledenverloop in vakbonden.* Ph.D. thesis, Vrije Universiteit, Amsterdam, The Netherlands.

Goslinga, S. and Klandermans, B. (2001), 'Union Membership in The Netherlands: Differences Between Traditional and 'New' Employees in Union Satisfaction, Union Commitment and Exit Behavior' in G. van Geys, H. De Witte and P. Pasture (eds), *Can Class Still Unite? The Differentiated Work Force, Class Solidarity and Trade Unions,* Ashgate, Aldershot, pp. 171-89.

Greenberger, D.B. and Strasser, S. (1986), 'Development and Application of a Model of Personal Control in Organizations', *Academy of Management Review,* Vol. 11, pp. 164-77.

Hartley, J., Jacobson, D., Klandermans, B. and Van Vuuren, T. (1991), *Job Insecurity: Coping with Jobs at Risk,* Sage Publications, London.

Klandermans, B. (1996), 'Ideology and the Social Psychology of Union Participation' in P. Pasture, J. Verberckmoes and H. De Witte (eds), *The Lost Perspective? Trade Unions between Ideology and Social Action in the New Europe. Volume 2,* Ashgate, Aldershot, pp. 259-74.

Lim, V.K.G. (1996), 'Job Insecurity and its Outcomes: Moderating Effects of Work-based and Nonwork-based Social Support', *Human Relations,* Vol. 49, pp. 171-94.

McShane, S.L. (1986), 'The Multidimensionality of Union Participation', *Journal of Occupational Psychology,* Vol. 59, pp. 177-87.

Meyer, J.P., Allen, N. and Smith, C. (1993), 'Commitment to Organizations and Occupations: Extension and Test of a Three-component Conceptualization', *Journal of Applied Psychology,* Vol. 78, pp. 538-51.

Rhoades, L., Eisenberger, R. and Armeli, S. (2001), 'Affective commitment to the organization: the contribution of perceived organizational support', *Journal of Applied Psychology,* Vol. 86, pp. 825-36.

Rothbaum, F., Weisz, J.R. and Snyder, S.S. (1982), 'Changing the World and Changing the Self: a Two-process Model of Perceived Control', *Journal of Personality and Social Psychology,* Vol. 42, pp. 5-37.

Shore, L.M., Tetrick, L.E., Sinclair, R.R. and Newton, L.A. (1994), 'Validation of a Measure of Perceived Union Support', *Journal of Applied Psychology,* Vol. 79, pp. 971-7.

Sverke, M., Hellgren, J. and Näswall, K. (2002), 'No security: a meta-analysis and review of job insecurity and its consequences', *Journal of Occupational Health Psychology*, Vol. 7, pp. 242-64.

Van Vuuren, T., Klandermans, B., Jacobson, D. and Hartley, J. (1991), 'Employees' Reactions to Job Insecurity' in J. Hartley, D. Jacobson, B. Klandermans and T. Van Vuuren, *Job Insecurity: Coping with Jobs at Risk*, Sage Publications, London, pp. 79-103.

Van Vuuren, C.V., Van Gastel, J.H.M. and Klandermans, P.G. (1988), 'Banen in gevaar: de beleving van onzekerheid over de arbeidsplaats', *Gedrag en Organisatie*, Vol. 1, pp. 14-29.

Weiss, H.M., Ilgen, D.R. and Sharbaugh, M.E. (1982), 'Effects of Life and Job Stress on Information Search Behaviors of Organizational Members', *Journal of Applied Psychology*, Vol. 67, pp. 60-6.

Note

1   The six public sector unions are: CFO, union for civil servants; ACP, union for policemen; ACOM, union for military personnel, Marechausseevereniging (MV), union for military police; KOV, catholic school teachers union; PCO, protestant school teachers union. The three private sector unions are: Hout- en Bouwbond CNV, union for construction workers; CNV Bedrijvenbond, union for the industry, food sector and transportation sector and Dienstenbond CNV, union for the services sector.

Chapter 6

Union Involvement during Downsizing and its Relation to Attitudes and Distress among Workers[1]

Kerstin Isaksson, Johnny Hellgren and Pär Pettersson

Introduction

The general aim of this chapter is to investigate the health and work-related consequences of the reorganisation and downsizing of the administration of a large retail company. A tradition of active unionism, with a large proportion of union members in the company, gave a unique opportunity to evaluate member satisfaction with union initiatives. The union tried to reduce damage to its members through representation on the company board and by raising demands in negotiations. The study compares four employment-status groups two years after the downsizing took place: persons who are still unemployed after being laid off, those who managed to get a new job, early retirees, and those who are still employed (survivors). The groups are compared with regard to attitudes towards company and unions, and predictors of distress.

Theoretical Background

Two perspectives or approaches have predominated in research into downsizing and personnel cutbacks (Kozlowski, Chao, Smith and Hedlund, 1993). The first is a purely *organisational* approach, including consideration of decision-making, strategic choice, efficiency, and so on (Cameron and Huber, 1997). The second has been to adopt an *individual perspective,* investigating reactions to, or coping with, the effects of downsizing (Mishra and Spreitzer, 1998).

There is however, a third perspective, which has remained largely undeveloped in this research arena. This is what might be called the *collective* approach, i.e. the adoption of an industrial-relations perspective to evaluate the influence, power and co-operative relations inherent in the downsizing process and how they affect the

1997; Shaw and Barrett-Power, 1997), but there have been relatively few studies so far.

Organisational Perspective

Personnel cutbacks may be either *proactive* (with long-term intra-organisation development in mind) or *reactive* (simply reacting to changes in the environment) (Kozlowski et al., 1993). Reactive cutbacks are often effected because a company has run into financial difficulties, threatening its survival. Proactive cutbacks, by contrast, have become increasingly common in highly profitable companies seeking to improve their market position by using downsizing as a strategy (Cameron and Huber, 1997). The distinction is crucial because the two approaches focus on different basic conditions, which eventually determine the line and course of possible actions.

Choice of downsizing strategy is governed largely by legal and ethical considerations, but also to some extent by weighing costs against skills (Mabon and Westling, 1996). Other factors, such as how rapidly a cost reduction has to be accomplished, and the need to exert control over the process are also important. In the company studied here, restructuring entailed a largely proactive process of change, which was designed - in the long term - to secure the profitability of the company. At the same time, the fact that profitability had been poor meant that there was also an element of reactivity.

With regard to efficiency, organisation researchers - at least in recent years - have adopted an increasingly critical stance towards the extent to which downsizing achieves the goals intended for it by management. Negative impacts on the persons who remain (so-called survivors) have been underestimated, and far too little attention has been paid to their reactions when retroactive evaluations are made (see e.g. Isaksson and Johansson, 2003). In extreme cases, downsizing can be a destructive process that sets off a downward spiral. It may even have negative effects on profitability, which may then trigger off new cutbacks (Kets de Vries and Balazs, 1997; Cascio, 1998).

Individual Perspective

The most common approach in this research arena has been an *individual* one. Over several decades research has concentrated on individuals leaving an organisation, i.e. the *persons made redundant*. The negative effects of unemployment, primarily with regard to psychological health, have been highlighted by previous research. However, research into unemployment has also shown that the 'period of anticipation', when employees have to wait for information on whether or not they are to be laid off, might be the most stressful (Joelsson and Wahlqvist, 1987; Ferrie, Shipley, Marmot, Stansfeld and Davey Smith, 1995). Survivors of downsizing often find themselves in a similar situation. It is common for them to be informed about an intention to reduce the number of employees, but further information about who will be affected is delayed. Systematic comparisons between survivors and the laid-off with regard to stress and health problems have not been made to any great extent. One exception is a study by Dekker and Schaufeli (1995), reporting that - after two months - the threat of redundancy appears to be more stressful for remaining (insecure) personnel than the actual unemployment experience.

However, studies of downsizing impacts on *remaining personnel* are accumulating, primarily from the USA. Brockner and colleagues (Brockner, 1988; Brockner, Grover, O'Mally, Reed and Glynn, 1993) dominated this research niche in the 1980s. Above all, they examined the attitudes of survivors to their work and to the company. Downsizing seems to have impacts on job satisfaction and motivation (see also Kets de Vries and Balazs, 1997). The findings of these and other studies clearly suggest that cutbacks reduce levels of job satisfaction and commitment at work, and often increase desire to leave the company (see e.g., Ashford, Lee and Bobko, 1989; Rosenblatt and Ruvio, 1996).

In previous research, the factors in the change-and-downsizing process that have been shown to be most significant in terms of the reaction of survivors are:
1. the degree of residual insecurity and extent of the threat of unemployment (Greenhalgh and Rosenblatt, 1984; Kozlowski et al., 1993);
2. whether or not employees regarded the downsizing process as fair (Brockner, 1988; Davy, Kinicki and Scheck, 1991);
3. the extent of the opportunities available to personnel to influence and participate in the process of change (Covin, 1993; Davy, Kinicki and Scheck, 1991; Barling and Kelloway, 1996);
4. how survivor work roles are structured i.e. if downsizing is followed by work intensification or work redesign (Parker, Chmiel and Wall, 1997).

Worry and stress during periods of reorganisation and downsizing have been shown to be strongly associated with inherent situational uncertainty, in particular in that job security is threatened by imminent personnel cutbacks. Job insecurity can be regarded as involving a discrepancy between desired and actual security (Jacobson, 1991). Perceived insecurity in any given situation varies between individuals, not only due to personality attributes but also as a product of other factors, such as the degree of social support offered inside and outside work (Lim, 1996). Most studies of the impacts of insecurity have shown negative short-term effects with regard to health and well being. A study by Heaney, Israel and House (1994) has shown long-term negative health effects in cases of chronic and long-term insecurity. Noer (1993) has described long-term effects in relation to a 'survivor syndrome', with distinctive features, such as stress, fatigue, and decreased motivation.

A study recently presented by Parker et al. (1997) indicated that strategic planning and the taking of special measures on behalf of surviving personnel might prevent the negative effects of personnel cutbacks. Despite work intensification, redesign and worker participation seemed to mitigate negative effects. The study, however, was performed in a situation where the personnel concerned had a relatively secure future. Accordingly, there is a need for replication under other circumstances for its findings to be confirmed.

Workgroup and Collective Perspective

There are several reasons for the neglect of research on unions and collective actions, the most critical perhaps being, that trade unions have declined in both membership and power over the last decades. They have struggled, sometimes desperately, to find ways of influencing cutbacks and other results of economic globalisation. The power of collective action and degree of union resistance are limited when the survival of a company is threatened. Proactive downsizing strategies, however, may give unions different action prospects (and thereby further justify research in this area). A collective perspective was especially relevant in this study, where co-operation between management and unions in the planning and conducting of a large personnel cutback could be evaluated in terms of both benefits for employees and attitudes towards company and union.

A common way of mitigating negative impacts on *persons made redundant* is for a company to offer various types of measures through which new employment is facilitated. Often, this takes the form of providing support and practical assistance in job seeking (outplacement assistance). In general, such schemes appear to have a positive effect, at least in that the laid-off are given training, and acquire new skills and self-confidence (Kozlowski et al., 1993; Burke and Nelson, 1998). They are then in a better position to acquire a new job, and are more motivated to do so (Caplan, Vinokur, Price and van Ryn, 1989). Price, van Ryn and Vinokur (1992) reported that the most beneficial effect of supportive measures was that they prevented depression during unemployment, rather than enabling employment. Measures of this kind, aimed at the laid-off, may also be supposed to have favourable effects with regard to attitudes among survivors, and even promote motivation during the period of change.

In sum, while it is evident that research has certainly expanded in this arena in recent years, it still has its limitations. Research reflecting how union participation and support to members affect attitudes and behaviour during and after downsizing is clearly insufficient. Hartley (1991) reported that people felt much more secure about their jobs when they could depend on a strong union. One critical precondition however, is, according to Hartley, a climate of trust between members and their union. The study by Dekker and Schaufeli (1995) reported no buffering effects of social support from unions or companies. A study by Mellor (1992) finally, indicated that severity of lay-off interacted with belief in union responsibility in predicting the willingness of remaining employees to work for the union following redundancies. The limited evidence available on workers' participation in management suggests that it is most effective in situations of job security (Strauss, 1992). Insecurity and the threat of unemployment seem to be the factors giving rise to the greatest strain. Control and influence over the process appear generally to have a positive effect on the attitudes of survivors and seem to buffer negative health outcomes (Barling and Kelloway, 1996). Examples of questions that need to be answered concern the effects of union participation in more or less secure situations. Collective action and the effects of union support in a threatened situation in the workplace surely need further exploration. This study makes a step in that direction, with a special focus on the effects of a trade-union strategy of engaging in co-operation with management to negotiate favourable agreements for its members.

Changes to the Central Administration of a Large Retail Company

Restructuring of the large retail company was initiated during the autumn of 1992 when details of the design of a new administrative organisation were first presented. The proposed restructuring was to entail substantial lay-offs among the 1,570 white-collar workers within the administration. In order to obtain a better understanding of the long-lasting restructuring and reorganisation of the company a pilot study was carried out. One critical part of this was to interview mangers, union representatives and union members. The information provided below is based on these interviews.

The company had a history of generally good relations with the unions, and a reputation as being something of a role model for personnel management. There was major confidence in the organisation's commitment to job security, and redundancies among white-collar employees on this scale had never previously been contemplated throughout the company's history. This may have contributed to personnel being relatively late to realise that this thoroughgoing change, with the personnel cutbacks it would entail, was in fact to be effected. Accordingly, the statement on over-manning and the scale of the forthcoming lay-off came as a shock.

A very large majority of employees were union members (about 90 per cent), and the unions had taken an active role in the structural changes, co-operating and participating in strategic planning through its representatives on the company board. The interviews revealed that they did not succeed in reducing the number of employees to be made redundant. Later on, the union worked hard to negotiate as favourable agreements as possible to mitigate the negative effects on personnel of the downsizing process. Decisions regarding lay-offs were based on Swedish labour-market legislation, following principles of seniority and competence. Senior employees (above 60 years of age) were offered early retirement, retaining 72 per cent of their salary until the age of 65. The union also negotiated that low-paid and part-time employees should be offered acceptable compensation in the case of early retirement.

A second result of trade-union demands made in the course of these discussions was that the company should take on a long-term commitment to help redundant personnel obtain new jobs. On this basis, plans were made at an early stage for an outplacement and counselling project. A total of 600 persons were regarded as surplus to requirements, of whom 200 were granted a negotiated early-retirement pension. The remaining 400 were transferred to the outplacement centre for the period of notice, one that could vary between three months and one year according to age and seniority. Participation was mandatory for all personnel given notice, and the primary aim was to find lasting job solutions.

Following the major structural change made to the organisation, a number of further reorganisations were effected to work processes and work content within the central administration, each of which entailed further rationalisation and personnel cutbacks. When our questionnaire was about to be administered, management had just announced that a reorganisation of buying operations would be implemented during the following year.

Aim and Research Questions

The general aim of this chapter was to examine the effects on personnel of the major restructuring and downsizing in a large retail company when two years had passed. Four groups, differently affected by the downsizing process, were compared in terms of attitudes towards company and union as well as distress: (1) persons who were given notice and had remained unemployed after spending their period of notice in the outplacement centre; (2) persons who were given notice, spent some time in the outplacement centre, but had managed to find a new job; (3) senior employees who left the company on early-retirement benefit, and finally; (4) 'survivors' of downsizing. Our first research question concerned differences between these groups in terms of organisational commitment, satisfaction with union involvement, satisfaction with outplacement assistance, and levels of distress symptoms after two years.

First of all, we expected that a crucial influence on commitment to company and union after downsizing would be the benefit or instrumental value obtained by each group. Satisfaction with union involvement is based on social exchange between union and member. A critical part of this is instrumental exchange, i.e. a cognitive assessment of the costs and benefits associated with union membership (Shore McFarlane, Tetrick, Sinclair and Newton, 1994). As shown in previous research (Guest, 1992), organisational commitment has several antecedents, but a social-exchange framework involving expectations of fair treatment and job security in exchange for loyalty is clearly relevant. Expectations of exchange and instrumental benefit generate the supposition that persons who had relatively favourable outcomes of downsizing (in this case, retained employment with the company, managed to get a new job after outplacement assistance or receive early-retirement benefit) would have more positive attitudes and be more loyal to both company and union than those who were still unemployed after two years.

Hypothesis 1: Survivors, early retirees and those who had obtained a new job after lay-off will have a generally more positive attitude towards both company and union than those who are still unemployed.

Moreover, an important consideration was that this was the first time in its history that the company had to lay off white-collar employees. In line with theories concerning breaches of expectations or psychological contracts (Rousseau, 1995), and earlier research (e.g. Noer, 1993), we expected that high distress levels and critical attitudes towards both company and union would be especially pronounced in this company, given its tradition of loyal personnel, long tenure and strong union influence. Further, the situation for survivors was still insecure, with further rumours of downsizing appearing. Under these circumstances we expected that negative reactions would be relatively long lasting, and at a similar level for both survivors and those who were still unemployed after lay off.

Hypothesis 2: Average level of distress will be at the same level for persons who are still unemployed and survivors of downsizing.

A further aspect to the research was to compare predictors of attitudes and distress across the four groups. It was supposed that the outcome of the process in terms of employment status and attitudes would lead to differences in predictors of distress across groups. For those who left the company, we expected that having obtained new employment or not, together with general satisfaction with outplacement counselling would be critical. By contrast, current work conditions were assumed to be critical for attitudes and well being of survivors of downsizing.

For several reasons, cross-sectional studies are especially vulnerable to confounding effects. One is that there is a lack of base-line measures, which makes it difficult to make inferences about selection effects (in relation to the various outcome categories). An effort was made to control for some possible confounders, such as age, tenure and health complaints, in the regression analysis. One reason for considering differential age effects was that legislation protecting employees with long tenure meant a greater threat of unemployment for younger persons. On the other hand, the large cutbacks and generally long tenure among personnel in this company increased the threat for older employees as well. The prevailing economic recession made the prospect of finding new employment especially poor for older employees. Further, large age variation provided a reason to introduce health complaints as a possible confounder.

Method

Data Collection

In December 1996, a questionnaire was administered to all remaining personnel within the company. At the same time, a questionnaire was sent to all persons who had accepted the offer of an early-retirement pension, and the redundant personnel who had been given notice. The questionnaires were sent by post to the home addresses of all respondents, together with a post-addressed envelope to the research team. Each questionnaire was accompanied by a letter explaining the purpose of the study and guaranteeing full confidentiality, and also by a letter from company management encouraging participation. A reminder to persons not returning their questionnaire was sent three weeks later.

Respondents and Non-respondents

Of redundant personnel (381), there were 212 (56 per cent) who returned their questionnaire to the research team. Their mean age was 45 (SD=11.8). Average length of previous employment at the company (KF) was 15 years, and 59 per cent were women. The group was subdivided according to current employment status. 126 persons had managed to get a new job, while the remaining 86 were unemployed.

Of the 182 early retirees, 119 (65 per cent) returned a completed questionnaire to the research team. Their mean age was 64 (SD=1.5), and they had an average length of previous employment at KF of 33 years. The gender distribution among early retirees was even.

Of the 786 survivors finally, there was a total of 555 (71 per cent) who returned their questionnaire to the research team. The average age of survivors was 49 (SD=8.85). Average length of previous employment was 22 years, and 69 per cent of respondents in this group were women.

Representativeness: Registry data from the company showed that the mean age of all employees at the time of administration of the first questionnaire was 47.2 years, that the average period of previous employment was 17.6 years, and that 53 per cent of employees were women. This indicates that older persons with relative short periods of prior employment had a higher questionnaire-response rate, and also, that women were somewhat overrepresented in the material. Selection effects could be expected, especially among those who had been laid off and left the company involuntarily. We know that principles of seniority were decisive in the lay-off process and the relatively high mean age among our respondents could be an indication of age selection. Results for these groups should be interpreted with caution.

Measuring Instruments

All but two of the variables encompassed by the study were measured on the same five-point scale (ranging from 1=do not agree at all, 5=agree entirely). The exceptions were distress (GHQ symptoms), which was measured on a 0-3 scale, and presence of somatic health complaints, where 1 refers to 'never or almost never' and 3 to 'always or almost always'. The analyses are based on mean values on indices, constructed for each scale, following recoding of negative statements. All reliability estimates (see Table 6.1 below) show a value in excess of 0.69, indicating that the instruments have satisfactory measurement properties (see e.g., Nunnaly, 1978). With regard to validity, the questionnaire items were developed after a pilot study and were discussed with representatives from both the company and the unions involved.

Attitudes towards Company and Union

Organisational commitment was measured using the mean value of two items on commitment or identification with the company ('KF has/has had a great personal value to me' and 'I am proud to be/to have been working for KF').

Satisfaction with union involvement was measured on the basis of three statements specially developed with the purposes of the study in mind ('In my view, the local union branch showed great involvement', 'In my view, the local union kept its members informed during the organisational change process', 'In my view, the central union branch showed great involvement').

Satisfaction with assistance offered to redundant personnel (essentially the outplacement project) was measured on the basis of two questions focusing on relevance and fulfilment of responsibilities ('I think that the company has taken great responsibility for redundant personnel through the Development Centre', 'I think that the outplacement centre has facilitated the prospect of getting a new job').

Health and Well-being

Distress (GHQ symptoms) was measured on the basis of twelve statements illuminating various aspects of well being/distress (e.g. 'In the light of current circumstances have you been feeling more or less all right in recent times?'). The scale was developed by Goldberg (1979) and has been widely used in occupational studies.

Health complaints A summary index was constructed on the basis of seven items on a symptom checklist (e.g. cardiovascular, musculoskeletal, and psychosomatic symptoms), forming a scale originally developed and tested by Andersson (1986). For this study, a later version, modified and previously used by Isaksson and Johansson (1997), was employed.

Current working conditions (measured only for survivors) Perceived job security was measured on the basis of three statements (e.g. 'I am worried about having to leave my job before I would like to'), concerning the individual's perception of employment security and continuity. The questions were developed by the research team (Hellgren, Sverke and Isaksson, 1999) and partly based on items in English developed by Ashford, Lee and Bobko (1989), which were translated into Swedish and then modified by the authors.

Quantitative workload was measured on the basis of responses to three statements (e.g. 'It happens quite often that I have to work under severe time pressure'), focusing on whether work was perceived as time-pressurised and stressful. The three statements are taken from Nystedt's (1992) four-affirmation scale.

Results

Table 6.1 shows correlation coefficients, descriptive statistics, and reliability estimates (as measured by Cronbach's α) for all personnel.

The table shows a lower mean value of satisfaction with union involvement (compared with organisational commitment) on a scale from 1 to 5. Satisfaction with outplacement assistance was generally high. Both organisational commitment and satisfaction with union involvement were found to be significantly related to age and tenure. Further, the attitude measures are all correlated with each other, as well as with the measure of distress. The measures of current work conditions (obtained only for survivors) were significantly associated with distress level and health complaints. The mean value of distress reported for all participants in the study was close to what Banks et al. (1980) found among employed persons in a study where the psychometric properties of the scale was tested in occupational settings.

Comparisons between Subgroups of Survivors and Redundant Personnel

The groups compared are the laid-off who had obtained new jobs ($\underline{n}$=126), the unemployed ($\underline{n}$=86), senior employees who left on early retirement ($\underline{n}$=119), and persons remaining in employment ($\underline{n}$=554). Table 6.2 shows the results of a MANOVA displaying univariate as well as stepdown F-values (Roy Bargmans), and also the values on Scheffé's post-hoc test.

As expected, there were significant differences between the early retirees ($\underline{M}$=64) and the other groups in terms of age and tenure with the company. Moreover, the early retirees attributed a more positive value to union involvement, and also displayed generally lower values of distress than the other groups. Early retirees and survivors have a more favourable view of involvement from the union than the two groups of laid-off persons. The mean ratings for all groups are at the lower end of the scale, indicating that attitudes were consistently rather negative. By contrast, satisfaction with the outplacement centre, which ran the operation to ease the occupational transition of laid-off personnel, was consistently fairly positive. The laid-off, who had obtained a new job, show the highest mean value, but unemployed persons and survivors also rated the centre quite highly. These three groups differ significantly from the early retirees, who reported low values. With regard to organisational commitment, all groups reported means at about the same level.

Roy Bargman's stepdown MANOVA was used to control for effects of correlated dependent variables. This procedure slightly changed some of the F-values in a downward direction (for tenure, union support, health complaints, and distress). However, the differences between groups regarding tenure, satisfaction with union involvement, outplacement assistance, and distress remained unchanged. Differences in terms of health complaints became statistically insignificant following application of this procedure, but the differences with regard to organisational commitment between laid-off persons with a new job and survivors became significant.

Table 6.1 Intercorrelations, means, standard deviations and reliability for all measures used (n=884)

Variables	1	2	3	4	5	6	7	8	9	10	M	SD	α
1. Age	-										49.0	10.8	-
2. Gender	0.16	-									0.6	0.5	-
3. Tenure	0.65	0.23	-								21.2	12.1	
4. Organisational commitment	0.19	0.06	0.21	-							3.2	1.1	0.69
5. Satisfaction with union involvement	0.29	0.06	0.23	0.27	-						2.5	1.1	0.88
6. Satisfaction with lay-off assistance	-0.05	-0.08	0.01	0.18	0.27	-					3.9	1.0	0.81
7. Health complaints	-0.16	-0.19	-0.14	-0.14	-0.18	-0.06	-				2.0	0.7	0.72
8. Distress (GHQ-12)	-0.09	-0.13	-0.04	-0.17	-0.18	-0.11	0.55	-			8.9	5.6	0.87
9. Perc. work load (n=553)	0.01	0.11	0.08	0.12	-0.03	-0.03	0.17	0.13	-		3.5	1.00	0.81
10. Perc. job insecurity (n=553)	-0.06	0.06	-0.09	0.02	0.00	0.06	-0.22	-0.30	0.05	-	3.0	1.2	0.79

$r=0.09$, $p<0.05$; $r=0.11$, $p<0.01$; $r=0.15$, $p<0.001$ (n=522)

Table 6.2 Differences between redundant personnel and survivors after downsizing (n=885)

Variables	New employment (n=126)		Unemployed (n=86)		'Survivors' (n=554)		Early retired (n=119)		F	Stepdown F	Post hoc
	M	SD	M	SD	M	SD	M	SD			
1. Age	44.0	11.2	46.0	12.5	48.0	8.8	64.0	1.5	121.1***	121.1***	4>1,2,3, 3>1
2. Tenure	13.0	10.6	17.0	12.3	22.0	10.3	33.0	10.2	69.8****	13.4****	4>1,2,3 - 3>1,2
3. Organisational commitment	3.0	1.2	3.1	1.2	3.2	1.1	3.2	1.2	1.0	2.7*	n.s.
4. Satisfaction with union involvement	2.1	1.1	2.3	1.2	2.4	1.0	3.3	1.4	26.1***	10.9***	4>1,2,3 - 3>1
5. Satisfaction with assistance	4.1	1.1	3.9	1.0	3.9	0.9	3.7	1.1	2.9*	4.9*	4<1,2
6. Health complaints	2.0	0.7	2.1	0.9	2.0	0.6	1.7	0.6	7.5***	1.8	n.s.
7. Distress (GHQ)	8.7	4.2	9.1	6.4	9.6	5.0	5.9	4.5	16.7***	13.3***	4<1,2,3

Predictors of Well-Being across Groups

Tables 6.3 and 6.4 show predictors of attitudes and distress for present and former employees respectively. Separate hierarchical regression analyses were conducted for those laid off and survivors with age, gender and tenure entered at the first step of the analysis, followed by the three attitude measures, and finally reported health complaints as the final step.

As expected, a slightly different picture emerged for the two groups. Table 6.3 shows results for those who were laid off.

First of all it emerged that having obtained new employment appeared to be important for attitudes towards the former employer only. Secondly, satisfaction with outplacement assistance appeared to be related both to positive attitudes as well as a lower level of distress after two years. Those who were negative or disappointed with the outplacement counselling reported higher levels of distress. It's interesting to note that satisfaction with assistance appeared to be more important for distress than whether the individual had managed to get a new job or not at the time of the study. Further, that attitudes towards former employer and the union were positively related. Finally, the occurrence of health complaints was significant as a predictor of distress symptoms.

The analyses aiming to identify significant predictors of attitudes and distress among surviving personnel were carried out in a slightly different manner. Here, we had data about present working conditions, which gave us a wider range of predictor variables. These were measures of perceived insecurity (threat of future layoffs) and perceived workload. Variables were first introduced in the same order as for the other group, i.e. age, gender, tenure at the first step as controls, followed by the attitudinal measures. Then, we introduced the two indicators of present work conditions, and finally reported health complaints as a control.

Table 6.4 shows significant associations between level of organisational commitment and attitude towards the union as well as with level of distress symptoms among survivors. Further, a high level of perceived insecurity was related to higher levels of reported distress. Finally, a high level of health complaints was also found to have an effect on reported distress in this group. Thus, the pattern of predictors of attitudes and distress was different among those who had continued to work for the company compared to the other group. Above all, a low level of organisational commitment was related to higher levels of distress in this group, which was not the case among redundant personnel. For those who lost their job during downsizing, satisfaction with assistance in finding a new job appeared as more critical for well being.

Discussion

With regard to our hypotheses, results were partly in line with expectations. All affected personnel had a relatively low mean value for satisfaction with union in-

Table 6.3 Predictors of attitudes and distress symptoms (GHQ-12) among persons laid-off (n=204)

Variables	Organisational commitment			Satisfaction with union			Distress symptoms		
	Step 1	Step 2	Step 3	Step 1	Step 2	Step 3	Step 1	Step 2	Step 3
1. Age	0.07	0.05	0.05	0.13	0.12	0.11	-0.06	-0.06	-0.02
2. Gender	0.00	0.02	0.02	0.18*	0.20**	0.19**	-0.01	-0.01	0.04
3. Tenure	0.28***	0.28***	0.28***	0.02	-0.09	-0.10	-0.05	-0.05	-0.01
4. New job	0.21**	0.21**	0.21**	-0.03	-0.08	-0.07	-0.07	-0.08	-0.09
5. Satisfaction with assistance		0.19***	0.20**		0.17**	0.15*		0.21**	-0.14*
6. Organisational commitment		-	-		0.23**	0.23***		0.04	0.02
7. Satisfaction with union involvement		0.21**	0.21***		-	-		-0.13	-0.05
8. Health complaints			0.03			-0.13*			0.59***
R^2 adjusted	0.13	0.21	0.21	0.05	0.13	0.14	0.00	0.05	0.37
R^2 change	0.13***	0.08***	0.00	0.05**	0.09***	0.02*	0.00	0.05**	0.32***

* $p<0.05$, ** $p<0.01$, *** $p<0.001$

Table 6.4 Predictors of attitudes and distress symptoms (GHQ-12) among survivors after downsizing (n=521)

Variables	Organisational commitment			Satisfaction with union			Distress symptoms		
	Step 1	Step 2	Step 3	Step 1	Step 2	Step 3	Step 1	Step 2	Step 3
1. Age	0.24***	0.20***	0.24***	0.14**	0.07	0.07	0.07	0.11**	0.12**
2. Gender	0.03	0.04	0.03	0.12	0.01	0.02	-0.15***	-0.13**	0.07
3. Tenure	-0.14***	-0.10**	-0.14***	-0.09*	-0.05	-0.05	0.03	0.00	-0.01
4. Satisfaction with assistance		0.06	0.06		0.25***	0.25***		-0.03	-0.04
5. Organisational commitment	—	—	—		0.22***	0.20***		-0.20***	-0.14***
6. Satisfaction with union involvement		0.22**	0.20***	-	-	-		-0.04	-0.01
7. Work load		0.13**	0.14**		0.03	-0.02		0.05	0.00
8. Job insecurity		0.01	0.04		0.00	0.02		0.27***	0.18***
9. Health complaints			-0.15***			-0.08			0.42***
R^2 adjusted	0.08	0.14	0.16	0.03	0.13	0.13	0.02	0.13	0.29
R^2 change	0.08***	0.07***	0.02	0.03**	0.12***	0.01	0.03**	0.10***	0.16***

* $p<.05$, ** $p<.01$, *** $p<.001$

volvement. As expected, persons who managed to remain employed and those who obtained the benefit of early retirement were more positive. On the other hand, those who had new employment did not seem to relate this to the union being involved in the process. Their level of satisfaction with the union was on the same, rather low level as that of the unemployed. Further, and contrary to expectations, attitudes towards the company, and the assistance received in the outplacement centre did not differ between subgroups. Thus, a relatively positive outcome in terms of employment status did not appear to be related to a higher level of commitment or satisfaction with assistance. Instead all groups reported similar, and generally high values and this appeared to be regardless of their own exchange.

The situation that survivors encounter following personnel cutbacks becomes apparent on comparison between them and personnel made redundant. Persons remaining in employment at the retail company after downsizing reported the highest values of minor psychological symptoms and on a similar level as those who were laid off in the process. Thus, our second hypothesis was supported. A question mark remains however, concerning those who had managed to get a new job and still had distress symptoms on a similar level as those who were unemployed.

As indicated by earlier studies, the results clearly confirm that continued employment in a company announcing further cutbacks can have negative health effects. The effect of the threat of unemployment was found to be severe, and appears to result in distress levels at the same level as that of unemployment itself.

The hypothesis of instrumental exchange in this case appeared to be relevant only for the union. Close co-operation between company and union did not lead to similar attitudes to the two. There are probably several reasons for this. One explanation may be that organisational commitment was initially at a much higher level than union commitment, a second that union members tend to have higher expectations, and attribute more of the blame for the outcome of downsizing to the union. Earlier research has reported that dual commitment towards company and union is in fact rare, and that the antecedents probably differ (Guest, 1992). Further research addressing the questions of union strategies and effects in insecure situations is clearly needed.

Among the predictors of distress, however, there was an interesting difference between the subgroups. Assistance after lay off was clearly the factor emerging as most important and related both to attitudes and distress among those who lost their job during the process of downsizing. Having obtained new employment was positively related to attitudes to the former employer but *not* to the union. For survivors, however, distress symptoms appeared to be more dependent on current working conditions, and also affected by present loyalty and commitment towards the company. Perception of job insecurity was an additional factor explaining variation in distress symptoms. Our results tend to support Noer's (1993) findings on the long-term term effects of downsizing. The survivor syndrome, and the continued worry and distress, found by Noer, were clearly evident in our study two years after downsizing had been implemented.

For trade unions it is also relevant to discuss perceptions of broken promises or failed expectations. Looking at mean attitudinal values, it seems that the unions lost support in negotiations in a situation where employment was clearly threatened. Co-operating with management in this case appears to have led to more critical reactions from employees to the trade union than to the company. Although survivors, and especially early retirees, had a higher evaluation, perception of support from unions was at a relatively low level, which indicates widespread dissatisfaction. This view was strongly supported by the results of interviews.

On the basis of our material, it is difficult to draw conclusions with regard to effects on persons who were laid off and forced to leave the organisation. They showed a more critical attitude to the union than the other groups. This applied to both those who had found a new job and those who were still unemployed. This makes their positive attitude to the outplacement centre rather surprising. The fairly positive response to the work of the centre, and the predictive value of this attitude in relation to well-being two years after lay-off, suggest that this type of activity can be regarded as having a positive impact both on individual well being and on attitudes towards former employer and union. The positive effects are likely to be effective both on persons made redundant and on the company (in the form of the goodwill of remaining personnel). The outplacement centre was the result of a union initiative and, in a two-year time perspective, its success appears to have been acknowledged and led to more positive evaluation.

Somewhat puzzling is that finding a new job was related to a positive view of the company but did not seem to affect on satisfaction with the union involvement in the process. Again, an explanation could be that members expect more from the union than from the company in terms of involvement and support. It may also be possible that the union should more clearly have informed its members of the positive results of negotiating in order to receive appropriate credit for it.

Limitations to the study include its cross-sectional nature, which means that questions of causality remain unclear. It is not possible to rule out explanations other than downsizing as causes of the reported outcomes. However, interviews with both union representatives and members tend to support our conclusions. The attitudinal measures are another weak point. Clearly, the value of the study would have been greater if more dimensions of attitudes and behaviours had been included.

Our findings might reasonably be supposed to be of interest to companies about to embark on major re-organisations and personnel cutbacks and to unions who are invited to participate. Perhaps the most important result is that perceptions of job insecurity (in that employees feel the threat of redundancy) have a distinct relation to symptoms of distress. The study provides reason critically to discuss the results presented by Parker, Chmiel and Wall (1997), who suggest that the negative effects of downsizing can be prevented by means of strategic planning, in particular because their study was conducted in a situation of relative job security. A recently conducted meta-analysis had clearly shown all kinds of negative consequences of job insecurity (Sverke, Hellgren and Näswall, 2002). Our findings add to this by suggesting that the presence or absence of continuing personnel cutbacks clearly modifies the impact of downsizing on surviving personnel.

References

Andersson, K. (1986), *Utveckling och prövning av ett frågeformulär rörande arbetsmiljö och hälsotillstånd (Development and test of a questionnaire on work environment and health)*, Rapport 1/1986, Yrkesmedicinska kliniken, Örebro, Sweden.

Ashford, S., Lee, C. and Bobko, P. (1989), 'Content, Causes and Consequences of Job Insecurity: A Theory-based Measure and Substantive Test', *Academy of Management Journal*, Vol. 32, pp. 803-29.

Banks, M., Clegg, C., Jackson, P., Kemp, N., Stafford, E. and Wall, T. (1980), 'The Use of the General Health Questionnaire as an Indication of Mental Health in Occupational Studies', *Journal of Occupational Psychology*, Vol. 53, pp. 187-94.

Barling, J. and Kelloway, K. (1996), 'Job Insecurity and Health: The Moderating Role of Workplace Control', *Stress Medicine*, Vol. 12, pp. 253-9.

Brockner, J. (1988), 'Scope of Justice in the Workplace: How Survivors React to Co-worker Layoffs', *Journal of Social Issues*, Vol. 46, pp. 95-106.

Brockner, J., Grover, S., O'Mally, M.N., Reed, T.F. and Glynn, M.A. (1993), 'Threat of Future Layoffs, Self-esteem and Survivors' Reactions: Evidence from the Laboratory and the Field', *Strategic Management Journal*, Vol. 14, pp. 153-66.

Burke, R.J. and Nelson, D. (1998), 'Mergers and Acquisitions, Downsizing and Privatization: A North American Perspective' in M.G. Gowing, J.D. Kraft and J.C. Quick (eds), *The New Organizational Reality: Downsizing, Restructuring and Revitalization*, APA, Washington, DC, pp. 21-54.

Cameron, K. and Huber, G. (1997), 'Techniques for Maintaining Organisations Effective' in D. Druckman, J. Singer and H. Van Cott (eds), *Enhancing Organisational Performance*, National Academy Press, Washington, DC, pp. 39-64.

Caplan, R., Vinokur, A., Price, R. and van Ryn, M. (1989), 'Job Seeking, Reemployment and Mental Health: A Randomized Field Experiment in Coping with Job Loss', *Journal of Applied Psychology*, Vol. 74, pp. 759-69.

Cascio, W. (1998), 'Learning from Outcomes' in M.G. Gowing, J.D. Kraft and J.C. Quick (eds), *The New Organizational Reality: Downsizing, Restructuring and Revitalization*, APA, Washington, DC, pp. 55-70.

Covin, T. (1993), 'Managing Workforce Reduction: A Survey of Employee Reactions & Implications for Management Consultants', *Organization Development Journal*, Vol. 11 (Spring), pp. 67-76.

Davy, J.A., Kinicki, A.J. and Scheck, C.l. (1991), 'Developing and Testing a Model of Survivors Responses to Layoffs', *Journal of Vocational Behavior*, Vol. 38, pp. 302-17.

Dekker, S. and Schaufeli, W. (1995), 'The Effects of Job Insecurity on Psychological Health and Withdrawal: A Longitudinal Study', *Australian Psychologist*, Vol. 30, pp. 57-63.

Ferrie, J., Shipley, M., Marmot, M.G., Stansfeld, S. and Davey Smith, G. (1995), 'Health Effects of Anticipation of Job Change and Non-employment: Longitudinal Data from the Whitehall II Study', *British Medical Journal,* Vol. 311, pp. 1264-9.

Goldberg, D. (1979), *Manual of the General Health Questionnaire,* NFER Nelson, London.

Greenhalgh, L. and Rosenblatt, Z. (1984), 'Job Insecurity: Towards Conceptual Clarity', *Academy of Management Review,* Vol. 9(3), pp. 438-48.

Guest, D. (1992), 'Employee Commitment and Control' in J. Hartley and G. Stephenson (eds), *Employment Relations,* Blackwell, Oxford, pp. 111-35.

Hartley, J. (1991), 'Industrial Relations and Job Insecurity: Learning from a Case Study' in J. Hartley, D. Jacobson, B. Klandermans and T. van Vuuren (eds), *Job Insecurity,* Sage, London, pp. 123-52.

Hartley, J. (1997), 'Challenge and Change in Employment Relations: Issues for Psychology, Trade Unions and Managers' in L.E. Tetrick and J. Barling (eds), *Changing Employment Relations,* APA, Washington DC, pp. 3-30.

Heaney, C., Israel, B. and House, J. (1994), 'Chronic Job Insecurity among Automobile Workers: Effects on Job Satisfaction and Health', *Social Science and Medicine,* Vol. 38, pp. 1431-7.

Hellgren, J., Sverke, M. and Isaksson, K. (1999), 'A Two-dimensional Approach to Job Insecurity: Consequences for Attitudes and Well-being', *European Journal of Work and Organizational Psychology,* Vol. 8, pp. 179-96.

Isaksson, K. and Johansson, G. (1997), *Avtalspension med vinst och förlust (Gains and losses through early retirement),* Folksam, Stockholm.

Isaksson, K. and Johansson, G. (2003), Managing Older Employees after Downsizing. *Scandinavian Journal of Management,* Vol. 19, pp. 1-15.

Jacobson, D. (1991), 'The Conceptual Approach to Job Insecurity' in J. Hartley, D. Jacobson, B. Klandermans and T. van Vuuren (eds), *Job Insecurity,* Sage, London, pp. 23-39.

Joelsson, L. and Wahlqvist, L. (1987), 'The Psychological Meaning of Job Insecurity and Job Loss', *Social Science and Medicine,* Vol. 25, pp. 179-82.

Kets de Vries, M. and Balazs, K. (1997), 'The Downside of Downsizing', *Human Relations,* Vol. 50(1), pp. 11-50.

Kozlowski, S., Chao, G., Smith, E. and Hedlund, J. (eds) (1993), 'Organizational Downsizing: Strategies, Interventions and Research' in C.L. Cooper and I.T. Robertson (eds), *International Review of Industrial and Organizational Psychology,* Vol. 8, pp. 263-331, Wiley, Chichester.

Lim, V. (1996), 'Job Insecurity and its Outcomes: Moderating Effects of Work-based and Nonwork-based Social Support', *Human Relations,* Vol. 49, pp. 171-93.

Mabon, H. and Westling, G. (1996), 'Using Utility Analysis in Downsizing Decisions', *Journal of Human Resource Costing and Accounting,* Vol. 1, pp. 19-30.

Mellor, S. (1992), 'The Influence of Layoff Severity on Post Layoff Union Commitment among Survivors: The Moderating Effect of the Perceived Legitimacy of a Layoff Account', *Personnel Psychology,* Vol. 45, pp. 578-600.

Mishra, A. and Spreitzer, G. (1998), 'Explaining how Survivors Respond to Downsizing: The Roles of Trust, Empowerment and Work Redesign', *Academy of Management Review,* Vol. 23, pp. 567-88.

Noer, D.M. (1993), *Healing the Wounds,* Jossey Bass, San Francisco, CA.

Nunnaly, J.C. (1978), *Psychometric Theory,* McGraw Hill, New York.

Nystedt, L. (1992), *Yrkesofficerares arbetsmiljö i armén* (FOA rapport nr C 50093-5.3), Försvarets Forskningsanstalt, Stockholm.

Parker, S.K., Chmiel, N. and Wall, T. (1997), 'Work Characteristics and Employee Well-being within a Context of Strategic Downsizing', *Journal of Occupational Health Psychology,* Vol. 3(4), pp. 289-303.

Price, R., van Ryn, M. and Vinokur, A. (1992), 'Impact of a Preventive Job Search Intervention on the Likelihood of Depression among the Unemployed', *Journal of Health and Social Behavior,* Vol. 33 (June), pp. 158-67.

Rousseau, D.M. (1995), *Psychological Contracts in Organizations: Understanding Written and Unwritten Agreements,* Sage Publications, Inc.

Rosenblatt, Z. and Ruvio, A. (1996), 'A Test of a Multidimensional Model of Job Insecurity: The Case of Israeli Teachers', *Journal of Organizational Behavior,* Vol. 17, pp. 587-605.

Shaw, J.B. and Barrett-Power, E. (1997), 'A Conceptual Framework for Assessing Organization, Work Group and Individual Effectiveness during and after Downsizing', *Human Relations,* Vol. 50, pp. 109-27.

Shore McFarlane, L., Tetrick, L. Sinclair, R. and Newton, L. (1994), 'Validation of a Measure of Perceived Union Support', *Journal of Applied Psychology,* Vol. 79, pp. 971-7.

Strauss, G. (1992), 'Workers Participation in Management' in J. Hartley and G. Stephenson (eds), *Employment Relations,* Blackwell, Oxford, pp. 291-313.

Sverke, M., Hellgren, J. and Näswall, K. (2002), 'No Security: A Meta-analysis and Review of Job Insecurity and its Consequences', *Journal of Occupational Health Psychology,* Vol. 7(3), pp. 242-64.

Note

[1] The study was financed by The Swedish Council for Work Life Research, the KF Group, The Salaried Employees' Union, and the Cooperative Employees Association. We gratefully acknowledge the active participation by former and present staff members, who shared their experiences with us.

Chapter 7

The Union Side of Downsizing: Investigating Members' Union Attitudes

Johnny Hellgren, Magnus Sverke and Caroline Stjernström

This chapter focuses on downsizing and how it may affect employees' attitudes toward their union. Downsizing is a topic that has received growing recognition along with the increased flexibility of the labour market, and numerous studies show strong negative reactions among the survivors. However, whereas the bulk of research suggests that downsizing may impair employees' well-being, attitudes toward the organisation, and performance (e.g., Burke and Cooper, 2000; De Witte, 1999; Isaksson, Hellgren and Pettersson, 2000; Kalimo, Taris and Schaufeli, 2003), less is known about how employees perceive their union in the downsizing process. The limited interest that has gone into understanding how union attitudes are affected by downsizing is surprising given that most layoffs take place in unionised workplaces (Mellor, 1992). Indeed, numerous institutions are likely to have an influence over how layoffs are being carried through - among them unions - and it could readily be assumed that employees in downsizing organisations will evaluate the role played by these different actors. For instance, employees who perceive that their union treats the members in a just and fair way and is capable of representing their interests are likely to express positive attitudes toward their union. In contrast, members' union attitudes could be expected to become more negative if the performance of the union is evaluated in a less favourable way (Hellgren and Chirumbolo, 2003).

The overall aim of the chapter is to shed more light on how downsizing may affect members' attitudes toward their union. We begin with a brief review of the downsizing literature and highlight the characteristics that typically make this type of organisational change burdensome for the employee. The following section focuses on factors that tend to reduce the negative consequences by providing employees more control over the process of change. Then we proceed to discuss how and why union attitudes may be affected. Next we present a study conducted in a Swedish emergency hospital undergoing downsizing, and report results on how the unionised employees' perceived their union. The concluding section puts the findings in relation to the literature and discusses implications for unions.

Downsizing

Downsizing refers to a planned elimination of possessions and jobs in an organisation, as a means to reduce labour costs and improve productivity (Cascio, 1993; Kozlowski, Chao, Smith and Hedlund, 1993). To downsize - or 'rightsize' (Hitt, Keats, Harback and Nixon, 1994) - organisations by permanent layoffs and offers of early retirement has become one of the most frequently used strategies for improving organisational effectiveness and competitive ability (Kalimo, Taris and Schaufeli, 2003). Indeed, over the past twenty years, rapidly changing economic conditions and market demands have forced organisations to reorganise in order to adapt to a new reality. Organisational actions, such as downsizing and other structural reforms (e.g., mergers, acquisitions, and privatisations), have been taken to effectively meet these changing conditions (for an overview, see Burke and Cooper, 2000).

However, downsizing differs from other types of structural reforms. For example, Kozlowski et al. (1993) identified two aspects that distinguish downsizing from other forms of organisational transformation. First of all, the decision to downsize is a deliberate and purposeful response to an increasingly uncertain and competitive environment. Second, this type of organisational change is specifically designed to improve cost-effectiveness. Along these lines, managers all over the world appear to have the greatest of expectations as to what can be achieved through entering a downsizing process. The presumed benefits of downsizing concern factors such as faster decision-making, greater flexibility, improvements in quality, and enhanced productivity (Freeman and Cameron, 1993).

In recent years the expected positive outcomes of this type of organisational transformation have been called into question since downsizing seems to be incompatible with good working conditions for the employees concerned and, in the long run, with the vitality of the organisation. Critics argue that layoffs result in the loss of human capital with crucial skills, and the disruption of organisational memory (Kets de Vries and Balazs, 1997; Pfeffer, 1998). Downsizing, though, does not only affect those who loose their jobs but also those remaining in the organisation, and the success or failure of a downsizing strategy ultimately depends on the reactions of the survivors of the process (Kozlowski et al., 1993). Research suggests that downsizing survivors cannot expect their employment in the organisation to be permanent and, therefore, they often perceive a less secure work environment (Roskies and Louis-Guerin, 1990). Indeed, one of the most cited consequences of organisational restructuring concerns increased uncertainty (Allen, Freeman, Russell, Reizenstein and Rentz, 2001).

Job insecurity, which represents the perhaps most frequently examined stressor involved in downsizing, refers to a 'powerlessness to maintain desired continuity in a threatened job situation' (Greenhalgh and Rosenblatt, 1984, p.438). It is considered a subjective phenomenon, based on the individual's perception of the situation (Sverke and Hellgren, 2002). Research has shown that the stress and insecurity associated with downsizing tends to have negative effects on employees' work-related attitudes (e.g., Ashford, Lee and Bobko, 1989; Hartley, Jacobson, Klandermans and van Vuuren, 1991) and well-being (e.g., De Witte, 1999; Hellgren and Sverke, 2003). Job insecurity can also result in resistance to change, reduced work effort, and turnover intentions (Hellgren, Sverke and Isaksson, 1999). A recent meta-analysis also shows that job insecurity perceptions have negative associations with work related attitudes as well as with health outcomes (Sverke, Hellgren and Näswall, 2002).

However, research suggests that job insecurity may not be the only stressor present in organisational downsizing (e.g., Parker, Chmiel and Wall, 1997). In developing a conceptual framework of downsizing, Shaw and Barrett-Power (1997) used the stress literature (Lazarus and Folkman, 1984) as a point of departure and defined downsizing as a 'constellation of stressor events ... which place demands upon the organisation, work groups, and individual employees' (p.111). As a consequence of the new organisational reality, where layoffs is a commonly used method to solve or prevent financial and competitive problems, the most immediate effect of a downsizing process is a reduced workforce which is expected to accomplish more in order to enhance efficiency - despite losses in human capital (Kets de Vries and Balazs, 1997). This, in turn, may give rise to both role overload (being assigned more tasks in the time available) and role ambiguity (the lack of environmental guidelines to direct one's behaviour in the organisation) as the employee experiences the policies and practices of the new organisation. Indeed, critics of downsizing go on to argue that - because more has to be done with fewer resources - downsizing typically leads to an accelerated work load, conflicting demands from various actors in the organisation, and less predictable goals and guidelines (Burke and Nelson, 1998; Kets de Vries and Balazs, 1997; Noer, 1993; Shaw, Fields, Thacker and Fisher, 1993).

Global Process Control

Our brief review of the downsizing literature suggests that uncertainty and stress involved in this type of organisational change may have negative consequences for the individual. In recent years, however, a growing body of research has examined if and how such negative effects can be reduced through fair treatment of the employees. This line of research underscores the importance of factors such as organisational justice (Brockner, 1990; Novelli, Kirkman and Shapiro, 1995), participation in the change process (Lind and Tyler, 1988; Parker, Chmiel and Wall, 1997), and control (Ashford, 1988; Barling and Kelloway, 1996). These constructs, which have emerged as important factors influencing survivors' work attitudes, performance, and well-being, can be summarised under the more general term global process control (Davy, Kinicki and Scheck, 1991). The basic idea underlying these research efforts is that employees' perceptions of justice, participation in decision-making, and control over the change process all will have beneficial consequences for employee work attitudes and well-being, and may even moderate the negative effects of downsizing-induced stress on such outcomes.

Justice is one of the aspects of global process control that appears to have important effects on downsizing survivors' reactions. It has been argued (Covin, 1993) that there is no 'win-win' situation in a downsizing process and, hence, people will be hurt. Organisational justice refers to employees' perceptions of fair treatment over the course of downsizing, for instance concerning who will be laid off and why (Thibaut and Walker, 1975). It appears that when survivors include the layoff victims in their evaluations of just and fair treatment from the organisation, then they tend to respond with impaired attitudes toward the organisation (Brockner, 1990). On the other hand, research suggests that positive evaluations of organisational justice associate with more favourable work attitudes and well-being, and may also decrease the stress associated with downsizing (Brockner, Tyler and Cooper-Schneider, 1992; Davy, Kinicki and Scheck, 1991; Elovainio, Kivimäki and Helkama, 2001). Moreover, meta-analysis results show that justice is positively related with several organisational attitudes (Colquitt, Conlon, Wesson, Porter and Ng, 2001).

Employee participation also contributes to the understanding of the consequences of downsizing. As noted by Covin (1993), the downsizing process is typically dictated by top management, with little or no employee participation. However, when employees are given the opportunity to influence the decisions concerning organisational change and its implementation, the transformation process generally is more likely to be successful, and negative consequences for employees tend to be fewer (for an overview, see Heller, Pusic, Strauss and Wilpert, 1998). For instance, Parker, Chmiel and Wall (1997) found that participation, that is, being kept informed and involved over the course of downsizing, was associated with improved job satisfaction and well-being. Participation has also been shown to moderate the effects of role stress among hospital employees undergoing organisational change (Pozner and Randolph, 1980).

In turn, it is also likely that employees feel a sense of control over the situation when they have an opportunity to influence the decisions being made. Employee workplace control thus represents yet another factor involved in what may be called global process control during organisational transformation. Typically, downsizing efforts focus more on productivity goals than on human effectiveness goals (Covin, 1993), but research suggests a positive effect of control on both individual and organisational outcomes of downsizing. For instance, Barling and Kelloway (1996) found that control perceptions had positive direct effects on various health indicators and work attitudes and, in addition, moderated the effects of job insecurity on physical health. Tetrick and LaRocco (1987) reported that control predicted job satisfaction, and moderated the relationship between job stress and satisfaction.

Consequences for Union Attitudes

To summarise the issues we have addressed so far, the literature suggests that the stressors associated with downsizing (e.g., job insecurity, role overload, role conflict, role ambiguity) generally tend to be negatively related with employees' organisational attitudes, well-being, and performance (e.g., Burke and Nelson, 1998; Parker, Chmiel and Wall, 1997; Pozner and Randolph, 1980; Shaw and Barrett-Power, 1997; Tombaugh and White; 1990). Apparently, then, downsizing can be characterised as a work environment issue - and, hence, a union issue. The literature also suggests that various aspects of global process control (e.g., organisational justice, participation in the change process, workplace control) may reduce the negative consequences of downsizing (Brockner, 1990; Hellgren and Sverke, 2001; Lind and Tyler, 1988; Barling and Kelloway, 1996). It follows that efforts to provide the employees with opportunities for global process control represent another important union issue (cf. Heller et al., 1998).

Despite the scarcity of research on the role of unions in organisational transformations, it could be expected that downsizing affects not only employees' attitudes toward their work and organisation, but also toward their union (Sverke and Hellgren, 2001). Unionised employees pay dues to their unions and in exchange they expect their union to represent their interests, work to improve their work environment, and protect their job security (Hellgren and Chrirumbolo, 2003). Indeed, surveys of member opinions repeatedly find that traditional union issues - such as protection against work environmental problems and job insecurity - receive top priorities and thus remain central elements on the labour movement agenda (e.g., Allvin and Sverke, 2000; Dworkin, Feldman, Brown and Hobson, 1988; Lind, 1996). This suggests that the way in which unions deal with stressors involved in downsizing is likely to be reflected in members' satisfaction with the union as well as in other individual evaluations of the union.

However, there is more to the picture than unions simply adjusting to the situation and working to protect the membership. Unions operate in the workplaces and have the potential to influence how downsizing is being implemented through representative, collective participation in the change process (Heller et al., 1998). A union can be conceived of as a 'secondary organisation', which is dependent on the primary organisation's (i.e., the company) way of taking action (Allvin and Sverke, 2000). This is an observation which has several implications.

First of all, because downsizing tends to affect employees' attitudes toward their organisation, it is also likely to affect their attitudes to the secondary organisation - the union - that operates within the primary organisation - the company. Previous research, which has found that both organisational and union attitudes are negatively related to downsizing stressors, provides support for this view (Hellgren and Sverke, 2001).

Second, because unions, through collective representation, generally have a say in the decision to downsize, the implementation of organisational change, and who will be affected by layoffs, employees may blame also the union for the transformations taking place. Indeed, research suggests that downsizing will influence members' perceptions of the union. For instance, Mellor (1992), in his seminal study of the role of unions in layoffs, found that when members experienced that their union was responsible - or to blame - for the changes taking place, they generally responded with negative attitudes toward the union. A more recent study (Isaksson, Hellgren and Pettersson, 1998) found that attitudes toward the union were more negative among downsizing survivors and laid off workers than among those who had received early retirement.

Third, it follows that when the union takes measures to make the implementation of a downsizing more just and fair, then they will be evaluated as responsible, at least partly, for this, and members' reactions will me more positive (Hellgren and Sverke, 2001). In other words, just like fair treatment from the organisation appears to have positive effects on employees' work attitudes (e.g., Brockner, Tyler and Cooper-Schneider, 1992) and well-being (Elovainio, Kivimäki and Helkama, 2001), factors associated with global process control are likely to have beneficial consequences also for union attitudes. In line with this, perceptions of workplace justice have been found to predict favourable attitudes toward the union (Aryee and Chay, 2001).

To summarise, all these factors may be decisive for employees' evaluations of the union and, hence, affect their union attitudes. Our focus in the present study is on three potential outcomes of organisational downsizing: union justice, union satisfaction, and union commitment. Union justice, which is a construct derived from the more general phenomenon of organisational justice (see Colquitt et al., 2001), refers to perceptions of fair treatment from the union. Union satisfaction reflects members' overall contentment with union performance and representation (Fiorito, Gallagher and Fukami, 1988). Union commitment can be described as an attachment to the union based on identification with its goals and values (Sverke and Kuruvilla, 1995).

The Survey

The data presented in this chapter are based on questionnaires from the staff of a Swedish emergency hospital undergoing organisational change. In the industrialised countries a far-reaching restructuring of the health care sector has recently been seen (Elias and Navon, 1996). Reorganisations with the double purpose of improving quality while simultaneously increasing cost-effectiveness have been present both in the private industry and in the public sector (Munson, 1995). In 1996, the Stockholm County Council (which is responsible for the health care in the capitol of Sweden), introduced a three-year retrenchment program, with the aim of reducing costs in health care services by 17 per cent. The cost reductions, which affected the emergency hospitals in the area differently, took place through reorganisations, layoffs, outsourcing, and natural attrition. The management at the hospital we surveyed adopted a long-term strategy to downsizing, and actions were taken to avoid negative impacts for the employees through strategic planning. The local unions were actively involved in the change process and they also had representatives in the managerial board (see Öhrming and Sverke, 2001, for further details).

In the present study, we investigated the importance of three different role stressors (role overload, role ambiguity, job insecurity) and three indicators of global process control (organisational justice, participation, control) for employees attitudes toward the union (union satisfaction, union justice, union commitment) over the course of downsizing. Completed questionnaires were returned by 58 per cent of the hospital staff. After correcting for missing data in any of the study variables, the analyses were based on 343 individuals. The respondents' mean age was 44 years, the average length of service in the organisation 13 years, and the majority (83 per cent) was female.

All variables except demographics were measured on five-point scales with anchors reading 'strongly disagree' and 'strongly agree'. After all the negatively phrased items were reverse-coded, variable indices were constructed by averaging over the scale items. In general, all scales exhibited reasonable internal consistency reliability. Intercorrelations, descriptive statistics, and reliability estimates for the study variables are presented in Table 7.1.

In order to assess the downsizing aspects we used three different measures. Role overload was measured with three items developed by Beehr, Walsh, and Taber (1976). Role ambiguity was assessed with a four-item index based on questions taken from Caplan (1971), and Rizzo, House and Lirtzman (1970). Job insecurity was operationalised using the Ashford, Lee and Bobko (1989) ten-item scale.

Global process control was also captured using three different measures. Organisational justice was assessed using a three-item index developed by Brockner, Tyler and Cooper-Schneider (1992). The degree of participation in the change process was measured with a slightly modified version of Mellor, Mathieu and Swim's (1994) three-item scale. Finally, control was measured with a reversed version of the Ashford, Lee and Bobko's (1989) three-item powerlessness scale (see also Barling and Kelloway, 1996, for details about the control measure).

The dependent union attitude variables were operationalised as follows. Union justice was measured using three items developed by Hellgren and Sverke (2001). Union satisfaction was assessed with a four-item index developed by Sverke and Sjöberg (1997), and union commitment was captured with nine questions from Sverke and Kuruvilla's (1995) value-based union commitment scale.

Findings

We used multiple regression analysis to examine the extent to which downsizing characteristics and indicators of global process control contributed to the variance in union attitudes. More specifically, separate regression models were used for the

Table 7.1 Correlations, descriptive statistics and reliability for all study variables

Variable	1	2	3	4	5	6	7	8	9	10	11	12	M	SD	Alpha
Demographics															
1. Age	1.00												44.00	9.33	–
2. Sex (female)	-0.06	1.00											0.83	0.38	–
3. Tenure	0.44	0.13	1.00										13.00	8.71	–
Downsizing															
4. Role overload	-0.07	-0.16	-0.16	1.00									3.74	0.97	0.81
5. Role ambiguity	0.06	-0.17	-0.03	0.28	1.00								1.79	0.78	0.78
6. Job insecurity	0.07	-0.13	0.03	0.11	0.32	1.00							1.74	0.73	0.85
Global process control															
7. Organisational justice	0.17	-0.07	0.17	-0.30	-0.20	-0.26	1.00						2.86	0.75	0.73
8. Participation	0.02	0.13	0.20	-0.33	-0.44	-0.28	0.36	1.00					3.31	1.09	0.80
9. Control	0.03	-0.02	0.11	-0.29	-0.35	-0.23	0.39	0.56	1.00				2.99	0.89	0.74
Union attitudes															
10. Union justice	0.02	0.01	0.05	-0.18	-0.19	-0.22	0.31	0.24	0.19	1.00			2.94	0.76	0.71
11. Union satisfaction	0.03	0.12	0.08	-0.21	-0.17	-0.08	0.11	0.22	0.06	0.58	1.00		2.98	0.77	0.64
12. Union commitment	0.09	0.04	0.11	-0.07	-0.04	-0.02	0.06	0.10	0.07	0.62	0.49	1.00	2.21	0.81	0.92

n=343 for r

prediction of union justice, union satisfaction, and union commitment. The results of the regression analyses are presented in Table 7.2.

Table 7.2   Results of multiple regression analysis predicting union justice, union satisfaction and union commitment

Predictor	Union justice	Union satisfaction	Union commitment
Demographics			
Age	-0.01	0.02	0.05
Sex (female)	-0.02	0.05	0.02
Tenure	-0.01	0.01	0.06
Downsizing			
Role overload	-0.06	-0.14*	-0.04
Role ambiguity	-0.05	-0.08	0.02
Job insecurity	-0.11*	-0.01	0.01
Global process control			
Organisational justice	0.22***	0.02	-0.01
Participation	0.10	0.19**	0.09
Control	-0.01	0.12	0.01
R^2 (adjusted)	0.11	0.06	0.00

n=343, * $p<0.05$, ** $p<0.01$, *** $p<0.001$

All of the measured demographics (age, sex, and tenure) were found to be unrelated to the union attitude variables. Union justice was predicted by one of the downsizing variables (job insecurity) and one of the process control variables (organisational justice). The relation between job insecurity and union justice was negative, which suggests that perceptions of job insecurity are associated with lower perceptions of union justice. Furthermore, the relation between organisational justice and union justice was found to be positive, thus indicating that favourable perceptions of organisational justice associate with positive evaluations of union justice as well. In total, the predictor variables accounted for eleven percent of the variation in union justice.

Union satisfaction was also predicted by one downsizing and one global process control variable. Role overload was negatively related to union satisfaction, thus implying that higher levels of overload are connected to lower satisfaction with the union. Participation was found to be positively associated with union satisfaction, which suggests that higher levels of perceived participation in the downsizing process are associated with higher levels of union satisfaction. Taken together, the predictor variables explained 6 per cent of the variation in the outcome variable.

Finally, the results reveal that all predictor variables were unrelated to union commitment. All the downsizing variables as well as the process control indicators failed to reach significance, and the model explained no variance in union commitment.

Discussion and Conclusions

The end of the twentieth century witnessed profound changes in the life of many organisations, not least in the health care sector as well as in the public sector in general. It is also likely that this trend will continue in the future (Sverke and Hellgren, 2002; Tetrick and Campbell Quick, 2003). The research reported here took place in a Swedish emergency hospital undergoing transformation where the organisation had to deal with changes like downsizing, outsourcing, and more frequent usage of contingent workers (for details, see Sverke, Hellgren and Öhrming, 1999; Öhrming and Sverke, 2001). The research question raised in this chapter was how downsizing related variables and various aspects of global process control affect union attitudes during organisational downsizing.

The results indicate that perceptions of job insecurity are negatively associated with union justice. This finding confirms previous results which suggest that perceptions of job insecurity may have detrimental consequences for employees' attitudes, not only toward the organisation as such but also toward the unions operating within the organisation. For example, Mellor (1992) reported that union members' attitudes toward their union might be affected in a negative way during layoffs if the members perceive the union's activities as illegitimate and unfair. One expression of this might be that union members who experience job insecurity may feel let down - or even betrayed - by the union, and that the situation facing them is unfair and not justified. It may also be that members are expecting the union to prevent such deteriorations of the work climate from happening. In line with this reasoning, research repeatedly finds protection of job security to be ranked as one of the most important union issues (Dworkin et al., 1988; Godard, 1997). This suggests that union policies concerning layoffs and reorganisations are important for members' reactions to downsizing related features such as job insecurity - and thereby also for their attitudes toward the union.

Our results also indicate that role stress is negatively associated with union satisfaction. The fact that downsizing survivors frequently find themselves in a situation where the organisation demands the reduced workforce to do the same amount of work as before the layoffs, indicates that we can expect the workload to increase among the survivors (Kets de Vries and Balazs, 1997; Shaw et al., 1993). This scenario could be regarded as a work environment problem and, thereby, as an issue for the union. Consequently, if the union is unable to counteract the increasing workload, the members may respond with a decreasing satisfaction with the union. Because one of the fundamental tasks of unions is to represent the interests of the membership, it appears important for the union to have an active role in the design of the members' immediate work environment - not least in situations of organisational restructuring (Hellgren and Sverke, 2001; Sverke and Hellgren, 2001).

We found participation in decision-making to have a positive impact on union satisfaction. This result implies that opportunities for participation and influence over the decisions being made tend to have positive consequences for the union involved. That is, if the climate in the organisation is participative and the employees are encouraged to have a voice in the process as well as being listened to, they may respond with an increase in their union satisfaction. This relation could also be the result of union demands and strategies for employee participation in decision-making, and thereby generate a positive evaluation of the union and its activities - something that would be reflected in member's satisfaction with the union.

In this study, however, we found no effect of the downsizing variables or the global process control variables on union commitment. One possible explanation for this may be that the union had succeeded in distinguishing its standpoints from those of the hospital management and thereby managed to keep members' commitment unaffected during the change process. This result is also in line with Mellor (1992), who reported only limited effects of downsizing on members' union commitment. Also Sverke and Sjöberg (1994) found that union commitment was unrelated to demographics and work characteristics but their study, however, was not conducted in a downsizing context.

Another plausible explanation to why we found effects on satisfaction, but not on commitment, concerns the different natures of these union attitudes. It may be argued that satisfaction is an affective response, which is more immediate and direct as compared to other union attitudes, such as union commitment (Hellgren and Chirumbolo, 2003; Kuruvilla, Gallagher and Wetzel, 1993). Union satisfaction, therefore, might function as a more direct indication of how well the union succeeds in preserving or restoring a good working environment for its members during organisational change. This could be taken to imply that a longer exposure to organisational turmoil may be required in order to have an impact on members' union commitment. To the extent that members' dissatisfaction with the union prevails, prolonged experiences of downsizing-induced stress may also affect more deeply rooted union attitudes, such as commitment - at least if members feel that their union is partly responsible for this work environment problem.

The fact that organisational justice predicted union justice may indicate that the union organisation is working as a suborganisation within the major organisation - a secondary organisation in Boglind's (1988) terms - and, thereby, may become intimately associated with the decisions and actions taken by the organisation. Support for this argument comes from studies that have found workplace justice perceptions to be related to union attitudes (e.g., Aryee and Chay, 2001). This, of course, is one of the double-sided characteristics of collective participation (Heller et al., 1998). It suggests that the union sometimes can benefit from being perceived as an organisation working together with the employer. However, it may also be that the union will face problems in order to distance itself from the employer, especially if the union is facing a situation where it is being blamed for negative changes taking place in the organisation. This problem emphasises the importance for unions to have clearly stated visions and policies if they want to reduce the risk of being perceived as one of the causal agents behind the company and its decisions concerning organisational transformation (Isaksson, Hellgren and Pettersson, 1998). Along similar lines, Mellor (1992) concluded in his study of members' perceptions of their union over the course of layoffs.

> Unions not only can but may need to use communications about the causes of a layoff as well, either to counteract the use of communications by the company or to increase their members' commitment after layoffs (Mellor, 1992, p.595).

In summary, this study shows that downsizing related variables (such as role overload and job insecurity) are negatively associated with union attitudes (union justice and union satisfaction). In addition, it shows that global process control variables (organisational justice and participation in decision-making) relate positively to the same union attitudes. In addition, the results reveal that union commitment was unrelated to the downsizing characteristics, the global process control variables, and the demographics. From a union perspective our findings indicate that characteristics of organisational downsizing and the way it is implemented may have important consequences for members' attitudes toward their union. In the long run, this could be expected to impact their future engagement in union activity. Indeed, research has shown that attitudes toward unions are of fundamental importance for the individual's willingness to retain membership and participate in union activity (Klandermans, 1986; Sverke, 1996).

However, given the cross-sectional nature of the study it is not possible to infer which variable influences the other. In the future, therefore, longitudinal research designs are needed to further examine the effects of organisational downsizing on union attitudes. Further, the high union density in Sweden (80 per cent) may obviously have an impact on the results obtained in this study. Therefore, some caution is warranted before inferring the results to other countries with different industrial relations characteristics, since it may be hazardous to generalise union related findings across countries (Heller et al., 1998). However, this is no reason for abandoning research on the role of unions in organisational change. On the contrary, this chapter illustrates that unions have an important role to play during organisational turmoil. By influencing the way in which downsizing is implemented and by working to provide opportunities for global process control, unions can also shape their members' attitudes.

References

Allen, T.D., Freeman, D.M., Russell, J.E., Reizenstein, R.C. and Rentz, J.O. (2001), 'Survivor Reactions to Organizational Downsizing: Does Time Ease the Pain?', *Journal of Occupational and Organizational psychology*, Vol. 74, pp. 145-64.

Allvin, M. and Sverke, M. (2000), 'Do New Generations Imply the End of Solidarity? Swedish Unionism in the Era of Individualization', *Economic and Industrial Democracy*, Vol. 21, pp. 71-95.

Aryee, S. and Chay, Y.W. (2001), 'Workplace Justice, Citizenship Behavior, and Turnover Intentions in a Union Context: Examining the Mediating Role of Perceived Union Support and Union Instrumentality', *Journal of Applied Psychology*, Vol. 86, pp. 154-60.

Ashford, S.J. (1988), 'Individual Strategies for Coping with Stress during Organizational Transitions', *Journal of Applied Behavioral Science*, Vol. 24, pp. 19-36.

Ashford, S.J., Lee, C. and Bobko, P. (1989), 'Content, Causes, and Consequences of Job Insecurity: A Theory-based Measure and Substantive Test', *Academy of Management Journal*, Vol. 4, pp. 803-29.

Barling, J. and Kelloway, K.E. (1996), 'Job Insecurity and Health: The Moderating Role of Workplace Control', *Stress Medicine*, Vol. 12, pp. 253-9.

Beehr, T.A., Walsh, J.T. and Taber, T.D. (1976), 'Relationship of Stress to Individually and Organizationally Valued States: Higher Order Needs as a Moderator', *Journal of Applied Psychology*, Vol. 61, pp. 41-7.

Boglind, A. (1988), *Medlemmen, Facket och Företaget (The Member, the Union, and the Company)*, SIF, Göteborg.

Brockner, J. (1990), 'Scope of Justice in the Workplace: How Survivors React to Co-worker Layoffs', *Journal of Social Issues*, Vol. 46, pp. 95-106.

Brockner, J., Tyler, T.R. and Cooper-Schneider, R. (1992), 'The Influence of Prior Commitment to an Institution on Reactions to Perceived Unfairness: The Higher They are, the Harder They Fall', *Administrative Science Quarterly*, Vol. 37, pp. 241-61.

Burke, R.J. and Cooper, C.L. (2000), *The Organization in Crisis: Downsizing, Restructuring, and Privatization*, Blackwell Publishers Inc., Oxford.

Burke, R.J. and Nelson, D. (1998), 'Mergers and Acquisitions, Downsizing, and Privatization: A North American Perspective' in M.K. Gowing, J.D. Kraft and J.O. Campbell Quick (eds), *The New Organizational Reality: Downsizing, Restructuring, and Revitalization*, pp. 21-45, American Psychological Association, Washington, DC.

Caplan, R.D. (1971), *Organizational Stress and Individual Strain: A Social-psychological Study of Risk Factors in Coronary Heart Diseases among Administrators, Engineers, and Scientists*, Institute for Social Research, University of Michigan, University Microfilms No. 72/14822, Ann Arbor, Michigan.

Cascio, W.F. (1993), 'Downsizing: What Do We Know? What Have We Learned?', *Academy of Management Executive*, Vol. 7, pp. 95-104.

Colquitt, J.A., Conlon, D.E., Wesson, M.J., Porter, C.O.L.H. and Ng, K.Y. (2001), 'Justice at the Millennium: A Meta-analytic Review of 25 Years of Organizational Justice Research', *Journal of Applied Psychology*, Vol. 86, pp. 425-45.

Covin, T.J. (1993), 'Managing Workforce Reduction: A Survey of Employee Reactions and Implications for Management Consultants', *Organizational Development Journal*, Vol. 11, pp. 67-76.

Davy, J.A., Kinicki, A.J. and Scheck, C.L. (1991), 'Developing and Testing a Model of Survivor Responses to Layoffs', *Journal of Vocational Behavior*, Vol. 38, pp. 302-17.

De Witte, H. (1999), 'Job Insecurity and Psychological Well-being: Review of the Literature and Exploration of Some Unresolved Issues', *European Journal of Work and Organizational Psychology*, Vol. 8, pp. 155-77.

Dworkin, J.B., Feldman, S.P., Brown, J.M. and Hobson, C.J. (1988), 'Workers' Preferences in Concession Bargaining', *Industrial Relations*, Vol. 27, pp. 7-14.

Elias, E. and Navon, M. (1996), 'Implementing Managed Care in a State Mental Health Authority: Implications for Organizational Change', *Smith College Studies in Social Work*, Vol. 66, pp. 269-92.

Elovainio, M., Kivimäki, M. and Helkama, K. (2001), 'Organizational Justice Evaluations, Job Control, and Occupational Strain', *Journal of Applied Psychology*, Vol. 86, pp. 418-24.

Fiorito, J., Gallagher, D.G. and Fukami, C.W. (1988), 'Satisfaction with Union Representation', *Industrial and Labor Relations Review*, Vol. 41, pp. 294-307.

Freeman, S.J. and Cameron, K. (1993), 'Organizational Downsizing: A Convergence and Reorientation Framework', *Organizational Science*, Vol. 4, pp. 10-29.

Godard, J. (1997), 'Beliefs about Unions and What They Should Do: A Survey of Employed Canadians', *Industrial & Labor Relations Review*, Vol. 50, pp. 621-39.

Greenhalgh, L. and Rosenblatt, Z. (1984), 'Job Insecurity: Toward Conceptual Clarity, *Academy of Management Review*, Vol. 3, pp. 438-48.

Hartley, J., Jacobson, D., Klandermans, B. and van Vuuren, T. (1991), *Job Insecurity: Coping with Jobs at Risk,* Sage, London.

Heller, F., Pusic, E., Strauss, G. and Wilpert, B. (1998), *Organizational Participation: Myth and Reality,* Oxford University Press, New York.

Hellgren, J. and Chirumbolo, A. (2003), 'Can Union Support Reduce the Negative Effects of Job Insecurity on Well-being?', *Economic and Industrial Democracy*, Vol. 2, pp. 271-89.

Hellgren, J. and Sverke, M. (2001), 'Unionized Employees' Perceptions of Role Stress and Fairness during Organizational Downsizing: Consequences for Job Satisfaction, Union Satisfaction and Well-being', *Economic and Industrial Democracy*.

Hellgren, J. and Sverke, M. (2003), 'Does Job Insecurity Lead to Impaired Well-being or Vice Versa? Estimation of Cross-lagged Effects Using Latent Variable Modelling', *Journal of Organizational Behavior*, Vol. 24, pp. 215-36.

Hellgren, J., Sverke, M. and Isaksson, K. (1999), 'A Two-dimensional Approach to Job Insecurity: Consequences for Employee Attitudes and Well-being', *European Journal of Work and Organization Psychology*, Vol. 8, pp. 179-95.

Hitt, M.A., Keats, B.W., Harback, H.F. and Nixon, R.D. (1994), 'Rightsizing-building and Maintaining Strategic Leadership: A Long-term Competitiveness', *Organizational Dynamics*, Vol. 23, pp. 18-32.

Isaksson, K., Hellgren, J. and Pettersson, P. (1998), *Strukturomvandling inom Svensk Detaljhandel: Uppföljning av Omorganisation och Personalminskning i KF/KDAB* (Structural Ttransformation in Swedish Retail Trade: Follow-up of a Reorganization and Layoff in KF/KDAB), Stockholm University, Reports from the Department of Psychology, No. 97/1998, Stockholm.

Isaksson, K., Hellgren, J. and Pettersson, P. (2000), 'Repeated Downsizing: Attitudes and Well-being for Surviving Personnel in a Swedish Retail Company' in K. Isaksson, C. Hogstedt, C. Eriksson and T. Theorell (eds), *Health Effects of the New Labour Market,* Kluwer, New York, pp. 85-101.

Kalimo, R., Taris, T.W. and Schaufeli, W.B. (2003), 'The Effects of Past and Anticipated Future Downsizing on Survivor Well-being: An Equity Perspective', *Journal of Occupational Health Psychology,* Vol. 2, pp. 91-109.

Kets de Vries, M.F.R. and Balazs, K. (1997), 'The Downside of Downsizing', *Human Relations,* Vol. 50, pp. 11-50.

Klandermans, B. (1986), 'Psychology and Trade Union Participation: Joining, Acting, Quitting', *Journal of Occupational Psychology,* Vol. 59, pp. 198-204.

Kozlowski, S., Chao, G., Smith, E. and Hedlund, J. (1993), 'Organizational Downsizing; Strategies, Interventions and Research Implications' in C. Cooper and I. Robertson (eds), *International Review of Industrial and Organizational Psychology,* Vol. 8, pp. 263-332.

Kuruvilla, S., Gallagher, D.G. and Wetzel, K. (1993), 'The Development of Members' Attitudes towards Their Unions: Sweden and Canada', *Industrial and Labor Relations Review,* Vol. 46, pp. 499-515.

Lazarus, R.S. and Folkman, S. (1984), *Stress Appraisal and Coping,* Springer, New York.

Lind, J. (1996), 'Trade Unions: Social Movement or Welfare Apparatus?' in P. Leisink, J. Van Leemput and J. Vilrokx (eds), *The Challenges to Trade Unions in Europe: Innovation or Adaptation,* Edward Elgar, Cheltenham.

Lind, E. and Tyler, T. (1988), *The Social Psychology of Procedural Justice,* Plenum, New York.

Mellor, S. (1992), 'The Influence of Layoff Severity on Post-layoff Union Commitment among Survivors. The Moderating Effect of the Perceived Legitimacy of a Layoff Account', *Personnel Psychology,* Vol. 45, pp. 579-600.

Mellor, S., Mathieu, J.E. and Swim, J.K. (1994), 'Cross-level Analysis of the Influence of Local Union Structure on Women's and Men's Union Commitment', *Journal of Applied Psychology,* Vol. 79, pp. 203-10.

Munson, C.E. (1995), 'Loss of Control in the Delivery of Mental Health Services', *Clinical Supervisor,* Vol. 13, pp. 1-6.

Noer, D. (1993), *Healing the Wounds: Overcoming the Trauma of Layoffs and Revitalizing Downsized Organizations,* Jossey-Bass, San Francisco.

Novelli, L.,Jr., Kirkman, B.L. and Shapiro, D.l. (1995), 'Effective Implementation of Organizational Change: An Organizational Justice Perspective' in C.L. Cooper and D.M. Rousseau (ed.), *Trends in Organizational Behavior,* Vol. 2, pp. 15-36.

Öhrming, J. and Sverke, M. (2001), *Bolagiseringen av S:t Göran: En Proaktiv Organisering* (Hospital Corporatization: Proactive Organisation), Studentlitteratur, Lund.

Parker, S.K., Chmiel, N. and Wall, T.D. (1997), 'Work Characteristics and Employee Well-being within a Context of Strategic Downsizing', *Journal of Occupational Health Psychology,* Vol. 4, pp. 289-303.

Pfeffer, J. (1998), *The Human Equation: Building Profits by Putting People First,* Harvard University Press, Boston, MA.

Pozner, B.Z. and Randolph, W.A. (1980), 'Moderators of Role Stress among Hospital Personnel', *Journal of Psychology*, Vol. 105, pp. 215-24.

Rizzo, J.R., House, R.J. and Lirtzman, S.I. (1970), 'Role Conflict and Ambiguity in Complex Organizations', *Administrative Sciences Quarterly*, Vol. 15, pp. 150-63.

Roskies, E. and Louis-Guerin, C. (1990), 'Job Insecurity in Managers: Antecedents and Consequences', *Journal of Organizational Behavior*, Vol. 11, pp. 345-59.

Shaw, J.B. and Barrett-Power, E. (1997), 'A Conceptual Framework for Accessing Organization, Work Group, and Individual Effectiveness during and after Downsizing', *Human Relations*, Vol. 50, pp. 109-27.

Shaw, J.B., Fields, W.M., Thacker, J.W. and Fisher, C.D. (1993), 'The Availability of Personal and External Coping Resources: Their Impact on Job Stress and Employee Attitudes during Organizational Restructuring', *Work & Stress*, Vol. 7, pp. 229-46.

Sverke, M. (1996), 'The Importance of Ideology in Trade Union Participation in Sweden: A Social-psychological Model' in P. Pasture, J. Verberckmoes and H. De Witte (eds.), *The Lost Perspective? Trade Unions between Ideology and Social Action in the New Europe, Vol. 2, Significance of Ideology in European Trade Unionism,* Perspectives on Europe, Avebury, Aldershot, pp. 353-376.

Sverke, M. and Hellgren, J. (2001), 'Exit, Voice, and Loyalty Reactions to Job Insecurity in Sweden: Do Unionized and Non-unionized Members Differ?', *British Journal of Industrial Relations*, Vol. 39, pp. 167-82.

Sverke, M. and Hellgren, J. (2002), 'The Nature of Job Insecurity: Understanding Employment Uncertainty on the Brink of a New Millennium', *Applied Psychology: An International Review*.

Sverke, M., Hellgren, J. and Näswall, K. (2002), 'No Security: A Meta-analysis and Review of Job Insecurity and Its Consequences', *Journal of Occupational Health Psychology*, Vol. 3, pp. 242-64.

Sverke, M., Hellgren, J. and Öhrming, J. (1999), 'Organizational Restructuring and Health Care Work: A Quasi-experimental Study' in P.M. le Blanc, M.C.W. Peeters, A. Büssing, and W.B. Schaufeli (eds.), *Organizational Psychology and Health Care: European Contributions,* Rainer Hampp Verlag, München.

Sverke, M. and Kuruvilla, S. (1995), 'A New Conceptualization of Union Commitment: Development and Test of an Integrated Theory', *Journal of Organizational Behavior*, Vol. 16, pp. 505-32.

Sverke, M. and Sjöberg, A. (1994), 'Dual Commitment to Company and Union in Sweden: An Examination of Predictors and Taxonomic Split Methods', *Economic and Industrial Democracy*, Vol. 15, pp. 531-64.

Sverke, M. and Sjöberg, A. (1997), 'Short-term Union Merger Effects on Member Attitudes and Behaviour' in M. Sverke (ed.), *The Future of Trade Unionism: International Perspectives on Emerging Union Structures,* Ashgate, Aldershot, pp. 347-60.

Tetrick, L.E. and Campbell Quick, J. (2003), 'Prevention at Work: Public Health in Occupational Settings' in J. Campbell Quick and L.E. Tetrick (eds), *Handbook of Occupational Health Psychology,* American Psychological Association, Washington, DC, pp. 3-17.

Tetrick, L.E. and LaRocco, J.M. (1987), 'Understanding, Prediction, and Control as Moderators of the Relationship between Perceived Stress, Satisfaction and Psychological Well-being', *Journal of Applied Psychology*, Vol. 74, pp. 538-43.

Thibaut, J. and Walker, L. (1975), *Procedural Justice: A Psychological Analysis,* Erlbaum, Hillsdale, NJ.

Tombaugh, J. and White, L.P. (1990), 'Downsizing: An Empirical Assessment of Survivors' Perceptions in a Post-layoff Environment', *Organizational Development Journal*, Vol. 8, pp. 32-43.

Chapter 8

We Get by with a Little Help from our Unions: Psychological Contract Violations and Downsizing

Magnus Sverke, Johnny Hellgren and Katharina Näswall

Several studies have brought up job insecurity as an increasingly serious problem in organisations (De Witte, 1999; Greenhalgh and Rosenblatt, 1984; Kinnunen, Mauno, Nätti and Happonen, 1999; Sverke and Hellgren, 2002). The growing number of studies on job insecurity can, to a great extent, be attributed to the increase in situations where job insecurity experiences are prevalent, such as periods of downsizing or restructuring (Burke and Nelson, 1998; Hellgren and Sverke, 2001; Hitt, Keats, Harback and Nixon, 1994). Definitions of job insecurity emphasise the subjective experience of a threat to the continuation of one's employment (Greenhalgh and Rosenblatt, 1984; Hartley, Jacobson, Klandermans, and van Vuuren, 1991; De Witte and Näswall, 2003). Job insecurity has also been described as a violation of the psychological contract the employee feels has been established between her or him and the employer, which guarantees continued employment if one works well (King, 2000). The increasing knowledge of job insecurity and psychological contract violations attributes impaired well-being and negative attitudes toward the organisation to the fear of job loss (Ashford, Lee and Bobko, 1989; Barling and Kelloway, 1996; Hartley et al., 1991). There is also evidence of negative consequences for the organisation where there is uncertainty, in that the employees react to job insecurity by taking different actions. In this chapter we focus on three forms of such actions described by Hirschman (1970) as exit, voice, and loyalty reactions to unsatisfactory situations. According to this framework, employees may exit from the organisation, use their voice by protesting against the organisational change, or express loyalty to the organisation in order to restore security in the future.

Research efforts have also been directed at identifying how negative consequences of downsizing and job insecurity can be mitigated. It has been suggested that several factors may reduce the impact of job insecurity, among them social support (Lim, 1996). Social support can come in several different forms. Despite the fact that downsizing and other forms of organisational change involving layoffs very often concern unionised employees (Mellor, 1992), little is known, however, about how attempts to deal with job insecurity may differ between unionised and non-unionised employees. Therefore, we have chosen to focus on the type of social support that is provided by the union (Dekker and Schaufeli, 1995), and ask to what extent unionised and non-unionised employees differ with respect to how they deal with experiences of job insecurity. Following Sverke and Hellgren (2001), we propose that workers who experience job insecurity and are members of a union will use different types of coping mechanisms (i.e., exit, voice, or loyalty) compared to insecure workers who are not members of a union. For instance, because union members may draw upon services, protection, and support provided by the union, they may be less inclined to individually voice their concerns or exit from the organisations. Without the collective support derived from union membership the employee will have more difficulty in coping with job insecurity (Dekker and Schaufeli, 1995; Sverke and Hellgren, 2001).

We begin our examination with a theoretical discussion of job insecurity and how it can be considered a violation of the psychological contract. The exit, voice, loyalty framework is described next in order to understand how these alternatives can be used to cope with job insecurity. In the following section we discuss how this framework relates to union membership before presenting the results. Our empirical investigations are based on data from a sample of nurses in a Swedish health care organisation undergoing downsizing.[1] After reporting our findings, in the final section we draw conclusions from the data and point to implications for both unions and management.

Job Insecurity and the Psychological Contract

There are several definitions of job insecurity, but common to most is that job insecurity is viewed as a stressor, which may have detrimental consequences for well-being and work-related attitudes (De Witte, 1999; Hartley et al., 1991; for meta-analysis results, see Sverke, Hellgren and Näswall, 2002). According to Greenhalgh and Rosenblatt (1984), job insecurity refers to a 'powerlessness to maintain desired continuity in a threatened job situation' (p.438). It has also been defined as the sense of threat to the continuation of the employment an employee experiences (Heaney, Israel and House, 1994). In line with the subjective nature of the phenomenon, job insecurity has been described as a 'perceptual phenomenon' (De Witte and Näswall, 2003; Jacobson, 1991), implying a difference between perceptions and objective reality. This perceptual nature of the experience, based on interpretations of the immediate work environment, would explain job insecurity as a discrepancy between the preferred security in the employment situation and what is actually experienced (Hartley et al., 1991). This discrepancy may give rise to feelings of job insecurity if the loss of employment is involuntary (Greenhalgh and Rosenblatt, 1984).

To understand job insecurity further, we have incorporated the framework used in theories on the psychological contract (e.g., Robinson, Kraatz and Rousseau,

1994; Rousseau, 1989). A psychological contract consists of a perception of mutual obligations between two actors, for instance the employee and the manager/ employer. The psychological contract defines those obligations the employee feels she or he has toward the employer, and what she or he can expect as a reward for fulfilling these obligations (Rousseau, 1989). One such reward can be job security in return for a work well done, which the employee may feel is implied by the employer (King, 2000). The experience of job insecurity will, according to this framework, be equivalent to the experience of a violation of the psychological contract (King, 2000). Such a contract violation may result in strong reactions in the employee (Rousseau, 1989), and impair the employee-employer relationship (Robinson, Kraatz and Rousseau, 1994).

Although fears of losing one's job are likely to increase in connection with corporate retrenchment - and with that experiences of violated psychological contracts - the subjective nature of the phenomenon suggests not only that the same objective situation can evoke dissimilar experiences but also that job insecurity can arise, and be an important factor, in seemingly unthreatened job situations (Näswall and De Witte, 2003; Rosenblatt and Ruvio, 1996). We can expect, however, that employees whose work situation is strongly affected by organisational change and who see their co-workers lose their jobs are more likely to experience high job insecurity. In contrast, those who are relatively unaffected by the transformation process would experience lower levels of insecurity (Heaney, Israel and House, 1994; Parker, Chmiel and Wall, 1997), since they do not feel that the psychological contract has been violated to the same degree as those going through organisational change.

Coping with Job Insecurity

The experience of stressful events (such as job insecurity and violation of a psychological contract) will prompt individuals to respond to them with various coping techniques (cf. Lazarus and Folkman, 1984). Hirschman (1970) provides one framework for understanding how various actors may respond to unsatisfactory conditions, such as the ones described, in a variety of institutional settings. The way that the employees act in trying to cope with the unsatisfactory event also serves to inform management about its failures (Hirschman, 1970). Although Hirschman's theory was developed primarily to describe how organisations respond to decline, organisational behaviour research undoubtedly has benefited from this framework; it has been helpful in enhancing the recognition and understanding of the different reactions individuals may display to unsatisfactory employment conditions (Farrell, 1983; Withey and Cooper, 1989). There are three alternatives for employees who find their work conditions unsatisfactory, according to Hirschman (1970). They can find a better job and quit (exit), stay and try to improve the situation (voice), or stay and remain supportive of the organisation (loyalty). These reactions to an unsatisfactory situation have been applied to the experience of a contract breach by Turnley and Feldman (1999), and are used in this chapter as well.

The major alternative to employees in a declining organisation (or customers of the same company, or citizens of a state in decline) is exit (Hirschman, 1970). For instance, dissatisfied customers can switch to another supplier and, similarly, employees who are dissatisfied with the security in their present position can choose to leave, or exit from, the job or the organisation (Hartley et al., 1991; Sverke and Hellgren, 2001). Indeed, job insecurity and violations of the psychological contract have been found to be related to withdrawal responses as manifested in intensified turnover intentions (Brockner, 1988; Davy, Kinicki and Scheck, 1997; Sverke and Goslinga, 2003; Hartley et al., 1991; Turnley and Feldman, 1999). Meta-analysis results provide strong support for the notion that job insecurity may make employees more inclined to quit their jobs (Sverke, Hellgren and Näswall, 2002). In the current chapter we have measured both exit from the job and exit from the organisation (see Appendix for further details).

A second reaction to attempt to bring about change to unsatisfactory situations, according to Hirschman (1970), is voice. Voice, as well as exit, has the potential to make management reconsider the unsatisfactory conditions and possibly redress their origins, especially if highly valuable employees express their concerns. Voice is a more political response than exit. It is also possible that, in reacting to unfavourable job situations, employees are likely to make attempts at changing the source of dissatisfaction prior to choosing the exit option (March and Simon, 1958). Voice is described by Hirschman (1970) as 'any attempt at all to change rather than to escape from an objectionable state of affairs' (p.30). Such a reaction is likely to be characteristic of individuals with substantial involvements in the organisation. When discussing voice as a reaction to a violation of the psychological contract, it is defined as an attempt to restore the relationship that has been damaged (Turnley and Feldman, 1999). Voice can also be conceived of as interest articulation, and it has been operationalised for instance as union membership (Freeman and Medoff, 1984), but it may also involve other actions and protests (Sverke and Goslinga, 2003). In Sweden, with an average rate of unionization exceeding 80 per cent (Kjellberg, 2001), union membership is part of everyday life and cannot in itself be described as a manifestation of voice. Therefore, we have decided to investigate and measure other forms of voice, and have operationalised voice as the expressions of disengagement in a change process and its goals, and protest against it (see Appendix).

A less dramatic, more passive form of coping response is loyalty. Hirschman (1970) described loyalty as the product of various factors that tie the individual to the organisation and thus make exit costly and voice troublesome. In this vein, loyalty may be the reaction of employees with lower status or less crucial skills in the organisation in their attempts to redress job insecurity. Loyalty can be manifested in improved performance or high levels of commitment to the organisation, and has also been measured as extra-role behaviour (Turnley and Feldman, 1999). However, both theoretical and empirical research on job insecurity calls this argument into question (for a discussion, see De Witte and Näswall, 2003). It has been found, for instance, that job insecurity typically is related with impaired organisational commitment (Ashford, Lee and Bobko, 1989; Brockner, Tyler and Cooper-Schneider, 1992; for meta-analysis results, see Sverke, Hellgren and Näswall, 2002). Studies have also found that the experience of violation of the psychological contract may decrease voluntary actions that would benefit the company (Robinson and Morrison, 1995). The issue of impaired loyalty as a consequence of job insecurity, or enhanced loyalty as an attempt to restore certainty, still needs to be empirically investigated. We have chosen to measure loyalty as organisational commitment and work intensity (see Appendix).

Union Membership

In the previous section we described three different ways of responding to job insecurity and psychological contract violations in order to cope with these stressful events. It is possible that other factors affect the relationship between these stressors and the outcomes, here manifested as coping reactions. As mentioned before, one of the possible moderating variables that have been suggested is social support (Lim, 1996). Social support can manifest itself in several different forms, from family, co-workers, or management (Lim, 1996). Another important source of social support is union membership (Dekker and Schaufeli, 1995), and in the present chapter we have chosen to focus on how this particular type of support can affect the relation between the psychological contract violation that job insecurity represents and the outcomes described above.

Even if social support from unions does nothing about the stressor itself - that is, it does not change the perceived insecure employment situation into a more favourable one - such support may have beneficial effects for the individual if it prevents the most negative reactions from occurring. This is an attractive idea, but despite the increasing awareness of job insecurity as an important factor in both unionised and non-unionised settings, little research has examined how being a union member relates to job insecurity and its outcomes. Also, despite the fact that unions often serve the function of collectively voicing members' concerns in unsatisfactory situations (e.g., in uncertain downsizing processes) (Freeman and Medoff, 1984), little is known of the potential buffering effects of union membership against negative consequences of downsizing for the survivors.

In more recent years, knowledge of the role unionization plays has increased to some extent, along with studies addressing what role the union has in a downsizing situation, where experiences of job insecurity and violations of the psychological contract are common. Research suggests that when union membership exists as an external coping resource, positive relationships tend to prevail between union membership and expressions of both loyalty (organisational commitment) and absence of voice (positive attitudes towards the organisational change). Yet no interaction effects of job insecurity and union membership on these reactions have been found (Shaw, Fields, Thacker and Fisher, 1993). A more recent study shows no buffering effect of social support derived from union membership, co-workers, and colleagues on the moderate effects of job insecurity on employee well-being (Dekker and Schaufeli, 1995). Still other research studies indicate that union members are less inclined to make use of exit or individual voice but tend to express more loyalty to the organisation in comparison with their non-unionised co-workers (Sverke and Hellgren, 2001).

Present Study

One major objective of the present chapter is to examine if unionised and non-unionised employees who experience job insecurity also differ in terms of how they cope with this employment uncertainty. More specifically, our goal is to evaluate if union membership has direct effects on the coping strategies and if it moderates the effects of job insecurity. In order to better clarify the different types of union members and non-unionised workers in this study, we provide a typology of job insecurity and union membership in Figure 8.1.

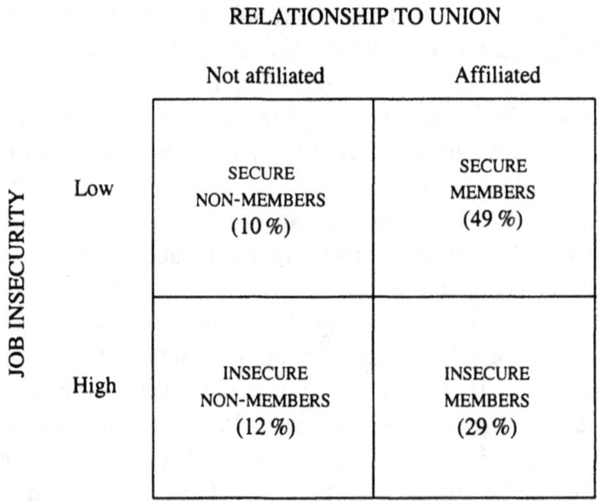

RELATIONSHIP TO UNION

		Not affiliated	Affiliated
JOB INSECURITY	Low	SECURE NON-MEMBERS (10 %)	SECURE MEMBERS (49 %)
	High	INSECURE NON-MEMBERS (12 %)	INSECURE MEMBERS (29 %)

Figure 8.1   A typology of union membership and job insecurity

The typology makes a distinction between high and low job insecurity and we used a mean split to obtain a dichotomous representation of our measure of job insecurity (see Appendix). By combining high and low levels of insecurity with affiliation/non-affiliation we get four different groups. *Insecure members* are those workers who belong to a trade union and feel that the probability of job loss is relatively high. Given that 78 per cent of the sample were unionised this group comprises a large proportion of the individuals surveyed (29 per cent). *Insecure non-members* (12 per cent) have similar experiences of job insecurity but are not affiliated to a union. The high level of job insecurity denoting these groups also implies frequent experiences of psychological contract violations. Whereas both groups are likely to engage in intense efforts to cope with the uncertainty, we believe there is a possibility that unionised and non-unionised employees differ in terms of the how they respond and cope. *Secure members* (49 per cent) and *secure non-members* (10 per cent) share similar experiences of low job uncertainty, which suggests that they will be less inclined to employ coping efforts as compared to insecure employees. They do differ with respect to formal relationships with labour organisations, however, something that could possibly manifest itself in the investments to cope with a relatively secure employment.

Findings

Before testing if members and non-members differ with respect to how they respond to job insecurity, let us first explore some descriptive statistics of the study variables. Table 8.1 reports mean values, standard deviations, and correlations for the total sample. As is evident from Table 8.1, the nurses in our study expressed low levels of perceived job insecurity (1.68 on the five-point scale), even though the health care organisation was going through downsizing. Again, we emphasise the subjective nature of the phenomenon, which suggests that the perception of job insecurity does not simply mirror the external situation (in this case, downsizing) but, rather, are coloured by the employee's personal characteristics (e.g., De Witte and Näswall, 2003; Greenhalgh and Rosenblatt, 1984). One such personal characteristic that has received growing recognition is employability (Klandermans and van Vuuren, 1999), and we note that hospitals in Sweden have difficulty attracting and retaining employees. Hence, the low level of job insecurity can, we argue, most likely be attributed to the favourable labour market of nurses at the time of data collection.

Despite the low mean value, job insecurity evidenced important relations with other variables. There was a negative correlation between job insecurity and union membership, thus indicating that the unionised nurses experienced less insecurity in comparison with their non-unionised colleagues. In addition, the fear of job loss was positively associated with both of the exit variables (organisational and job withdrawal) as well as with both of the voice variables (disengagement in the downsizing goal and protest against the downsizing process). This is consistent with previous research, which has suggested that insecure workers are more inclined to turnover (e.g., Davy, Kinicki and Scheck, 1997) and to express negative attitudes toward the organisational change (Shaw et al., 1993). While job insecurity, also in accordance with previous research (e.g., Ashford, Lee and Bobko, 1989), evidenced a negative correlation with one of the loyalty variables (organisational commitment), however, it was unrelated to work intensity.

Table 8.1   Means (M), standard deviations (SD), and correlations for the study variables

Variable	M	SD	1	2	3	4	5	6	7	8	9	10
1. Age	39.93	10.22	1.00									
2. Gender (woman)	0.86[a]	--	0.09	1.00								
3. Job insecurity	1.68	0.68	0.02	-0.05	1.00							
4. Union membership	0.78[a]	--	0.19	0.23	-0.18	1.00						
Exit variables												
5. Organisational withdrawal	2.01	1.18	-0.09	-0.23	0.21	-0.22	1.00					
6. Job withdrawal	2.50	1.15	-0.18	-0.14	0.23	-0.17	0.70	1.00				
Voice variables												
7. Disengagement in the downsizing goal	2.85	0.72	-0.19	-0.12	0.28	-0.20	0.42	0.39	1.00			
8. Protest against the downsizing process	3.21	0.79	-0.13	-0.06	0.30	-0.16	0.31	0.29	0.71	1.00		
Loyalty variables												
9. Organisational commitment	2.78	0.81	0.18	0.10	-0.13	0.17	-0.46	-0.38	-0.56	-0.46	1.00	
10. Work intensity	4.52	0.48	0.10	0.19	-0.07	0.17	-0.14	-0.09	-0.22	-0.10	0.33	1.00

[a] The number after the decimal point indicates the percentage scoring 1.
-- not applicable
For r>0.12, p<0.05

On a bivariate level our results also point to a potential importance of union membership. Union membership was negatively related to all the forms of exit and voice included in our study, while it evidenced positive correlations with the two forms of loyalty. These results are congruent with the Shaw et al. (1993) study, which found union membership to be positively related to organisational commitment (i.e., loyalty) and positive attitudes towards an ongoing organisational restructuring (i.e., low levels of voice). The findings also replicate previous research which has suggested that unionised workers, as compared to their non-unionised counterparts, are more inclined to remain with their organisation (e.g., Bender and Sloane, 1999), to hold more favourable opinions towards an ongoing organisational restructuring and to express more loyalty to their organisation (Shaw et al., 1993; Sverke and Hellgren, 2001; cf. Freeman and Medoff, 1984).

The correlational results thus provide preliminary evidence for the proposition that union members and non-members differ in their attempts to deal with job insecurity by engaging in exit, voice, and loyalty activities in divergent ways. In order to test this proposition in a multivariate framework, we also employed multivariate analysis of variance procedures with covariates (MANCOVA). We combined the dichotomised job insecurity measure with the union membership variable to operationalise the typology presented in Figure 8.1. Main and interaction effects of job insecurity and union membership were then estimated for all the exit, voice, and loyalty variables simultaneously. Since such effects may be under the influence of demographic characteristics, we also controlled for age and gender. We obtained significant multivariate effects of the covariates (age and gender), job insecurity, and union membership, but not of the insecurity by membership interaction. This suggests that, on an overall level, there are differences in the levels of the exit, voice, and loyalty variables that can be attributed to both job insecurity and union membership, even after controlling for age and gender. The non-significant interaction term indicates, however, that union membership does not moderate the effects of job insecurity.

Table 8.2 presents mean values in exit, voice, and loyalty for insecure members, secure members, insecure non-members, and secure non-members. It also reports the results of the follow-up univariate F tests.

An examination of the results for exit shows that job insecurity had significant univariate effects on the inclination to withdraw from both the organisation and the job. This is to some extent a replication of previously conducted studies where support has been found for an association between job insecurity and turnover intentions (e.g., Brockner, 1988; Davy, Kinicki and Scheck, 1997). It adds to these previous studies with the suggestion that those employees experiencing job insecurity not only consider quitting the organisation, but also look for a position with more security in the same company. Based on this, we want to point out the relevance of a distinction between different forms of withdrawal intentions (cf. Cohen, 1998). Our results also suggest that union members are less inclined to use the exit option in comparison with their co-workers who are not associated with a union. Regardless of their level of job insecurity, union members expressed mean values

Table 8.2 Mean values in exit, voice, and loyalty reactions, and tests for direct and interaction effects of union membership and job insecurity

	Members		Non-members		Effects (F)[a]			Covariates (F)[a]	
	Secure	Insecure	Secure	Insecure	Insecurity	Union	I x U	Age	Gender
Exit									
Organisational withdrawal	1.70	2.15	2.43	2.57	4.00*	6.47*	0.56	0.68	10.59***
Job withdrawal	2.25	2.62	2.62	3.08	6.90**	2.67	0.02	6.85**	2.94
Voice									
Disengagement in the downsizing goal	2.69	2.92	2.94	3.27	7.77**	4.54*	0.12	7.20**	1.90
Protest against the downsizing process	3.00	3.38	3.25	3.62	11.79***	3.02	0.04	3.69	0.07
Loyalty									
Organisational commitment	2.81	2.82	2.52	2.40	0.20	5.48*	0.22	7.82**	1.29
Work intensity	4.57	4.56	4.37	4.37	0.06	4.07*	0.02	1.16	6.86**

[a] d.f.=1,294

* p<0.05, ** p<0.01, *** p<0.001

in both organisational and job withdrawal that were substantially and significantly lower than for non-members. Whereas this finding is congruent with previous research (e.g., Bender and Sloane, 1999; D'Amico, 1984; Sverke and Hellgren, 2001), we did not find support for the idea that union membership moderates the negative effects of job insecurity on members' willingness to remain.

The levels of the voice variables were generally higher in comparison with the exit variables, a finding which supports the notion that dissatisfied workers tend to change the situation through voicing their concerns prior to considering exit (cf. March and Simon, 1958). For members as well as non-members, the levels of both disengagement in the downsizing goal and protest against the downsizing process were higher among nurses experiencing high insecurity than among those feeling more secure. However, whereas job insecurity had significant univariate effects on both voice variables, union membership reached significance only for disengagement in the downsizing goal. In contrast to the non-affiliated employees, the union members in our study typically stated that they to a lesser extent were disengaged in the goals of the downsizing. This finding, which is congruent with the Shaw et al. (1993) conclusion that union membership tends to be positively associated with more favourable attitudes towards an ongoing organisational restructuring (i.e., low levels of voice), suggests that members may be less inclined than non-members to express individual voice to redress employment uncertainty (cf. Sverke and Hellgren, 2001).

The results for the loyalty variables followed a somewhat different pattern. Job insecurity showed no significant univariate effect on organisational commitment or work intensity. The Hirschman (1970) framework suggests that one obvious way to restore security and redress one's attractiveness in the organisation is to express enhanced loyalty to the organisation. Stress theory (e.g., Lazarus and Folkman, 1984) and conceptualizations of the psychological contract (e.g., Rousseau, 1989), on the other hand, would suggest that insecure workers tend to distance themselves from the source of stress or the party they feel is responsible for violating the psychological contract. Hence, our finding takes a position in-between and highlights the need for more theoretical and empirical work on the relationship between job insecurity and various forms of loyalty. However, we did find significant effects of union membership on both organisational commitment and work intensity, thus confirming previous research that has uncovered positive relations between unionization and positive attitudes toward the organisation (Freeman and Medoff, 1984; Shaw et al., 1993). The unionised nurses in our sample reported higher levels of both organisational commitment and work intensity in comparison with their non-unionised colleagues.

Implications

We opened this chapter by observing that job insecurity has become an increasingly important factor in modern working life. To view job insecurity as a violation of the psychological contract between employer and employee (King, 2000) implies, we argued, that this subjectively experienced risk of involuntary loss of one's job is likely to have detrimental consequences for both the individual and the organisation. We also raised the questions of whether such consequences differ between union members and their non-unionised colleagues and, more specifically, if union membership serves as a source of support that may protect members from the most negative consequences.

First of all, our results contribute to the growing body of research that has uncovered relationships between job insecurity and the propensity to use the exit option (e.g., Hellgren, Sverke and Isaksson, 1999; Turnley and Feldman, 1999) as well as the tendency to voice dissatisfaction with downsizing (e.g., Shaw et al., 1993; Sverke and Hellgren, 2001). Our empirical data indicate that perceptions of job insecurity are primarily related to coping strategies in the exit and voice domains, but not to loyalty reactions. From a psychological contract point of view (e.g., Robinson, Kraatz and Rousseau, 1994; Rousseau, 1989), these findings illustrate that employees react to contract violations by distancing themselves from the party that is perceived to be responsible for the contract breach. From the perspective of the exit, voice, loyalty framework (Freeman and Medoff, 1984; Hirschman, 1970), our results also support the view that dissatisfied employees tend to make use of the voice option prior to considering exit. Mean values in the voice variables (disengagement in the downsizing goal, protest against the downsizing process) were, on average, higher compared to the exit variables (organisational and job withdrawal). Interestingly, however, job insecurity was unrelated to both forms of loyalty. It has been argued (King, 2000) that white-collar workers (e.g., nurses) who experience contract violations in terms of job insecurity may be hesitant to express disloyalty to the organisation, at least in overt forms, which could explain the lack of effects in present sample as well.

Some caution is warranted, though, in interpreting the results for job insecurity. Most likely, the reactions to job insecurity are related to economic fluctuations, and our study was conducted when there was a limited supply of nurses on the labour market. Their high employability might thus explain why they appeared willing to make use of exit and reported that they voiced their concerns. In a less favourable situation, expressions of loyalty may be the only realistic option, that is, as a means to show one's attractiveness to the current employer in the absence of better alternatives.

While our study partly replicates previous results, it also expands research on job insecurity by considering the role of the union. Indeed, only a limited number of studies have investigated how, or if, union membership influences employee reactions to downsizing. The most significant finding of the present study, however, refers to the relationships between union membership and the coping strategies. Even if we did not find support for the idea that membership moderates the negative effects of job insecurity (i.e., there was no significant insecurity by membership interaction), there were substantial differences between unionised and non-unionised employees in terms of how they engaged in exit, voice, and loyalty activities.

In contrast to the non-affiliated nurses, union members in our sample reported a lower propensity to exit from the organisation. Moreover, they displayed mean values in the loyalty variables (organisational commitment and work intensity) that were substantially higher than for non-members. These findings thus parallel previous research, which has found union membership to be positively related with loyalty to the organisation (e.g., Shaw et al., 1993; Sverke and Hellgren, 2001) and negatively associated with turnover intentions (e.g., Bender and Sloane, 1999; D'Amico, 1984). Hence, our results suggest that union membership not only may reduce exit but also may lead to increased loyalty (and in the long run perhaps to enhanced productivity). Such beneficial consequences of union presence were observed already by Freeman and Medoff (1984) and Hirschman (1986), and have obvious practical implications for management. The message is that management should not fear union presence as a factor which may lead employees to express rivalling loyalty to the union - on the contrary, and in contrast to what might perhaps be expected, union members tend to remain with their organisation and express loyalty to it even in the context of downsizing. One potential explanation to these results, derived from research on dual commitment to company and union, is that a co-operative industrial relations climate - a characteristic of the Swedish industrial relations system - will facilitate employee expressions of loyalty to both the union and the employer (cf. Magenau, Martin and Peterson, 1988; Sverke and Sjöberg, 1994).

Furthermore, our data also suggest that unionised employees, in contrast to the non-members, are less inclined to use the voice option. Members expressed less disengagement in the downsizing goal than non-members (even if there was no effect of union membership on protests against the downsizing process). This finding supports previous research, which has found that members are less prone to individually voice negative opinions about organisational restructurings such as downsizing (Shaw et al., 1993; Sverke and Hellgren, 2001). Against our finding, and in the light of previous difficulties assessing voice (e.g., Withey and Cooper, 1989), it could be claimed that our operationalisation failed to capture the essence of voice. We argue, however, that our finding rather illustrates that unionised workers - merely because they belong to a union that represents their interests - benefit from collective forms of voice expressed by their unions and, hence, feel less need to engage in individualised voice activities. This explanation is in congruence with the notion that union presence in itself may be a voice function (Freeman and Medoff, 1984). Along this line, union membership can be described as a factor that reduces the need for individual voice and, also, reduces negative effects for the organisation. Indeed, union presence at the workplace serves to direct members' concerns to management attention, through one - representative or indirect - channel (Sverke and Goslinga, 2003; Heller, Pusic, Strauss and Wilpert, 1998). From the management perspective this has the double advantage of avoiding a plethora of individualised forms of voice, and of increasing the chance to express a collectively derived strategy to management (Freeman and Medoff, 1984).

To conclude, the results reported in the present chapter suggest that non-affiliated workers tend primarily to engage in exit and voice activities while union members are more prone to cope with job insecurity by expressing loyalty to the organisation. However, a few limitations to this conclusion deserve commentary. First, it should be recalled that even though we found support for positive effects of union membership, this variable did not moderate the effects of job insecurity. Given the small number of individuals in the non-member groups, however, this study had little power to identify a significant interaction effect. Consequently, future research is warranted to further investigate the potential moderating role of union membership. Second, our study was conducted in a single union in a country with a high degree of unionization. Clearly, additional research is needed to investigate to what extent the results can be generalised to occupations with a less favourable situation on the labour market and to countries with a less dominant role of the unions. In addition, our study has highlighted one aspect of downsizing. While we failed to detect an interaction between membership and job insecurity it is conceivable that union membership could have a moderating effect on other characteristics of downsizing.

Bearing these limitations in mind, our results indicate that non-members are more prone to use exit and voice activities in a downsizing situation, possibly because they feel that they are capable of handling the situation on their own (cf. Allvin and Sverke, 2000). In contrast, union members tend to remain loyal to the organisation in similar situations. One potential explanation for this could be that they can rely on the collective social support provided by union membership (Dekker and Schaufeli, 1995). Given that there hardly exist any studies on how unionised and non-unionised employees differ in their reactions to downsizing, we believe that this chapter could be a valuable contribution to further understanding the role of union membership with respect to the psychological contract violation which downsizing represents.

Appendix: Description of measures used

Variable	Number of items	Source	Sample item	Response mode	Reliability (alpha)
Age	1	--	--	years	--
Gender (woman)	1	--	--	0=man 1=woman	--
Job insecurity	10	Ashford et al. (1989)	'It is likely that I may be laid off permanently'	1-5[a]	0.83
Union membership	1	--	--	0=non-member 1=member	--
Exit variables					
Organisational withdrawal	3	Cohen (1998)	'I am actively looking for other jobs outside this organisation'	1-5[a]	0.88
Job withdrawal	3	Cohen (1998)	'I am actively looking for another assignment'	1-5[a]	0.79
Voice variables					
Disengagement in the downsizing goal	8	Hollenbeck et al. (1989)	'Quite frankly, I don't care if I achieve the goals of the organisation's cost savings or not' (reverse coded)	1-5[a]	0.83
Protest against the downsizing process	6	Sverke and Hellgren (2001)	'The measures that have been taken to save money in the organisation are not acceptable'	1-5[a]	0.84

Variable	Number of items	Source	Sample item	Response mode	Reliability (alpha)
Loyalty variables					
Organisational commitment	8	Allen and Meyer (1990)	'This organisation has a great deal of personal meaning to me'	1-5[a]	0.83
Work intensity	5	Brown and Leigh (1996)	'When there's a job to be done, I devote all my energy to getting it done'	1-5[a]	0.70

[a] 1=strongly disagree, 5=strongly agree

References

Allen, N.J. and Meyer, J.P. (1990), 'The Measurement and Antecedents of Affective, Continuance and Normative Commitment to the Organization', *Journal of Occupational Psychology*, Vol. 63, pp. 1-18.

Allvin, M. and Sverke, M. (2000), 'Do New Generations Imply the End of Solidarity? Swedish Unionism in the Era of Individualization', *Economic and Industrial Democracy*, Vol. 21, pp. 71-95.

Ashford, S.J., Lee, C. and Bobko, P. (1989), 'Content, Causes, and Consequences of Job Insecurity: A Theory-based Measure and Substantive Test', *Academy of Management Journal*, Vol. 4, pp. 803-29.

Barling, J. and Kelloway, K.E. (1996), 'Job Insecurity and Health: The Moderating Role of Workplace Control', *Stress Medicine*, Vol. 12, pp. 253-9.

Bender, K.A. and Sloane, P.J. (1999), 'Trade Union Membership, Tenure and the Level of Job Insecurity', *Applied Economics*, Vol. 31, pp. 123-35.

Brockner, J. (1988), 'The Effects of Work Layoffs on Survivors: Research, Theory, and Practice' in B.M. Staw and L.L. Cummings (eds), *Research in Organizational Behavior*, Vol. 10, pp. 213-55, JAI Press, Greenwich, CT.

Brockner, J., Tyler, T.R. and Cooper-Schneider, R. (1992), 'The Influence of Prior Commitment to an Institution on Reactions to Perceived Unfairness: The Higher They are, the Harder They Fall', *Administrative Science Quarterly*, Vol. 37, pp. 241-61.

Brown, S.P. and Leigh, T.W. (1996), 'A New Look at Psychological Climate and its Relationships to Job Involvement, Effort, and Performance', *Journal of Applied Psychology*, Vol. 81, pp. 358-68.

Burke, R.J. and Nelson, D. (1998), 'Mergers and Acquisitions, Downsizing, and Privatization: A North American Perspective' in M.K. Gowing, J.D. Kraft and J.C. Quick (eds), *The New Organizational Reality: Downsizing, Restructuring, and Revitalization*, pp. 21-54), American Psychological Association, Washington, DC.

Cohen, A. (1998), 'An Examination of the Relationship between Work Commitment and Work Outcomes among Hospital Nurses', *Scandinavian Journal of Management*, Vol. 14, pp. 1-17.

Davy, J.A., Kinicki, A.J. and Scheck, C.L. (1997), 'A Test of Job Security's Direct and Mediated Effects on Withdrawal Cognitions', *Journal of Organizational Behavior*, Vol. 18, pp. 323-49.

D'Amico, R. (1984), 'Industrial Feudalism Reconsidered', *Work and Occupations*, Vol. 11, pp. 407-37.

Dekker, S.W.A. and Schaufeli, W.B. (1995), 'The Effects of Job Insecurity on Psychological Health and Withdrawal: A Longitudinal Study', *Australian Psychologist*, Vol. 30, pp. 57-63.

De Witte, H. (1999), 'Job Insecurity and Psychological Well-being: Review of the Literature and Exploration of Some Unresolved Issues', *European Journal of Work and Organizational Psychology*, Vol. 8, pp. 155-77.

De Witte, H. and Näswall, K. (2003), "Objective' vs. 'Subjective' Job Insecurity: Consequences of Temporary Work for Job Satisfaction and Organizational Commitment in Four European Countries', *Economic and Industrial Democracy*, Vol. 24, pp. 149-88.

Farrell, D. (1983), 'Exit, Voice, Loyalty, and Neglect as Responses to Job Dissatisfaction: A Multidimensional Scaling Study', *Academy of Management Journal*, Vol. 26, pp. 596-607.

Freeman, R.B. and Medoff, J.L. (1984), *What Do Unions Do?*, Basic Books, New York.

Greenhalgh, L. and Rosenblatt, Z. (1984), 'Job Insecurity: Toward Conceptual Clarity', *Academy of Management Review*, Vol. 3, pp. 438-48.

Hartley, J., Jacobson, B., Klandermans, B. and van Vuuren, T. (1991), *Job Insecurity: Coping with Jobs at Risk*, Sage, London.

Heaney, C.A., Israel, B.A. and House, J.S. (1994), 'Chronic Job Insecurity among Automobile Workers: Effects on Job Satisfaction and Health', *Social Science & Medicine*, Vol. 38, pp. 1,431-7.

Heller, F., Pusic, E., Strauss, G. and Wilpert, B. (1998), *Organizational Participation: Myth and Reality*, Oxford University Press, New York.

Hellgren, J. and Sverke, M. (2001), 'Unionized Employees' Perceptions of Role Stress and Fairness During Organizational Downsizing: Consequences for Job Satisfaction, Union Satisfaction and Well-being', *Economic and Industrial Democracy*, Vol. 22, pp. 543-67.

Hellgren, J., Sverke, M. and Isaksson, K. (1999), 'A Two-dimensional Approach to Job Insecurity: Consequences for Employee Attitudes and Well-being', *European Journal of Work and Organizational Psychology*, Vol. 8, pp. 179-95.

Hitt, M.A., Keats, B.W., Harback, H.F. and Nixon, R.D. (1994), 'Rightsizing-building and Maintaining Strategic Leadership: A Long-term Competitiveness', *Organizational Dynamics*, Vol. 23, pp. 18-32.

Hirschman, A.O. (1986), *Rival Views of Market Society*, Viking, New York.

Hirschman, A.O. (1970), *Exit, Voice, and Loyalty: Responses to Decline in Firms, Organizations, and States*, Harvard University Press, Cambridge, MA.

Hollenbeck, J.R., Williams, C.R. and Klein, H.J. (1989), 'An Empirical Examination of the Antecedents of Commitment to Difficult Goals', *Journal of Applied Psychology*, Vol. 74, pp. 18-24.

Jacobson, D. (1991), 'Toward a Theoretical Distinction between the Stress Components of the Job Insecurity and Job Loss Experiences' in S.B. Bacharach (ed.), *Research in the Sociology of Organizations*, Vol. 9, pp. 1-19, JAI Press, Greenwich, CT.

King, J.E. (2000), 'White-collar Reactions to Job Insecurity and the Role of the Psychological Contract: Implications for Human Resource Management', *Human Resource Management*, Vol. 39, pp. 79-92.

Kinnunen, U., Mauno, S., Nätti, J. and Happonen, M. (1999), 'Perceived Job Insecurity: A Longitudinal Study among Finnish Employees', *European Journal of Work and Organizational Psychology*, Vol. 8, pp. 243-60.

Kjellberg, A. (2001), *Fackliga organisationer och medlemmar i dagens Sverige (2nd revised ed.)* (Unions and members in contemporary Sweden), Arkiv, Lund.

Klandermans, B. and van Vuuren, T. (1999), 'Job Insecurity: Introduction', *European Journal of Work and Organizational Psychology*, Vol. 8, pp. 145-53.

Lazarus, R.S. and Folkman, S. (1984), *Stress Appraisal and Coping*, Springer, New York.

Lim, V.K.G. (1996), 'Job Insecurity and its Outcomes: Moderating Effects of Work-based and Non-work-based Social Support', *Human Relations*, Vol. 49, pp. 171-94.

Magenau, J.M., Martin, J.E. and Peterson, M.M. (1988), 'Dual and Unilateral Commitment among Stewards and Rank-and-file Union Members', *Academy of Management Journal*, Vol. 31, pp. 359-376.

March, J.G. and Simon, H.A. (1958), *Organizations*, Wiley, New York.

Mellor, S. (1992), 'The Influence of Layoff Severity on Post-layoff Union Commitment among Survivors: The Moderating Effect of the Perceived Legitimacy of a Layoff Account', *Personnel Psychology*, Vol. 45, pp. 579-600.

Näswall, K. and De Witte, H. (2003), 'Who Feels Insecure in Europe? Predicting Job Insecurity from Background Variables', *Economic and Industrial Democracy*, Vol. 24, pp. 189-215.

Parker, S.K., Chmiel, N. and Wall, T.D. (1997), 'Work Characteristics and Employee Well-Being within a Context of Strategic Downsizing', *Journal of Occupational Health Psychology*, Vol. 4, pp. 289-303.

Robinson, S.L., Kraatz, M.S. and Rousseau, D.M. (1994), 'Changing Obligations and the Psychological Contract: A Longitudinal Study', *Academy of Management Journal*, Vol. 37, pp. 137-52.

Robinson, S.L. and Morrison, E.W. (1995), 'Organizational Citizenship Behavior: A Psychological Contract Perspective', *Journal of Organizational Behavior*, Vol. 16, pp. 289-98.

Rosenblatt, Z. and Ruvio, A. (1996), 'A Test of a Multidimensional Model of Job Insecurity: The Case of Israeli Teachers', *Journal of Organizational Behavior*, Vol. 17, pp. 587-605.

Rousseau, D.M. (1989), 'Psychological and Implied Contracts in Organizations', *Employee Rights and Responsibilities Journal*, Vol. 2, pp. 121-39.

Shaw, J.B., Fields, W.M., Thacker, J.W. and Fisher, C.D. (1993), 'The Availability of Personal and External Coping Resources: Their Impact on Job Stress and Employee Attitudes during Organizational Restructuring', *Work & Stress*, Vol. 7, pp. 229-46.

Sverke, M. and Goslinga, S. (2003), 'The Consequences of Job Insecurity for Employers and Unions: Exit, Voice, and Loyalty', *Economic and Industrial Democracy*, Vol. 24, pp. 241-70.

Sverke, M. and Hellgren, J. (2001), 'Exit, Voice, and Loyalty Reactions to Job Insecurity in Sweden: Do Unionized and Non-unionized Members Differ?', *British Journal of Industrial Relations*, Vol. 39, pp. 167-82.

Sverke, M. and Hellgren, J. (2002), 'The Nature of Job Insecurity: Understanding Employment Uncertainty on the Brink of a New Millennium', *Applied Psychology: An International Review*, Vol. 51, pp. 23-42.

Sverke, M., Hellgren, J. and Näswall, K. (2002), 'No Security: A Meta-analysis and Review of Job Insecurity and its Consequences', *Journal of Occupational Health Psychology*, Vol. 7, pp. 242-64.

Sverke, M. and Sjöberg, A. (1994), 'Dual Commitment to Company and Union in Sweden: An Examination of Predictors and Taxonomic Split Methods', *Economic and Industrial Democracy*, Vol. 15, pp. 531-64.

Turnley, W.H. and Feldman, D.C. (1999), 'The Impact of Psychological Contract Violations on Exit, Voice, Loyalty, and Neglect', *Human Relations*, Vol. 52, pp. 895-922.

Withey, M.J. and Cooper, W.H. (1989), 'Predicting Exit, Voice, Loyalty, and Neglect', *Administrative Science Quarterly*, Vol. 34, pp. 521-39.

Note

[1] Questionnaires were sent to all 438 nurses employed by the organization, and we obtained a response rate of 68.5 per cent (n=300). The majority of nurses (78 per cent) belonged to Swedish Federation of Salaried Employees in Public Health Services (Vårdförbundet), affiliated with the Swedish Confederation of Professional Employees (TCO). Details about the measures used in the present chapter can be found in the Appendix.

Chapter 9

Responses to Downsizing under Different Adjustment Regimes: A Two-Country Comparison

Axel van den Berg and Anthony Masi[1]

Introduction

Downsizing has practically become a way of life in corporate North America (Mishra, Spreitzer and Mishra, 1998; Peak, 1995). In the United States, corporate restructuring and downsizing have been the order of the business day throughout the 1990s (Koretz, 1997; Madrick, 1995; Neumark, 2000). In Canada a recent survey found that 53 per cent of 1,000 establishments surveyed had permanently reduced their workforces during a two-year period in the mid-1990s, by an average of as much as 15 per cent. With the possible exception of Great Britain, European enthusiasm for the 're-engineering' of corporations has thus far appeared more muted. There are, however, definite signs that the trend is taking hold on the continent as well, even in allegedly resistant Germany (The Economist, 1998).

But there are some indications that the rage for 'rightsizing', to use a currently favoured euphemism (Morrall, 1998), may have peaked at last in North America (Ramsey, 1997; The Internal Auditor, 1997). A growing body of literature on the 'downside of downsizing' expresses varying degrees of scepticism about the long-run economic benefits of workforce reductions (Mishra, Spreitzer and Mishra, 1998; Mabert and Schmenner, 1997; Roach, 1996; Peak, 1996; Madrick, 1995; McElroy, Morrow and Rude, 2001; Kets de Vries and Balazs, 1997). Several factors have been suggested to explain lower than expected gains, including increased workloads, loss of critical talent and skills and even rising disability costs (see Auman and Draheim, 1997). But the most often mentioned factor by far is that of the decreased morale and 'organisational commitment' among the 'survivors' of downsizing (Frazee, 1997; Peak, 1995; Klein, 1997; Armstrong-Stassen, 1998; Wager, 2001). Such losses of employee morale can undermine performance and productivity to such a degree as to effectively wipe out all economic gains from the reduced payroll, it is argued (see e.g., O'Donnell and Hubiak, 1997; Abbasi and Hollman, 1998; Bishop and Scott, 1997; Kim, 2003).

This does not mean, of course, that downsizing as a way to reduce costs is inherently self-defeating. The crucial intervening variable is the *degree of anxiety or insecurity* among the remaining employees that it produces. This degree of insecurity is, according to the literature, partly the result of the manner in which management handles the downsizing episode, and in particular the degree to which it is able to retain its employees' trust through appropriate communication. Thus, such diagnoses are invariably accompanied by a plethora policy recommendations on how to improve communication between management and the employees so as to (re-)build trust, commitment and confidence among employees (Gottlieb and Conkling, 1995; Morrall, 1998; Mishra, Spreitzer and Mishra, 1998; Ramsey, 1997; Blohowiak, 1995; James and Tang, 1996; Frazee, 1996; Louchheim, 1991/1992; Knudsen, Johnson, Martin and Roman, 2003; Cameron, Bright and Caza, 2004; Kets de Vries and Balazs, 1997; Jalajas and Bommer, 1999). This is perhaps not so surprising, since such recommendations have long been among the mainstays of management theory, partly inspired by the now somewhat faded Japanese model of lifetime employment (cf. Baruch, 1998).

Somewhat more curiously, however, given its supposed sensitivity to the 'human' side, this literature tends to pay very little if any attention to the *socio-institutional* context of downsizing. That is, the analyses and arguments are presented in entirely universalistic terms, suggesting that the effects will be the same anywhere and everywhere. But there are some strong reasons for questioning the validity of this (usually implicit) assumption.

Other things being equal, one would expect the effect of downsizing on the anxiety and sense of employment insecurity of 'survivors' to be affected not only by the quality of social relations within the firm but also by the (un-)attractiveness of the perceived alternatives open to its workers *outside* it. After all, the prospect of losing one's job must look quite different to a worker who has some confidence that s/he will find a similar job or at least be assured of an adequate income in the event, than to a worker who has no such hopes (see also Kline and Goldenberg, 1999).[2]

There are marked differences between different countries in the nature and combinations of socio-economic institutions and traditions that are likely to affect the outside options and constraints facing workers. The 'Anglo-Saxon' model with relatively weak job protection, modest income support, little in the way of active labour market policy and relatively weak but adversarial unions, is often contrasted with the 'Continental' model of strong job protection, generous governmental income and other support programmes and strong but relatively co-operative unions. One would expect such very different 'adjustment regimes' quite powerfully to condition workers' and unions' responses to managerial attempts at downsizing.

As a matter of fact, a number of critics of the allegedly indiscriminate American labour-cost cutting approach have argued for the long-term economic superiority of a 'European' high-value-added/high-wage strategy for precisely those reasons. They have argued that some degree of employment and earnings security is an integral part of a security-for-flexibility bargain. From this perspective, the relative security of employment and income serves to *reduce* labour's resistance to a variety of industrial changes. It is also thought to enhance workers' readiness and suitability for production requiring high levels of skill and versatility (e.g., Sengenberger, 1991; Sengenberger and Campbell, 1994; Jessop, 1993; Mahnkopf, 1992; Streeck, 1992; see also van den Berg, Furåker and Johansson, 1997, Chapter 4; Hall and Soskice, 2001).

But in most of these arguments it is assumed that so-called 'external' flexibility, that is, the ability to downsize, must be sacrificed for other, presumably more important forms of flexibility, particularly 'functional' and work-time flexibility (cf. Smith, Masi, van den Berg and Smucker, 1995). There is one important exception to this rule, however: the original 'Swedish Model'. This intricate system of coordinated government and union policies was designed in the 1950s by Gösta Rehn and Rudolf Meidner, two economists associated with the powerful blue collar union central LO (for *Landsorganisationen i Sverige*). It was explicitly intended to encourage *external* flexibility in return for the kinds of security provided by 'active' labour-market policies (training, mobility support, relief work), low unemployment and 'solidaristic' wage-policy. The framers and advocates of what also became known as the 'Rehn-Meidner Model' were quite explicit in their assumption that it should be possible to reconcile workers and unions to an *accelerated* pace of economic change, including faster winding down of uncompetitive industries and firms, if they could be assured of equivalent work or, as a last resort, at least generous income support, in case of job loss.

A central presupposition, then, of the celebrated Swedish approach is that a certain degree of external security, mainly in the form of assured employability[3] and/or generous income support, can significantly *reduce* the amount of anxiety among workers facing the possibility of mass redundancy (see e.g., Esping-Andersen, 1985, pp.229-30; Heclo and Madsen, 1987, pp.49-50; Meidner, 1986; Muszynski, 1985, p.295; Rehn, 1984, 1985). Note that this set of policies essentially promoting structural change and mobility, including, presumably, downsizing on efficiency grounds, was formulated and promoted by Sweden's most powerful *union* federation. Indeed, and very much contrary to what appears to be the traditional position and reputation of labour unions elsewhere - particularly in the Anglo-Saxon world with its strongly adversarial labour relations tradition - Sweden's union leaders have taken great pride in their strong commitment to economic efficiency even at the expense of the short-term interests of some of their own constituencies (see e.g., Öhman, 1974; van den Berg, 2001; van den Berg, Masi, Smucker and Smith, 2000). At the very least, this suggests that the role played by labour unions in dealing with and mediating downsizing may vary considerably from country to country.

Since the publication of Freeman and Medoff's (1984) influential survey of what unions do in the US, the traditional view that unions are inherently an obstacle to efficiency-enhancing structural and technological change has been seriously questioned. Rather than merely serving as rent-seeking organisations, as they had been depicted by most neoclassical economists, Freeman and Medoff argued that unions provide workers with a collective 'voice'. Such a voice, they reasoned, may very well *contribute* to efficiency rather than detract from it as it can serve to improve communication between labour and management. The argument here complements that of the management literature concerning downsizing reviewed above. Since unions may serve as conduits for improved labour-management communication, their presence should *mitigate* the negative effect of exposure to downsizing on the remaining workers' anxieties about their own employment situation.

On the other hand, as Freeman himself clearly recognises (see e.g., Freeman, 1992), whether or not the union plays such a constructive role in negotiating change depends very much on the quality of labour relations as a whole which, in turn, is to some considerable degree a function of the larger socio-institutional context and *its* history (cf. e.g., Gallie, 1983; van den Berg, Furåker and Johansson, 1997, Chapter 9). Where this context is conducive to highly adversarial labour relations, as is often said to be the case in the Anglo-Saxon countries, one would expect such a constructive union stance to be less prominent than in more 'neocorporatist' settings such as those to be found in many countries on the European continent. Consequently, it is quite possible that whereas unions help to mitigate the anxiety-producing effects of downsizing in the latter type of context they may *exacerbate* such effects in a more adversarial environment.

Hypotheses

We have then, three different, but not necessarily mutually exclusive, hypotheses about conditions affecting the effect of downsizing on the morale of 'survivors'. The human resource management literature suggests that *the quality of* labour-management relations constitutes a crucial intervening variable. It determines the amount of trust between employer and employee which, in turn, is important in mitigating the degree of anxiety and sense of insecurity during and after the painful period of downsizing and industrial re-engineering, it is argued. Hence, we have:

Hypothesis 1: The better the quality of labour-management relations, the smaller the negative effect of downsizing on 'surviving' workers' anxiety with respect to their employment prospects.

On the other hand, proponents of the kind of reasoning underlying the Swedish Model sketched out above suggest that the degree of *external* (employment and/or income) security has a major effect on how workers respond to downsizing of their own employer. In environments with high levels of such security, downsizing should affect workers' worries about the prospect of losing their jobs much less dramatically than where they face the likelihood of significant unemployment and income loss. The second hypothesis, then, is:

Hypothesis 2: The greater the degree of external (employment and/or earnings) security the smaller the negative effect of downsizing on 'surviving' workers' anxiety with respect to their employment prospects.

Finally, following the sort of argument that we briefly reviewed at the end of the preceding section, one would expect that labour unions would have some intervening effect as well on the relationship between downsizing and workers' anxieties. But the direction and strength of such an effect would seem to depend in large part on the broader labour-relations context. This gives our third hypothesis:

Hypothesis 3: Labour unions have an ameliorating effect on 'surviving' workers' anxiety where labour relations are cooperative and an exacerbating effect where those relations are adversarial.

Now, as noted already, these three hypotheses are not necessarily mutually exclusive. It is entirely possible that *both* the quality of local industrial relations *and* external security *and* the quality of overall labour relations significantly affect the effect of downsizing on the 'survivors' employment anxiety. But even then, it would be of more than mere academic interest to find out the relative strengths of these intervening variables. For in a sense, they represent two quite different policy alternatives: the pursuit of the 'social contract' at the firm level *versus* at the societal level.

In this article we report findings from comparative research conducted in Sweden and Canada. For several reasons, the two countries make for particularly good comparative cases for addressing our present hypotheses. Swedish labour theorists have done more than merely theorise about the desirability of shifting the burdens of rationalisation from individual workers to society as a whole. Although the degree to which their 'Model' was actually implemented may be debatable (see e.g., Eklund, 2001), there is no question that Sweden has gone further than most countries in providing to its workers the kind of 'external' security under consideration here. By contrast, Canada is among the more free-market oriented of the industrialised countries when it comes to labour markets. While not quite as limited as in the United States or, now, in New Zealand, Canadian welfare and income maintenance programs for workers are fairly modest by Northern European standards in terms of benefit levels, duration and eligibility. Moreover, until the early 1990s Canadian unemployment levels have been among the highest of the advanced industrial countries and certainly considerably higher than Sweden's. The two countries also provide a useful contrast for addressing our third hypothesis which emphasises the importance of differences in labour relations traditions and institutions. With the partial exception of the province of Québec, the Canadian labour movement and, consequently, Canadian labour relations have a strong 'Anglo-Saxon' orientation. Among other things, this means that virtually all forms of collective bargaining take place at the firm level, or at most at the industry level. Traditionally, Canadian unions also adopt a typically Anglo-Saxon, militant stance towards employers. By contrast, Sweden is one of Europe's most 'neo-corporatist' countries as far as industrial relations and general socioeconomic policy is concerned. Until the early 1980s collective bargaining was tightly coordinated at the national level, on both the unions' and the employers' side. Since then some decentralization has taken place, but the Swedish collective bargaining system still remains one of the most coordinated in the world. The forementioned federation of manual workers' unions, the LO, has from the beginning played a leading part in the construction and maintenance of the 'Swedish Model' and it has, consequently, also taken a much more positive and constructive position with respect to cooperation with the employers in restructuring and modernizing the economy, as we noted already. In other words, in terms of the social-institutional character of labour relations the two countries provide precisely the kind of contrast between relatively conflictual and relatively cooperative traditions that are invoked in our third hypothesis (for more comparative detail, see van den Berg, Furåker and Johansson, 1997, Chapter 2).

On the other hand, in terms of the structure of their economies, there is a number of striking similarities between Canada and Sweden, no doubt in part due to geographic and climatological similarities. Both countries have come to specialise in resource- and communication-based industries. They are also both relatively small countries (in terms of population!) characterised by heavy trade dependence, specialising in resource- and communication-based industries that are dominated by relatively large, export-oriented companies. As a result, many Canadian and Swedish industries compete more or less directly with one another on an increasingly integrated world market (in e.g., pulp and paper, steel, telecommunications, automobiles). These similarities help to eliminate at least some major potential confounding factors in a two-country comparison.

Thus, Canada and Sweden offer a highly favourable combination of socio-institutional contrast and industrial similarity for testing our Hypotheses. According to our first hypothesis the degree to which downsizing causes 'surviving' employees to worry about their own employment prospects should primarily be a function of the quality of labour-management relations at the firm level, in Sweden as well as in Canada. If Hypothesis 2 is valid, downsizing should have a significantly more negative effect on workers' employment worries in relatively 'insecure' Canada than in Sweden. Our third hypothesis, finally, predicts that due to the generally adversarial character of labour relations in Canada the presence of a union will have a negative effect whereas in neocorporatist Sweden the effect should be positive.

Data and Findings

Variables

The quantitative data presented here are drawn from two representative national samples of the populations chosen for analysis, one each in Canada (November

1992) and Sweden (March 1993). The populations for these subsamples were all blue-collar workers employed in the manufacturing sector of their respective countries at the time of the surveys. Our questions were piggybacked onto the monthly labour force surveys in the two nations. For details on the sampling frames see van den Berg et al. (1998) and van den Berg, Furåker and Johansson (1997). Because of differences in the practices of the two national statistical bureaux, the useable sample sizes are unequal: 779 for Canada, 1205 for Sweden. Questions cover recent experience with downsizing and being fired, fears and worries about one's employment prospects, attitudes towards employers, attitudes towards a variety of workplace changes, the quality of labour relations, confidence in union leadership and unions' and managers' responses. In addition, we will report some of the results of a closely related research project involving semi-structured interviews with management and employee representatives of 44 Canadian and 29 Swedish manufacturing plants in three industries (steel, pulp and paper, and telecommunications equipment) conducted between 1991 and 1993.

Our specific research concerns as reflected in our questionnaire (see van den Berg, Furåker and Johansson, 1997, pp.258-60) were with issues of labour market flexibility. However, we also collected information on respondents' experiences with technological changes in the workplace, recent spells of unemployment, and a variety of attitude scales dealing with, among other things, the perception of labour market conditions, industrial relations, and especially anxieties and insecurities with regard to current employment and future employment prospects. The labour force surveys also provided us with some useful socio-demographic and economic information on respondents. As a result, we are able to examine the effects of both general contextual factors, presumably representing external (in-)security, *and* those of the perceived quality of local industrial relations on the relationship between downsizing and workers' worries about their employment prospects. In addition, we have at our disposal a number of variables measuring important *other* forms of workplace change and socio-economic characteristics that permit us to explore in greater depth the nature of the downsizing-insecurity nexus.

One of our questions directly asked respondents to indicate how worried they were about the prospect of becoming unemployed during the next two years. In this article we will treat this (Worrunem) as our main dependent variable. Thus, as the starting point for our analysis we note that there is a modest, but statistically significant, difference in Worrunem between Canadians and Swedes. Just over 46 per cent of Canadians are (either 'very' or 'rather') worried about becoming unemployed and approximately 39 per cent of Swedes expressed this concern.

Table 9.1 presents a first group of independent variables for both countries with the usual significance tests for the difference between means. These are a number of background variables that may be important in assessing the nature of the relationship between downsizing and worker worries. As with our dependent variables, we chose to dichotomise all variables presented below. This contributes to the simplicity and clarity of our presentation and also renders our statistical analyses as rigorous as possible. This procedure does entail the loss of a certain amount of potentially interesting and important information. But on the other hand, it makes rejection of the null hypotheses more difficult, thus increasing the robustness of our statistical tests, which is, we feel, desirable when dealing with attitudes.

Table 9.1   Socio-economic background variables

Variable	Canadian (n=779)		Swedish (n=1,205)		T-test for difference
	Mean	SE	Mean	SE	T
Firmmed	0.3976	0.0176	0.4631	0.0144	-2.885**
Firmsml	0.3528	0.0171	0.3054	0.0133	2.187*
Older	0.6000	0.0176	0.5700	0.0143	1.2790
Woman	0.1900	0.0141	0.2300	0.0122	-2.2520*
Bott2_5D	0.4115	0.0176	0.3602	0.0138	2.3030*

* $p<0.05$, ** $p<0.01$

Definitions of the variables:

Firmmed   Firm for which R works is medium-sized (1=yes, 0=no).

Firmsml   Firm for which R works is small-sized (1=yes, 0=no).

Older   Respondent is between 45 and 64 years of age (1=yes, 0=no).

Woman   Respondent's sex (1=woman, 0=man).

Bott2_5D   Respondent is in the bottom 40% of the earnings distribution of the national sample (1=yes, 0=no).

As Table 9.1 shows, a slightly smaller proportion of Canadian respondents (40 per cent) worked for medium-sized enterprises (50 to 499 employees), than was the case for the Swedes (46 per cent). The figures are reversed for small firms (Firmsml) with 35 per cent of Canadians so employed as compared to almost 31 per cent of the Swedish respondents, while about one-fifth in both countries worked for large firms with 500 employees or more. The age structure of the samples is almost identical with 60 per cent of the Canadians and 57 per cent of the Swedes being over age 45 (Older). Because of the way in which the earnings and income questions were asked - and not because of some greater equality in Sweden - the breakdown by categories yielded 41 per cent of Canadians, but only 36 per cent of the Swedes in the bottom 'two-fifths' of the earnings distribution (Bott2_5d).

Several of our questions attempted to ascertain the extent to which individuals had experienced changes in their workplace and in their labour market situations over the few years prior to the surveys. Table 9.2 provides the descriptive statistics and t-tests for the differences between our Canadian and Swedish respondents on five indicator variables. In both Canada (52 per cent) and Sweden (48 per cent), about one-half of all respondents said that new machinery or equipment had been installed in their workplaces recently (Chngmach). However while nearly two-fifths of Canadians (38 per cent) said that such changes in machinery had affected their own jobs, less than one-third of Swedes claimed this to be the case (Chngwork). Independently of changes in machinery or equipment, slightly more Canadians (33 per cent) than Swedes (29 per cent) had their work tasks (and organisation) changed in the recent past (Chngtask).

Table 9.2   Objective experiences with change in the workplace

Variable	Canadian (n=779)		Swedish (n=1,205)		T-test for difference
	Mean	SE	Mean	SE	T
Chngmach	0.5188	0.0179	0.4822	0.0144	1.593
Chngwork	0.3817	0.0174	0.3178	0.0134	2.904**
Chngtask	0.3333	0.0169	0.2871	0.0130	2.163*
Firmdown	0.3672	0.0173	0.5751	0.0143	-9.283**
Laidoff	0.3446	0.0170	0.1867	0.0112	7.734**

*$p<0.05$, **$p<0.01$

Definitions of the variables:

Chngmach There have been changes in the machinery at workplace (1=yes, 0=no).
Chngwork There have been machinery changes affecting respondent's own job (1=yes, 0=no).
Chngtask There have been changes in tasks assigned to respondent's own job (1=yes, 0=no).
Firmdown The number of employees at the workplace has been reduced (1=yes, 0=no).
Laidoff Respondent has experienced being laid off from principal job at any time in the last 3 years (1=yes, 0=no).

But the principal change variables for our purposes are Firmdown (reduction in the number of employees at the respondent's workplace in past three years) and Laidoff (respondent has been laid off him/herself in the past three years). Firmdown measures, of course, the extent to which respondents have been exposed to downsizing in their respective workplaces. It will serve as our fundamental independent variable. Laidoff measures the experiences of individuals who are *both* victims and 'survivors' of downsizing, since, at the time of the surveys they were once again employed. It will, therefore, be of particular interest to explore what effect *it* has on the workers' sense of employment insecurity, especially in the presence of the intervening variables referred to in our hypotheses. As can be seen in Table 9.2, Canada and Sweden differ significantly on these two measures. While 37 per cent of Canadians claimed that their workplaces had downsized, as many as 58 per cent of the Swedes reported the same. The exact opposite pattern, however, presents itself with regard to having actually been laid-off from one's principal job in the last three years. Just over one-third of our Canadian respondents (34 per cent), but less than one-fifth of the Swedes (19 per cent), said that they had suffered that fate.

Tables 9.3 and 9.4 show the variables that we will be using as indicators for the principal variables to test our three hypotheses. For Hypothesis 1, we are most concerned with the quality of local labour-management relations in the workplace. As shown in Table 9.3, we have three variables to measure these aspects. With regard to having some say or influence over the way in which technological changes are introduced in the workplace (Somesay), less than half of the Canadians (47 per cent) but almost two-thirds (65 per cent) of the Swedes claim to have a 'voice'. It is interesting to note, however, that nearly identical percentages of Canadians (65 per cent) and Swedes (66 per cent) thought that their local level industrial relations situation was good or very good (Irgood). We also asked individuals if, when employers say they have to downsize their workforce this is often done 'to make their employees more co-operative' or almost always due to 'economic problems'. In other words, this variable directly measures the amount of trust between employee and employer with respect to the very question of downsizing. Here, too, it is interesting to note how little difference we found between the two countries. About one fifth of both Canadians (19 per cent) and Swedes (18 per cent) indicated the first, sceptical, response (Downskp1).

Table 9.3   Industrial relations and 'trust' variables

Variable	Canadian (n=779)		Swedish (n=1,205)		T-test for difference
	Mean	SE	Mean	SE	T
Somesay	0.4703	0.0179	0.6548	0.0137	-8.187**
Irgood	0.6418	0.0172	0.6614	0.0136	-0.895
Downskp1	0.1922	0.0141	0.1834	0.0112	0.489

* p<0.05, ** p<0.01

Definitions of the variables:

Somesay   Workers have influence in the implementation of technological change in the workplace (1=much or some say, 0=no say).

Irgood   Opinion concerning workplace industrial relations (1=good or very good, 0=other response).

Downskp1 Opinion concerning employer motives for potential downsizing (1=threat to induce cooperation, 0=any other reason).

In Table 9.4 we present the independent variables with which we will attempt to test our second and third hypotheses. According to Hypothesis 2, the degree of (in)security about one's own employment prospects is the primary factor affecting the relation between downsizing and worries. The first two variables in Table 9.4 indicate how likely respondents thought it was that they would lose their jobs (Jobloss1), and become unemployed (Bcunemp1), in the next two years. As with our other variables, we dichotomised these so that the figures in the Table indicate the proportions who answered 'very' or 'rather likely' to the question at hand. To our surprise, on these two variables the differences between the Canadian and Swedish respondents are neither large nor statistically significant, with just about one-fifth of each sample thinking it likely that they would lose their jobs and likely that they would become unemployed as a result. Perhaps less surprisingly, these two variables are also highly correlated with each other ($r=0.774$) and both loaded as a single factor in a principal components analysis with scores over 0.9. Consequently, to avoid multicollinearity we decided that in the remaining statistical analyses for this study, we would create a composite variable, Lossunrc which is dummy-coded so that a score of 1 indicates that either or both Bcumemp1 or Jobloss1 was a concern of the respondent and 0 indicates neither to be. As can be seen from Table 9.4, just over one-quarter (26 per cent) of the Canadian sample had values of 1 on this composite variable, while just over one-fifth of the Swedes did (22 per cent).

Table 9.4   Insecurity and anxieties in the workplace and labour market

| Variable | Canadian (n=779) | | Swedish (n=1,205) | | T-test for difference |
	Mean	SE	Mean	SE	T
Jobloss1	0.2115	0.0146	0.1967	0.0115	0.803
Bcunemp1	0.2316	0.0151	0.1768	0.0110	2.932
Lossunrc	0.2636	0.0158	0.2191	0.0119	2.250*
Findtuff	0.6731	0.0168	0.8257	0.0109	-7.611**
Labxpoor	0.3506	0.0171	0.3950	0.0141	-2.003*
Bargunit	0.6300	0.0174	0.9200	0.0077	-15.628**

* $p<0.05$, ** $p<0.01$

Definitions of the variables:

Jobloss1   Likelihood that present job will be lost (1=likely or very likely, 0=any other not likely response).

Bcunemp1   Likelihood that respondent will become unemployed (1=likely or very likely, 0=any other not likely response).

Lossunrc   Likelihood of either job loss *or* becoming unemployed (1= one or other or both likely, 0=neither one nor the other likely).

Findtuff   Perceived difficulty to find an equivalent job (1=difficult or very difficult, 0=not difficult).

Labxpoor   Perception of functioning of government employment offices (1=poor or very poor, 0=other response).

Bargunit   Respondent's trade union status (1=LO in Sweden or any TU in Canada, 0=non-member).

The next two variables in Table 9.4 were also intended to measure the amount of external employment insecurity. The first indicates the proportion of respondents who thought it would be 'difficult' or 'very difficult' for them to find employment with at least the same conditions they enjoyed on their present job. Again to our surprise, more than four out of five Swedes (83 per cent) turned out to be pessimistic on this score, while 'only' two out of three Canadians felt that it would be tough to replicate their present employment situation. The final external insecurity variable in Table 9.4, Labxpoor, deals with the perception of our interviewees concerning the effectiveness of government employment offices. Here, too, the results are surprising in view of the enormous importance that the architects of the 'Swedish Model' attached to 'active' labour market policies. In both countries between one-third and two fifths of the respondents thought these agencies were poor or very poor in terms of their ability to find jobs for those seeking work, 35 per cent in Canada and 40 per cent in Sweden.

The last variable in Table 9.4, finally, is meant to address Hypothesis 3 at least indirectly. It simply distinguishes those whose job contract is covered by a collective agreement concluded with a labour union from all others. This turned out to be the most sensible way of measuring the effective presence of a union since, depending on legislation and tradition, being covered by a collective agreement and being member of a union need not coincide. It should be clear from Table 9.4 that this variable might have some effect in Canada, where 63 per cent of respondents were covered by a collective agreement and therefore 37 per cent were *not*, but that it does not produce a statistically analyzable distribution for Sweden since there almost all employees (92 per cent) are represented by unions. Indeed, for the Swedish sample the variable only reflects whether the respondent is a member of an LO-affiliated union and therefore may actually under-represent the percentage with some form of coverage.

Downsizing and unemployment worries: a combined analysis Our dependent or criterion variable, then, is binary (dichotomously coded 1=worries, 0=does not worry about the prospect of unemployment). Further, in addition to our principal independent variables measuring exposure to downsizing, we are interested in the potential effects of several predictors (control variables). Consequently, the most appropriate statistical method for analysis is the multiple logistic regression model (cf. Hosmer and Lemeshow, 1989; Norušis, 1997; Menard, 1995). Following the three hypotheses that we have discussed above, in Table 9.5 we present six different models for the pooled Swedish and Canadian samples.

Model 1 in Table 9.5 serves as our base model in which we try to estimate the degree of worry about possible unemployment (Worrunem) by our country dummy (1=Canada; 0=Sweden) and the respondents' socio-demographic background variables. As can be seen from the column labelled Model 1, the logistic regression coefficient for the country dummy is statistically significant (p<0.0001). The exponentiated logistic regression coefficient (Exp-B) or the log-odds is provided together with the standard error in the cells underneath the coefficient itself. The interpretation of the log-odds is relatively straightforward: it approximates how much more or less likely it is for the outcome (in this case being worried about unemployment) to occur among Canadians than Swedes. In other words, Canadians are 1.35 times more likely than Swedes to be worried about becoming unemployed. The only background factor to be statistically significantly related to Worrunem is being in the bottom two-fifths of earners, which increases the probability of worrying about unemployment by 1.36 times.

The question, then, is whether and to what extent this difference between the two countries in terms of average amount of worrying can be explained as a result of the differences between the two samples reported in Table 9.2. It is entirely possible that the differences in worries about future unemployment between our national groups, even after considering relevant socio-demographic characteristics, is mostly, or even entirely, the result of differences in the actual *amounts* and/or *kinds* of workplace change experienced by them. Model 2, the second column of Table 9.5, regresses Worrunem on the Canadian dummy, five background factors, *and* the five variables meant to assess each respondent's experiences with change. While Chngwork did not have a statistically significant regression coefficient, both Chngtask and Chngmach were significant. Those who had experienced changes in the tasks assigned to them (Chngtask) were 1.2 times as likely as those who did not experience such reorganisations to worry about becoming unemployed. By contrast, the exponentiated coefficient for Chngmach indicates that those people who have experienced the introduction of new machinery or equipment in their workplaces rather than in their own jobs are only 77 per cent as likely to report being worried as those who, all other factors being equal, have *not* seen such workplace change. But the coefficients for the last two variables in Model 2 are for our purposes by far the most interesting. Employees whose firms had recently downsized were twice as likely (Firmdown, Exp-B=2.03) to report being worried than those who had not, and more than twice as likely if they themselves had experienced a recent layoff (Laidoff, Exp-B=2.15). Clearly, then, 'surviving' a downsizing episode and/or experiencing a layoff oneself does contribute significantly to worries about one's future prospects. At the same time it should be noted that neither the effect of being Canadian nor that of low income is in any way weakened in Model 2.

Now that we have been able to establish the degree to which the experience of being laid off and/or of downsizing in one's immediate environment elicit worrying (controlling only for country and background variables) we can proceed to test our three hypotheses. In Models 3 through 5 we introduce the intervening variables from Tables 9.3 and 9.4, grouped according to the respective hypothesis. The idea is to examine whether and to what extent the effect of downsizing on worker insecurity is attenuated by those variables, as predicted by the hypotheses. In Model 3 we attempt to test Hypothesis 1. Having good local level industrial relations (Irgood), having some influence over the way in which changes are introduced into the workplace (Somesay), and the degree of trust that workers have in management (the reciprocal of Downskp1) are all expected to reduce Worrunem. Our results are

Table 9.5 Logistic regression models for Worrunem, Swedish–Canadian sample (n=1,984) (Exp-B in parentheses)

	Model 1	Model 2	Model 3	Model 4	Model 5	Model 6
Constant	-0.5819****	-1.1260****	-0.8776****	-1.7278****	-1.5830****	-1.8825****
Canadian	0.2985**	0.3546***	0.3086**	0.4022***	0.5061****	0.4884****
	(1.3479)	(1.4256)	(1.3615)	(1.4950)	(1.6589)	(1.6297)
Firmmed		–	–	–	–	–
Firmsml		–	–	–	0.2745*	0.2757
					(1.3158)	(1.3174)
Older			–	–	–	–
Woman			–	–	0.2032	–
					(1.2253)	
Bott2_5D	0.3050**	0.3290**	0.3536**	0.3186**	0.3277**	0.3384**
	(1.3567)	(1.3896)	(1.4242)	(1.3752)	(1.3878)	(1.4028)
Chngmach		-0.2566*	-0.2557*	–	-0.2910**	-0.2179
		(0.7737)	(0.7744)		(0.7475)	(0.8042)
Chngwork		–	–	–	–	–
Chngtask		0.1853	0.1717*	0.1968	0.2007	0.1985
		(1.2036)	(1.1873)	(1.2175)	(1.2222)	(1.2196)
Firmdown		0.7056****	0.6708****	0.5696****	0.6877****	0.5319****
		(2.0251)	(1.9559)	(1.7676)	(1.9892)	(1.7021)
Laidoff		0.7664****	0.7698****	0.5681****	0.7281****	0.5416****
		(2.1519)	(2.1594)	(1.7649)	(2.0712)	(1.7187)
Somesay		–	–			–
Irgood			-0.2874**			-0.2251*
			(0.7502)			(0.7984)

Table 9.5 (continued)

	Model 1	Model 2	Model 3	Model 4	Model 5	Model 6
Downskpl1 Findtuff			--	**0.5432******		**0.5018******
				(1.7215)		(1.6516)
Labxpoor Lossunrc				--		--
				1.2145****		**1.1899******
				(3.3685)		(3.2867)
Bargunit					**0.4998******	**0.4060****
					(1.6484)	(1.5008)
Initial log likelihood function	2,696.6433					
Efficiency	59.83%	62.80%	63.01%	67.46%	63.65%	68.25%
Pseudo-R^2	30.99%	36.10%	36.45%	44.16%	37.58%	45.45%
-2LL	2,668.358	2,550.092	2,534.692	2,415.533	2,537.338	2,339.399
Goodness fit	1,984.581	1,987.246	1,984.855	1,990.468	1,992.039	1,995.537
Model Chi^2	28.285	146.552	161.951	281.110	159.305	297.244
d.f.	6	11	14	14	12	18
Step significance	0.0001	0.0000	0.0000	0.0000	0.0000	0.0000

p-values: <0.10=bold, <0.05=bold*, <0.01=bold**, <0.001=bold***, <0.0001=bold****.
p-values based on Wald statistic: $W_k^2 = (b_k/\text{s.e. of } b_k)^2$, following a Chi-square distribution.

not very encouraging for the hypothesis. The introduction of these variables has virtually no effect on the coefficients and log-odds of the effects of downsizing and being laid off. It is true that those employees who consider the relation with their employers to be good are statistically significantly less likely to be worried, but this is not the case for those who claim that have some say in decisions about the introduction of technological change (Somesay). But even more damaging for Hypothesis 1 is the fact that the effect of scepticism about management's motives when proposing to downsize is not statistically significant. This is a heavy blow to the hypothesis because this variable represents the most direct test of the theory on which it is based.

Model 4 subjects Hypothesis 2 to the test. Here we introduce our three external (in-)security variables. The results are somewhat more positive for this hypothesis but not overwhelmingly so. Controlling for the respondents' expected difficulty to find an equivalent job (Findtuff), their judgement of labour exchanges' effectiveness (Labxpoor) and the composite probability of job loss/unemployment variable (Lossunrc) does have a somewhat weakening effect on the *degree* to which downsizing and being laid off produce worries - the log-odds drop from around 2 to 1.76 - but the original effects do not appear to have lost any of their statistical significance. If one expects to lose one's job and/or become unemployed one is more than three times more likely to be worried (Exp-B=3.3685) than if one does not have such expectations which is, of course, not really very surprising.

Model 5 is our direct test of Hypothesis 3, the importance of trade unions in ameliorating worries where industrial relations are good, but exacerbating them where they are bad. As can be seen in the penultimate column of Table 9.5, the presence of a union has a direct *negative* effect: it increases the likelihood of workers' worrying about their employment prospects by a factor of 1.65. On the other hand, union presence apparently has no effect at all on the degree to which downsizing and being laid off affect being worried. The coefficients and Exp-B's for these variables have returned to the magnitudes and significance levels that they had in Models 2 and 3.

For the sake of completeness and to check for possible interaction effects we present Model 6 in the last column of the table, a regression in which we have included all variables together. There are no surprises in the results. The effects of downsizing and being laid off are somewhat reduced, as was the case in Model 4, but there are no noteworthy changes in any of the other coefficients.

Canada versus Sweden: separate logistic regressions Thus far, we have established that the effect of the country variable, as well as the two principal experiences with recent workplace changes, Firmdown and Laidoff, continue to have statistically significant coefficients, even in the presence of other variables. This remains the case even when these controls themselves are strong predictors of Worrunem, such as Lossunrc or the perception that equivalent employment would be hard to find. We also ascertained that for our joint sample, good local industrial relations mitigates worries, while the presence of collective bargaining units tends to exacerbate them. The next logical step is to explore whether or not the same factors operate to produce worries about unemployment prospects for our two country samples separately. After all, the persistence of the strong country effect suggests that it might strongly condition the potential effects of the other independent variables. The only way to verify this is to disaggregate the sample into its Swedish and Canadian components and rerun the regression models on each. To avoid unnecessary repetition we report the detailed regression results in two tables in the Appendix (Table A1 for Canada; A2 for Sweden). Table 9.6, which we shall discuss here in greater detail, presents a summary of the results as well the most complete two-country model from Table 9.5 for easy comparison.

Table 9.6   Comparison of multiple logistic regression for Worrunem, Model 6, significant variables only, point estimates for Exp-B given

	Two-countries	Canada	Sweden
Canadian	1.6297		
Firmmed			
Firmsml	1.3174		
Older			
Woman			1.4133
Bott2_5D	1.4028	2.0517	
Chngmach	0.8042		
Chngwork		0.6913	
Chngtask	1.2196	1.7623	
Firmdown	1.7021	1.7810	1.7572
Laidoff	1.787	2.0041	1.5422
Somesay			
Irgood	0.7984		0.7260
Downskp1			
Findtuff	1.6516	1.6262	1.6969
Labxpoor			
Lossunrc	3.2867	3.7937	3.0997
Bargunit	1.5008	1.8125	
Efficiency	68.25%	69.19%	68.96%
Pseudo-R^2	45.45%	42.58%	49.25%

As can be seen in Table 9.6, there are four variables that are consistently statistically significant across the three analyses. Not surprisingly, thinking that one is likely to lose a job and/or to become unemployed (Lossunrc) makes people three to nearly four times more likely to worry about unemployment. Further, for those who think that finding equivalent employment will be difficult (Findtuff), the propensity to worry goes up by more than 1.6 times in all three models. In addition, if you yourself have had the experience of being let go from your principal job in the last three years (Laidoff), then you are 1.5 times more likely to worry about unemployment in Sweden but over 2 times more likely in Canada. Finally, those individuals whose firms have downsized (Firmdown) are consistently around 1.7 times more likely to be worried than their counterparts whose workplaces have not experienced such cutbacks.

But from the perspective of the theoretical arguments that inform this article the factors on which the Canadian and Swedish models *differ* are more interesting. In Canada, but not in Sweden, several workplace change variables are statistically significantly related to the propensity to worry about unemployment. If you yourself have had to adapt to new machinery in order to do your job (Chngwork), then the probability of being among the worriers in our sample is actually only 69 per cent of what it is for those who have not had to make such adjustments. On the other hand, if you have recently experienced a re-organisation of your work role unrelated to any new equipment, then the chances that you will be among the worriers increases by 1.8 times. Two other variables are significant in Canada but not in Sweden. The presence of a trade union (Bargunit) increases Worrunem by 1.8 times. Finally, being in the bottom forty percent of the earnings distribution more than doubles (2.1 times) the probability that the Canadian respondent will be a worrier.

On the other hand, there are two variables that are statistically significant in Sweden but not in Canada. First, those individuals who thought that the local level industrial relations situation at their workplaces were good or very good (Irgood) were only three-quarters as likely (0.73) to be worried about unemployment as those who were not so enthused about the quality of local labour relations. Second, Swedish women (Woman) were about 1.4 times more likely than the men to be classified as worrying about unemployment.

It is also worth noting that several predictor variables turned out *not* to be significant in *any* of our three models summarised in Table 9.6. Surprisingly enough, distrust of employers who threaten with downsizing (Downskp1) turned out not to have a significant effect in any of our models. The same can be said, perhaps a little less surprisingly, for older workers, for workers in middle-sized firms and for those who have a negative view of government employment centres' ability to find new work for those in need of jobs. We return to these results below.

Theoretical Implications

Now let us return to the theoretical questions with which we started. Does downsizing appear to have the demoralizing effect on 'surviving' workers that some of the literature claims it does? Is such an effect significantly attenuated by good labour-management relations? Is it greatly affected by the degree of (in-)security facing workers in the external labour market? Is the presence of a trade union a positive or a negative factor? Which, if any, of these intervening factors is more important in attenuating the effect of downsizing on the worries of those left behind?

No doubt our results can be interpreted in more than one way but they provide, in our opinion, enough of a basis to render the following general conclusions at least plausible. First, there is no doubt that *exposure to downsizing as such* has a considerable negative impact on the degree to which 'survivors' worry about their own employment prospects. This effect remains robust and virtually unaffected even by the presence of a host control variables that theoretically might be expected to significantly influence it. This can be seen from the remarkable strength and constancy of *both* downsizing variables across all models we tested. Working for a firm that had suffered through significant downsizing in the preceding three years (Firmdown) renders one between 1.7 and 2 times more likely to worry about becoming unemployed oneself than not having had that experience. And this effect remains virtually unchanged in either statistical significance or magnitude across the pooled models presented in Table 9.5 as well as in the separate-country equations of Table 9.6. The same can be said for the laid-off variable: those who had been laid off at some time during the preceding three years were from 1.5 to 2 times more likely to worry than their luckier colleagues. To put it differently, *neither* the quality of local labour-management relations *nor* the degree of insecurity about external labour market prospects, *nor* the presence of a trade union, *nor* even all other socioeconomic differences that should be picked up by the country dummy affect this fundamental relation between downsizing and survivor employment worries to any significant degree.

But this conclusion requires some qualification. Of the three groups of variables that we introduced separately, two had no noticeable influence *whatsoever* on the effect of downsizing on worries. To be sure, the introduction of the third group, the external insecurity variables, did not reduce the level of significance of that effect either but it did somewhat reduce its magnitude. In other words, a sense of security about one's prospects on the external labour market did to some extent mitigate the worrying effect of downsizing. This provides at least some *prima facie* support for our second ('Swedish') hypothesis.

This general impression is further reinforced by our regression results for the two countries separately, in particular when one considers the *differences* between the two. Several variables had an effect on worries about unemployment in one country but not in the other. In Canada but not in Sweden, Chngwork, having experienced substantial change in the equipment used in one's own job in recent years, has a *positive* effect, that is, it *reduces* the degree to which one worries about becoming unemployed (Exp-B=0.61). On the other hand, the experience of having had one's job tasks changed *apart from changes in equipment*, appears to have a considerable *negative* effect, making it 1.83 times more likely that one will worry about becoming unemployed than if one's work tasks have *not* changed substantially in the recent past. Again, in Sweden there appears to be no such effect. One plausible interpretation of these intriguing differences is that the introduction of new equipment indicates to the worker a comforting willingness on the part of his/her employer to invest in one's person and job. On the other hand, being subjected to work reorganisations that involve no such investments on the part of one's employer may well spell trouble. The reasoning sounds plausible enough and one would expect it to hold fairly generally. Yet the interesting thing about our findings is that they seem to hold *only for Canada*. Receiving new equipment to work with does not seem to have the same comforting effect in Sweden, nor do reorganisations appear to have the same negative effects. In the more externally secure Swedish context, workers do not appear to be as relieved of their anxieties by new investment nor as apprehensive about organisational change involving no new investments as workers are in Canada's less hospitable external environment.

Something similar may account for the fact that workers in the bottom 40 per cent of the income distribution in Canada are twice as likely to worry about their employment prospects as their better-off fellow countrymen. Again, in Sweden, with its celebrated social safety net and relatively compressed income distribution, we find no such difference among high and low income workers. Finally it is worth noting that the coefficients and log-odds for the downsizing- and even more so for the laid-off variable are consistently somewhat or even considerably higher in Canada than in Sweden. Taken together, all these results do seem to indicate that the external labour market is viewed as less threatening and risky in Sweden than in Canada and that this has a clear influence on the degree to which workers worry about the possibility of unemployment and downsizing. In other words, a number of our findings appear to underwrite Hypothesis 2 fairly consistently.

Another intriguing finding in Table 9.6 is the fact that the presence of a labour union *increases* the amount of worrying among Canadian workers while there is no such effect at all in Sweden. The latter is not surprising since there virtually all respondents (and more than 80 per cent of *all* employees) were part of some collective bargaining unit. But what interests us here is the fact that in Canada the union apparently has a *negative* effect on workers' anxiety. This might point to a partial confirmation of our third hypothesis: in the Canadian historical-institutional context of relatively militant, conflictual relations between unions and employers the presence of a union increases the worries and sense of insecurity of the workers about their employment prospects.

This interpretation receives some support from the results of the factory interviews, alluded to earlier, which we conducted with some 150 employer and employee representatives in three major industries (steel, pulp and paper and telecommunications equipment) in Sweden and Canada at about the same time our surveys were conducted. While we cannot here report at length on our findings from those interviews (for this, see Smith et al., 1995; 1997; Smucker, Masi, Smith and van den Berg, 1998; van den Berg, Furåker and Johansson, 1997, Chapter 6; van den Berg et al., 2000), the degree to which they correspond to the quantitative results reported here is striking.

In these factory interviews, too, we found that redundancies and downsizing caused considerable anxieties in both countries, irrespective of differences in labour-market regimes and quality of labour relations, and notwithstanding certain systematic interindustry differences. More interestingly, however, the roles played by the unions in the process of coping with changes of various kinds turned out to be quite different in the two countries. While unions in Sweden appeared often to be relatively cooperative and sometimes even more favourably disposed towards change than their rank-and-file, Canadian unions were frequently described as defensive, adversarial and often much less accommodative than their ordinary members. In fact, one often got the impression that the union was the cause of a fair amount of unrest in some of the Canadian settings whereas it appeared to be mostly a stabilizing factor in Sweden. Such findings fit rather well, of course, with what we know about the different traditions of the Anglo-Saxon, adversarial Canadian labour movement and the neocorporatist, almost technocratic Swedish unions (see also van den Berg, Furåker and Johansson, 1997, Chapter 2). And it would certainly appear to be in keeping with our statistical finding that being part of a bargaining unit in Canada *raises* the level of employment anxiety among workers.

All in all, then, at the very least our results cannot be said to have refuted Hypotheses 2 and 3. Most of our findings either support them or else are at least compatible with them. The same cannot be said about our Hypothesis 1. It is difficult to find any support for the thesis that the quality of local labour-management relations and especially employees' trust of employers significantly influence the degree to which downsizing generates anxiety among left-over employees. Introduction of control variables measuring the perceived quality of labour-management relations and trust between workers and employers had no effect whatsoever on the degree to which downsizing or having been laid off caused employees to worry about their future employment. A relatively good relationship with the employer as perceived by the employees had a weak attenuating direct effect on the anxiety of the employees, but only in Sweden. But much more damaging for the hypothesis is the fact that neither having a say nor mistrust of employers threatening to downsize had any effect at all. Especially the latter finding would appear to us to be rather fatal for Hypothesis 1 since it is the most direct test of that hypothesis that one can imagine.

Conclusion

The human resource management literature has recently come to emphasise the 'downside of downsizing'. In particular, it is claimed that the negative effects on the morale of the workers who have 'survived' the downsizing exercise may be so harmful to overall productivity as to outweigh whatever immediate economic gains the workforce reductions may bring. The main mechanism by which downsizing is said to have such negative effects is by arousing insecurity and worries among the 'survivors' about their own employment prospects. However, this effect can be substantially attenuated or even eliminated, it is claimed, by the successful cultivation of good labour-management relations that elicit trust and commitment among the 'surviving' workers.

On the other hand, a number of political economists critical of the 'free-market' model allegedly practised in the United States have argued that a crucial factor in helping allay the fears and anxieties caused by industrial restructuring is the degree of employment and/or income security available to workers *outside* their current place of employment. In addition, there is a whole literature emphasizing the importance of the role played by labour unions, suggesting that in a relatively constructive context the presence of a union can exert a considerable mitigating influence on the negative effects of industrial restructuring, whereas in a more adversarial environment the union can also have the effect of heightening the anxieties caused by restructuring.

In this article we report findings from a Swedish-Canadian comparison of blue-collar manufacturing workers having been exposed to various kinds of change, including downsizing. The results provide strong support for the claim that experience with downsizing, irrespective of a variety of controls, has a strong negative effect on survivor employment worries everywhere. At the same time, there is also some evidence suggesting that the degree of externally provided security has a considerable impact both on the total amount of anxiety *and* on how exactly various other factors affect it. There are also some indications in our results that support the thesis that under relatively conflictual circumstances the presence of a labour union can lead to increased worries on the part of employees about their employment prospects. On the other hand, the thesis that the quality of labour-management relations is of decisive importance is not borne out by our data. Good relations with one's employer do not appear to have much of a mitigating effect on the worries of employees, and where they have such an effect it appears to be highly context-dependent.

Of course, we hardly expect our negative findings to be taken as a definitive refutation of what is arguably the theoretical core of the entire management literature. Such a refutation requires a huge mass of cumulative negative evidence, as Kuhn (1970) has so famously argued. However, we do think we have at least made a case for paying more attention to the larger socio-economic environment in studying the effects of downsizing, and workplace change more generally, on workers than has hitherto been the case especially in the management literature which has tended to treat the firm as a relatively isolated unit. Neither theory nor, at least in the present case, empirical evidence would seem to justify the assumption that the nature of local labour relations are of primordial importance or that they can be studied, let alone harnessed, in isolation from the socio-economic and institutional environment of which they are a part.

On the other hand, we have not, of course, made any definitive case for the importance of the external security factor either. Rather, our findings are suggestive of *some* mitigating or at least modifying effect of this factor on the impact of industrial change. How important it is and exactly how it operates remain to be established by more detailed studies using a variety of methodologies in different settings. It would be particularly interesting to see what factors affect survivor insecurity, and how they do, in the socio-economic settings of other advanced industrialised countries which in many respects tend to cluster somewhere in the middle on the continuum of between Sweden and Canada.

Appendix

Table A1. Logistic regression models for Worrunem, Canadian sample (n=779) (standard errors and Exp-B are given in parentheses below regression coefficients)

	Model 1	Model 2	Model 3	Model 4	Model 5	Model 6
Constant	-0.4718*	-0.9212****	-0.6854*	-1.5271****	-1.3597****	-1.6961****
	(0.1898)	(0.2417)	(0.2714)	(0.2892)	(0.2700)	(0.3453)
Firmmed	-0.0596	0.0687	0.0508	0.0780	0.1216	0.1144
	(0.1876)	(0.1979)	(0.2006)	(0.2077)	(0.1998)	(0.2120)
	(0.9421)	(1.0711)	(1.0521)	(1.0812)	(1.1293)	(1.1212)
Firmsml	0.0598	0.1094	0.0836	0.1106	0.3661	0.3048
	(0.1935)	(0.2071)	(0.2089)	(0.2188)	(0.2195)	(0.2327)
	(1.0616)	(1.0711)	(1.0872)	(1.1169)	(1.4422)	(1.3563)
Older	0.1567	0.1010	0.0913	-0.0280	-0.0169	-0.1306
	(0.1526)	(0.1610)	(0.1622)	(0.1697)	(0.1653)	(0.1752)
	(1.1697)	(1.1063)	(1.0956)	(0.9724)	(0.9832)	(0.8776)
Woman	-0.1386	-0.2084	-0.2686	-0.1844	-0.0858	-0.1123
	(0.1958)	(0.2069)	(0.2104)	(0.2168)	(0.2103)	(0.2236)
	(0.8706)	(0.8119)	(0.7644)	(0.8316)	(0.9178)	(0.8937)
Bott2_5D	0.6275****	0.6374***	0.7003****	0.6642***	0.6511***	0.7187****
	(0.1615)	(0.1717)	(0.1754)	(0.1793)	(0.1738)	(0.1844)
	(1.8730)	(1.8916)	(2.0144)	(1.9430)	(1.9177)	(2.0517)
Chngmach		-0.2658	-0.2548	-0.1483	-0.3799*	-0.2329
		(0.1856)	(0.1875)	(0.1954)	(0.1897)	(0.2012)
		(0.7666)	(0.7751)	(0.8621)	(0.6839)	(0.7923)

Table A1 (continued)

	Model 1	Model 2	Model 3	Model 4	Model 5	Model 6
Chngwork		-0.4872*	-0.4385*	-0.4955*	-0.5001**	-0.4791*
		(0.1906)	(0.1934)	(0.2008)	(0.1920)	(0.2038)
		(0.6143)	(0.6450)	(0.6093)	(0.6065)	(0.6193)
Chngtask		0.4089*	0.4140*	0.4998**	0.4918**	0.5666**
		(0.1715)	(0.1746)	(0.1784)	(0.1753)	(0.1846)
		(1.5051)	(1.5129)	(1.6484)	(1.6352)	(1.7623)
Firmdown		0.8040****	0.7904****	0.5986***	0.7664****	0.5771***
		(0.1624)	(0.1653)	(0.1711)	(0.1645)	(0.1752)
		(2.2344)	(2.2044)	(1.8196)	(2.1520)	(1.7810)
Laidoff		0.8898****	0.9075****	0.7435*****	0.8057*****	0.6952*****
		(0.1643)	(0.1668)	(0.1728)	(0.1670)	(0.1772)
		(2.4347)	(2.4782)	(2.1032)	(2.2383)	(2.0041)
Somesay			-0.3237*			-0.2509
			(0.1608)			(0.1697)
			(0.7235)			(0.7781)
Irgood			-0.1966			-0.0954
			(0.1678)			(0.1778)
			(0.8216)			(0.9090)
Downskp1			0.1106			0.0902
			(0.1982)			(0.2091)
			(1.1169)			(1.0944)
Findtuff				0.5681**		0.4863**
				(0.1791)		(0.1840)
				(1.7650)		(1.6262)

Table A1   (continued)

	Model 1	Model 2	Model 3	Model 4	Model 5	Model 6
Labxpoor				-0.1110		-0.0987
				(0.1697)		(0.1724)
				(0.8949)		(0.9060)
Lossunrc				**1.3780******		**1.3333******
				(0.1928)		**(0.1951)**
				(3.9671)		**(3.7937)**
Bargunit					**0.7145******	**0.5947****
					(0.1827)	**(0.1944)**
					(2.0431)	**(1.8125)**
Initial log likelihood function	1,075.769					
Efficiency	57.16%	64.19%	62.47%	69.17%	65.28%	69.19%
Pseudo-R^2	20.09%	33.25%	29.90%	42.58%	35.41%	42.58%
-2LL	1,058.752	989.854	982.531	923.386	974.135	909.882
Goodness fit	779.044	776.012	772.633	786.848	776.746	786.242
Model Chi^2	17.017	85.915	93.238	152.383	101.634	165.887
d.f.	5	10	13	13	11	17
Step Significance	0.0045	0.0000	0.0000	0.0000	0.0000	0.0000

p-values: <0.10=bold, <0.05=bold\$, <0.01=bold**, <0.001=bold***, <0.0001=bold****.

p-values based on Wald statistic: $W_k^2 = (b_k/\text{s.e. of } b_k)^2$, following a Chi-square distribution.

Table A2. **Logistic regression models for Worrunem, Swedish sample (n=1,205) (standard errors and Exp-B are given in parentheses below regression coefficients)**

	Model 1	Model 2	Model 3	Model 4	Model 5	Model 6
Constant	**-0.1968***	**-1.0782****	**-0.8551****	**-1.6869****	**-1.2195****	**-1.5986****
	(0.1443)	**(0.1931)**	**(0.2185)**	**(0.2486)**	**(0.2933)**	**(0.3495)**
Firmmed	-0.0329	0.0936	0.1161	0.0912	0.0923	0.1055
	(0.1522)	(0.1576)	(0.1588)	(0.16310)	(0.1576)	(0.1639)
	(0.9676)	(1.0981)	(1.1232)	(1.0955)	(1.0967)	(1.1113)
Firmsml	0.0101	0.2021	0.2539	0.2513	0.2235	0.3045
	(0.1661)	(0.1760)	(0.1778)	(0.1821)	(0.1791)	(0.1859)
	(1.0101)	(1.2239)	(1.2890)	(1.2857)	(1.2504)	(1.3559)
Older	-0.1117	-0.1434	-0.0964	**-0.2257**	-0.1494	-0.1872
	(0.1208)	(0.1248)	(0.1268)	**(0.1305)**	(0.1251)	(0.1327)
	(0.8943)	(0.8664)	(0.9081)	**(0.7980)**	(0.8613)	(0.8993)
Woman	**0.3761***	**0.4204****	**0.4020***	**0.3646***	**0.4160****	**0.3459***
	(0.1511)	**(0.1560)**	**(0.1569)**	**(0.1616)**	**(0.1561)**	**(0.1625)**
	(1.4567)	**(1.5226)**	**(1.4947)**	**(1.4399)**	**(1.5159)**	**(1.4133)**
Bott2_5D	0.0748	0.1196	0.1148	0.0817	0.1183	0.0827
	(0.1371)	(0.1408)	(0.1417)	(0.1458)	(0.14080)	(0.1465)
	(1.0777)	(1.1271)	(1.1216)	(1.0820)	(1.1255)	(1.0862)
Chngmach		-0.2227	-0.2285	-0.1751	-0.2239	-0.1804
		(0.1430)	(0.1439)	(0.1478)	(0.1430)	(0.1486)
		(0.8004)	(0.7957)	(0.8394)	(0.7994)	(0.8349)
Chngwork		0.0430	0.0496	0.0789	0.0461	0.0829
		(0.1539)	(0.1545)	(0.1588)	(0.1540)	(0.1592)
		(1.0440)	(1.0509)	(1.0820)	(1.0472)	(1.0864)

Table A2 (continued)

	Model 1	Model 2	Model 3	Model 4	Model 5	Model 6
Chngtask		0.0279	0.0145	-0.0093	0.0226	-0.0230
		(0.1424)	(0.1432)	(0.1471)	(0.1426)	(0.1478)
		(1.0283)	(1.0146)	(0.9907)	(1.0228)	(0.9773)
Firmdown		0.6810****	0.6448****	0.6002****	0.6727****	0.5637****
		(0.1303)	(0.13140)	(0.1344)	(0.1309)	(0.1359)
		(1.9759)	(1.9056)	(1.8224)	(1.9595)	(1.7572)
Laidoff		0.6952****	0.6866****	0.4389**	0.6903****	0.4332**
		(0.1548)	(0.1558)	(0.1647)	(0.1550)	(0.1657)
		(2.0041)	(1.9870)	(1.5510)	(1.9942)	(1.5422)
Somesay			-0.0652			-0.0067
			(0.13170)			(0.1365)
			(0.9368)			(0.9933)
Irgood			-0.3627**			-0.3202*
			(0.1336)			(0.1383)
			(0.6958)			(0.7260)
Downskp1			0.1976			0.1423
			(0.1571)			(0.1627)
			(1.2184)			(1.1530)
Findtuff				0.5366**		0.5288**
				(0.1790)		(0.1804)
				(1.7102)		(1.69969)
Labxpoor				0.0738		0.0574
				(0.1290)		(0.1298)
				(1.0766)		(1.0591)

Table A2   (continued)

	Model 1	Model 2	Model 3	Model 4	Model 5	Model 6
Lossunrc				**1.1530******		**1.1313********
				(0.1532)		**(0.1541)**
				(3.1676)		**(3.0997)**
Bargunit					0.1592	0.1122
					(0.2476)	(0.2579)
					(1.1726)	(1.1187)
Initial log likelihood function	1,609.9251					
Efficiency	61.16%	63.98%	63.90%	67.80%	63.98%	68.96%
Pseudo-R^2	36.49%	41.11%	40.98%	47.35%	41.11%	49.25%
-2LL	1,599.966	1,542.515	1,531.948	1,471.346	1,542.097	1,464.341
Goodness fit	1,205.178	1,207.277	1,207.270	1,210.623	1,207.678	1,213.710
Model Chi^2	9.959	67.410	77.977	138.579	67.828	145.584
d.f.	5	10	13	13	11	17
Step Significance	0.0764	0.0000	0.0000	0.0000	0.0000	0.0000

p-values: <0.10=bold, <0.05=bold*, <0.01=bold**, <0.001=bold***, <0.0001=bold****.

p-values based on Wald statistic: $W_k^2 = (b_k / \text{s.e. of } b_k)^2$, following a Chi-square distribution.

References

Abbasi, S.M. and Hollman, K.W. (1998), 'The Myth and Realities of Downsizing', *Records Management Quarterly*, Vol. 32(2), April, pp. 31-7.

Armstrong-Stassen, M. (1998), 'The Effect of Gender and Organizational Level on How Survivors Appraise and Cope with Organizational Downsizing', *The Journal of Applied Behavioral Science*, Vol. 34(2), June, pp. 125-42.

Auman, J. and Draheim, B. (1997), 'The Downside to Downsizing', *Benefits Canada*, Vol. 21(5), May, pp. 31-3.

Baruch, Y. (1998), 'The Rise and Fall of Organizational Commitment', *Human Systems Management*, Vol. 17(2), pp. 135-43.

Bishop, J.W. and Scott, K.D. (1997), 'How Commitment Affects Team Performance', *HRMagazine*, Vol. 42(2), February, pp. 107-11.

Blohowiak, D.W. (1995), *How's All the Work Going to Get Done?*, Career Press, Franklin Lakes, NJ.

Cameron, K.S., Bright, D. and Caza, A. (2004), 'Exploring the Relationships Between Organizational Virtuousness and Performance', *American Behavioral Scientist*, Vol. 47(6), February, pp. 766-90.

Davies, H. (1995), 'Don't Downsize the Soul of the Organisation too', *Personnel Management*, Vol. 1(21), October 19, pp. 29.

Eklund, K. (2001), 'Gösta Rehn and the Swedish Model: Did We Follow the Rehn-Meidner Model too Little Rather than too Much?' in Milner and Wadensjö (eds), *Gösta Rehn, the Swedish Model and Labour Market Policies, International and National Perspectives*, Chapter 3, Ashgate, Aldershot, pp. 53-72.

Esping-Andersen, G. (1985), *Politics Against Markets*, Princeton University Press, Princeton.

Frazee, V. (1996), 'When Downsizing Brings your Employees Down', *Personnel Journal*, Vol. 75(3), March, pp. 126-7.

Frazee, V. (1997), 'What Happens a Year or More after the Jobs Have Been Cut?', *Workforce*, Vol. 76(3), March, p. 21.

Freeman, R.B. (1992), 'Is Declining Unionization of the US Good, Bad, or Irrelevant' in L. Mishel and P.B. Voos (eds), *Unions and Economic Competitiveness*, M.E. Sharpe, Armonk, NY, pp. 143-69.

Freeman, R.B. and Medoff, J.L. (1984), *What Do Unions Do?*, Basic Books, New York.

Gallie, D. (1983), *Social Inequality and Class Radicalism in France and Britain*, Cambridge University Press, Cambridge.

Gottlieb, M.R. and Conkling, L. (1995), *Managing the Workplace Survivors: Organizational Downsizing and the Commitment Gap*, Quorum Books, Westport, Conn.

Hall, P. and Soskice, D. (eds) (2001), *Varieties of Capitalism: The Institutional Foundations of Comparative Advantage*, Oxford University Press, Oxford.

Heclo, H. and Madsen, H. (1987), *Policy and Politics in Sweden: Principled Pragmatism*, Temple UP, Philadelphia.

Hosmer, D.W. and Lemeshow, S. (1989), *Applied Logistic Regression*, Wiley-Interscience, New York.

Jalajas, D.S. and Bommer, M. (1999), 'The Influence of Job Motivation versus Downsizing on Individual Behavior', *Human Resource Development Quarterly*, Vol. 10(4), Winter, pp. 329-41.

James, T.A.W. and Tang, T.L.P. (1996), 'Downsizing and the Impact on Survivors - a Matter of Justice', *Employment Relations Today*, Vol. 23(2), Summer, pp. 33-41.

Jessop, B. (1993), 'Towards a Schumpeterian Workfare State? Preliminary Remarks on Post-Fordist Political Economy', *Studies in Political Economy*, Vol. 40, pp. 7-39.

Kets de Vries, M.F.R. and Balazs, K. (1997), 'The Downside of Downsizing', *Human Relations*, Vol. 50, January, pp. 11-50.

Kim, W.B. (2003), 'Economic Crisis, Downsizing and 'Layoff Survivor's Syndrome'', *Journal of Contemporary Asia*, Vol. 33(4), pp. 449-64.

Klein, M. (1997), 'Downsides of Downsizing', *American Demographics*, Vol. 19(2), February, p. 23.

Kline, T. and Goldenberg, S. (1999), 'The Downsizing Experience and Gender: Similarities and Differences', *North American Journal of Psychology*, Vol. 1(1), June, pp. 135-55.

Knudsen, H.K., Johnson, J.A., Martin, J.K. and Roman, P.M. (2003), 'Downsizing Survival: The Experience of Work and Organizational Commitment', *Sociological Inquiry*, Vol. 73(2), May, pp. 265-83.

Koretz, G. (1997), 'Big Payoffs from Layoffs', *Business Week*, No. 3,515, February, p. 30.

Kuhn, T. (1970), *The Structure of Scientific Revolutions*, Second ed., University of Chicago Press, Chicago.

Louchheim, F.P. (1991/1992), 'Four Lessons from Downsizing to Build Future Productivity', *Employment Relations Today*, Vol. 18(4), Winter, pp. 467-75.

Mabert, V.A. and Schmenner, R.W. (1997), 'Assessing the Roller Coaster of Downsizing', *Business Horizons*, Vol. 40(4), July/August, pp. 45-53.

Madrick, J. (1995), 'Corporate Surveys Can't Find a Productivity Revolution, Either', *Challenge!*, Vol. 38(6), November/December, pp. 31-4.

Mahnkopf, B. (1992), 'The 'Skill-oriented' Strategies of German Trade Unions: Their Impact on Efficiency and Equality Objectives', *British Journal of Industrial Relations*, Vol. 30(1), March, pp. 61-81.

Martin, A. (1984), 'The Shaping of the Swedish Model' in P. Gourevitch (ed.), *Union and Economic Crisis: Britain, West Germany and Sweden*, Allen and Unwin, London, pp. 190-359.

McElroy, J.C., Morrow, P.C. and Rude, S.N. (2001), 'Turnover and Organizational Performance: A Comparative Analysis of the Effects of Voluntary, Involuntary, and Reduction-in-force Turnover', *Journal of Applied Psychology*, Vol. 86(6), December, pp. 1294-9.

Meidner, R. (1986), 'Swedish Union Strategies Towards Structural Change', *Economic and Industrial Democracy*, Vol. 7, pp. 85-97.

Menard, S. (1995), *Applied Logistic Regression Analysis*, Sage, Newbury Park.

Milner, H. and Wadensjö, E. (eds) (2001), *Gösta Rehn, the Swedish Model and Labour Market Policies, International and National Perspectives*, Ashgate, Aldershot.

Mishra, K.E., Spreitzer, G.M. and Mishra, A.K. (1998), 'Preserving Employee Morale during Downsizing', *Sloan Management Review*, Vol. 39(2), Winter, pp. 83-95.

Morrall, A. Jr. (1998), 'A Human Resource Rightsizing Model for the Twenty-First Century', *Human Resource Development Quarterly*, Vol. 9(1), Spring, pp. 81-8.

Muszynski, L. (1985), 'The Politics of Labour Market Policy' in G.B. Doern (ed.), *The Politics of Economic Policy*, University of Toronto Press, Toronto, pp. 251-305.

Neumark, D. (ed.) (2000), *On the Job: Is Long-term Employment a Thing of the Past?*, Russell Sage Foundation, New York.

Norušis, M.J. (1997), *SPSS: Professional Statistics 7.5*, SPSS Inc., Chicago.

O'Donnell, S.J. and Hubiak, W.A. (1997), 'Downsizing: A Pervasive Form of Organizational Suicide', *National Productivity Review*, Vol. 16(2), Spring, pp. 31-6.

OECD (1997), *Employment Outlook*, Chapter 5: 'Is Job Insecurity on the Increase in OECD Countries?'.

Öhman, B. (1974), *LO and Labour Market Policy since the Second World War*, Prisma, Stockholm.

Peak, M.H. (1995), 'Employees are Our Greatest Asset and Worst Headache!', *Management Review*, Vol. 84(11), November, pp. 47-51.

Peak, M.H. (1996), 'All pain, no gain', *Management Review*, Vol. 85(7), July, pp. 1.

Ramsey, R.D. (1997), 'Growth after downsizing', *Supervision*, Vol. 58(3), March, pp. 5-7.

Rehn, G. (1984), *Cooperation between the Government and Workers' and Employers' Organisations on Labour Market Policy in Sweden*, The Swedish Institute for Social Research, Stockholm.

Rehn, G. (1985), 'Swedish Active Labor Market Policy: Retrospect and Prospect', *Industrial Relations*, Vol. 24(1), Winter, pp. 62-89.

Roach, S.S. (1996), 'The Hollow Ring of the Productivity Revival', *Harvard Business Review*, Vol. 74(6), November/December, pp. 81-9.

Rutherford, T.D. (1998), 'Still in Training? Labor Unions and the Restructuring of Canadian Labor Market Policy', *Economic Geography*, Vol. 74(2), April, pp. 131-48.

Sengenberger, W. (1991), 'Intensified Competition, Industrial Restructuring and Industrial Relations', *Internation Labor Relations Review*, Vol. 131(2), pp. 139-54.

Sengenberger, W. and Campbell, D. (eds) (1994), *Creating Economic Opportunities: The Role of Labour Standards in Industrial Restructuring*, International Institute for Labour Studies, Geneva.

Smith, M.R., Masi, A.C., van den Berg, A. and Smucker, J. (1995), 'External Flexibility in Sweden and Canada: A Three Industry Comparison', *Work, Employment and Society*, Vol. 9(4), pp. 689-718.

Smith, M.R., Masi, A.C., van den Berg, A. and Smucker, J. (1997), 'Insecurity, Labour Relations, and Flexibility in Two Process Industries: A Canada/Sweden Comparison', *Canadian Journal of Sociology*, Vol. 22, pp. 31-64.

Smucker, J., Masi, A.C., Smith, M.R. and van den Berg, A. (1998), 'Labour Deployment within Plants in Canada and Sweden: A Three-Industry Comparison', *Relations Industrielles/Industrial Relations*, Vol. 53(3), Summer, pp. 430-57.

Streeck, W. (1992), *Social Institutions and Economic Performance: Studies of Industrial Relations in Advanced*, Sage Publications, London.

The Economist (1998), 'Restructuring Corporate Germany', *The Economist*, November, pp. 63-4.

The Internal Auditor (1997), 'Downsizing Reaches 90s low', Vol. 54(6), December, pp. 15-6.

van den Berg, A. (2001), 'Can Security Enhance Efficiency? Testing an Assumption Underlying the Rehn Model by Comparing Canada and Sweden' in H. Milner and E. Wadensjö (eds), *Gösta Rehn, the Swedish Model and Labour Market Policies, International and National Perspectives*, Chapter 6, Ashgate, Aldershot, pp. 101-16.

van den Berg, A., Furåker, B. and Johansson, L. (1997), *Labour Market Regimes and Patterns of Flexibility: A Sweden-Canada Comparison*, Arkiv, Lund.

van den Berg, A., Masi, A.C., Smith, M.R. and Smucker, J. (1998), 'To Cut or Not to Cut: A Cross-National Comparison of Attitudes toward Wage Flexibility', *Work and Occupations*, Vol. 25(1), February, pp. 49-73.

van den Berg, A., Masi, A.C., Smucker, J. and Smith, M.R. (2000), 'Manufacturing Change: A Two-Country, Three-Industry Comparison', *Acta Sociologica*, Vol. 43(2), June, pp. 139-56.

Wager, T.H., 'Consequences of Work Force Reduction: some Employer and Union Evidence', *Journal of Labor Research*, Vol. 22(4), Fall, pp. 851-62.

Notes

[1] Department of Sociology, McGill University, Montreal. The research on which this chapter reports was funded by a grant from the Swedish *Humanistiska och Samhällsvetenskapliga Forskningsråd* (HSFR), as well as additional support from the Quebec *Fonds pour la formation de Chercheurs et l'Aide à la Recherche* (FCAR) and Statistics Canada. It is part of a larger joint comparative research project supported by both Swedish and Canadian funding agencies, including the Social Sciences and Humanities Research Council of Canada (SSHRCC). The authors of the present article are indebted to Bengt Furåker (University of Gothenburg) and Leif Johansson (University of Umeå), Joseph Smucker (Concordia University) and Michael R. Smith (McGill University) for collaborating with us in obtaining the Swedish funding and for their contributions in designing and helping to carry out the research, often under exceedingly difficult circumstances. In addition, we owe Joseph Smucker for his contribution to an earlier version of this chapter.

[2] Along these lines, a recent OECD *Employment Outlook* reports that the intercountry differences in perceived employment insecurity seem to be explicable by actual differences in expected losses from job loss between countries (OECD, 1997, Chapter 5).

[3] Interestingly, 'employability' is rapidly becoming the management buzzword of the day, among other things as something of a substitute for long-term employment in dealing with morale problems due to downsizing (e.g. Davies, 1995). But here it is conceived as something offered at the firm-level only, of course. Nevertheless, the underlying reasoning is identical to that of the framers of the Swedish Model.

Chapter 10

Job Insecurity, Union Attitudes and Workers' Union Participation: Conclusions and Suggestions for Practice and Research

Hans De Witte

In the introductory chapter to this volume, job insecurity has been defined as a subjective concern about the future existence of the actual job, or of valued job features of this job. During the last decades, a research tradition arose, documenting the harmful effects of job insecurity for the well-being of individual workers, and its negative impact on their organisational attitudes and behaviours (e.g. Klandermans and van Vuuren, 1999; Sverke and Hellgren, 2002; Sverke, Hellgren and Näswall, 2002). In this growing body of research, however, surprisingly little scholars have been analysing whether job insecurity is related to the attitudes of workers towards unions, or whether it impacts on their participation in unions. This topic is quite important, since unions are cornerstones of industrial democracy, and since they often have a crucial role to play in negotiations between employers and employees during downsizing or restructuring processes. Job insecurity might impose new and specific threats to trade unions. Dealing with these threats in a constructive way thus constitutes an important challenge for the European union movement (and abroad).

In this volume, eight contributions from European psychologists and sociologists are presented, who try to answer aspects of this broad research question. They discuss results of research on the impact of job insecurity on union participation (such as joining a union), and on the consequences of union involvement in a restructuring process on attitudes towards unions, such as satisfaction, commitment and justice. The various contributions in this volume do not focus on job insecurity as such, or on its consequences on other aspects (such as well-being). In several chapters, however, interesting findings are reported on antecedents and consequences of job insecurity too, transcending the prime focus of this book. Since they add to previous research in this area, it seems worthwhile to discuss them as well.

Structural Antecedents of Job Insecurity

One of these additional findings relates to the *antecedents* of job insecurity. It is interesting to note that at least three chapters in this volume contain results on this issue. The definition of job insecurity as a subjective perception (see Chapter 1), gave rise to some controversy in the literature regarding the origins of this perception (see e.g. De Witte, 2004). Is it a purely 'subjective' phenomenon, merely reflecting personality traits (such as negative affectivity or locus of control) or is it related to 'objective reality' by reflecting a weak and problematic position on the labour market? This dichotomy could be summarised as 'personality or structural position?'. Research of course supports both views simultaneously (e.g. van Vuuren, Klandermans, Jacobson and Hartley, 1991). Various findings in this volume, however, strengthen the relevance of the view that job insecurity reflects the labour market position of individual workers, thus strengthening the structural view.[1]

The results of Nätti et al. in Finland (Chapter 2), Steijn in the Netherlands (Chapter 3) and van den Berg and Masi in Canada and Sweden (Chapter 9) first of all show that the perception of job insecurity is associated with positional and organisational variables, which reflect the (weak and vulnerable) position of the individual on the labour market. They find that perceptions of insecurity are higher among blue-collar workers, workers in manufacture and construction and workers in the private sector. These characteristics are all indicators of a weak labour market position. Even more important are a temporary employment contract, the fact that one has been unemployed in the past, and the experience of lay-offs in the organisation in the past. These experiences as well as working on a temporary contract also emphasise the vulnerability of the actual position. This interpretation is corroborated by the finding of van den Berg and Masi (Chapter 9) that the perceived difficulty to find an equivalent job increases worrying over job loss.

Most associations with individual characteristics mentioned above have already been reported before (e.g. van Vuuren et al., 1991). New, and thus extending the findings of previous research, are the associations with variables at a macro level that are reported in Chapters 2, 3 and 9. The comparison of Canada with Sweden in Chapter 9 first of all suggests that job insecurity is higher in a country with relatively weak job protection, modest income support and a limited active labour market policy (e.g. Canada). The findings in Chapter 2 on Finland (and to a lesser extent also Chapter 3 on the Netherlands) also show an association at the aggregate level between the unemployment rate and the perception of job insecurity over time: an increase in unemployment in the country seems to increase feelings of insecurity among workers. The impact of changes in the Finnish economy is also witnessed in the finding that the associations of job insecurity and positional variables change over time. Striking in that respect is the increase of insecurity in services and the public sector at times of economic decline in these sectors. Taken together, these findings clearly corroborate the assumption expressed in so many introductions of this volume, that job insecurity reflects economic hardship. It is worthwhile to stress this conclusion, because the assumption of an association between insecurity and economic changes has often been made, but has rarely been empirically substantiated.

Consequences of Job Insecurity for Individuals and Organisations

Some chapters also contain information on the *consequences* of job insecurity for individuals and the organisation. The results regarding health and well-being are most straightforward. In Chapter 6, Isaksson et al. report an association of job insecurity with distress symptoms and health complaints. The negative correlation between job insecurity and job satisfaction reported by Kerkhof et al. in Chapter 4, adds to the conclusion that job insecurity has negative consequences for health and well-being. These findings are in line with previous research, and show that these conclusions can be generalised across countries (e.g. Klandermans and van Vuuren, 1999; Sverke and Hellgren, 2002; Sverke, Hellgren and Näswall, 2002).

Surprising, however, is the absence of negative associations with organisational variables in most chapters. Kerkhof et al. fail to report significant correlations in Chapter 4 between job insecurity and organisational commitment or trust in the works council. This could be due to the rather specific characteristics of their sample (civil servants in municipalities). Isaksson et al. (Chapter 6) also fail to report a negative association between job insecurity and organisational commitment among survivors. Here too, however, the sample is limited to workers of just one specific organisation. In yet another Swedish organisation (an emergency hospital undergoing organisational change) Sverke et al. (Chapter 8) do find a negative association between job insecurity and a variety of organisational variables, such as withdrawal and disengagement, but again not with organisational commitment. These findings suggest that the context in which workers experience job insecurity could play an important role in deciding whether or not organisational attitudes will be affected (depending on e.g. the relationship between employers and unions, and on cultural and structural characteristics of the organisation). The findings also suggest that organisational commitment might be more sensitive to this context than other organisational variables.

Job Insecurity and Union Membership

As discussed in Chapter 1, trade union participation is not a one-dimensional phenomenon. For purposes of review, and following Klandermans (1996), we distinguished four types: union membership, voting in union elections, participation in actions and becoming a union activist. In this volume, most studies focus on the first type of participation: union *membership*. This is perhaps not surprising, as this aspect is more easily examined (e.g. just one question on membership needs to be added to a survey). An analysis of the possible impact of job insecurity on union membership figures is rather important for unions too, because membership constitutes the cornerstone of their power in mobilizing workers and in negotiations with employers and governments.

Three chapters are devoted to the analysis of the association of job insecurity and union membership: the trend study of Nätti et al. in Finland (Chapter 2), the trend study of Steijn in the Netherlands (Chapter 3) and the two-country comparison of van den Berg and Masi (Chapter 9).[2] Their results reveal an association with insecurity and union membership at a macro (national) and micro (individual) level. Nätti et al. first of all demonstrate that the unionization rate in Finland increased in parallel with unemployment: a higher rate of unemployment in the country was accompanied by an increase in membership over time. This finding at an aggregate level did translate into similar findings at the level of individuals. In Finland, workers who witnessed dismissals in their organisation, or became unemployed in the past, were more often member of a union.[3] Direct evidence on the association of job insecurity and membership of a union is found in Finland, the Netherlands and Canada too. In these three countries, workers who felt insecure (or worried) about their jobs were more often member of a trade union. Steijn in the Netherlands (Chapter 3) adds to this by reporting that this association is similar for both blue and white collar workers, suggesting a similar 'collective coping strategy' for both social classes. Nätti et al. (Chapter 2) add to this by showing that also temporary workers who experience job insecurity and/or prefer permanent work are more likely to join unions. Taken together, these findings suggest that insecurity seems to increase (rather than decrease) union membership in Europe. The need to look for support and protection when one feels vulnerable on the labour market seems to be the rationale behind this phenomenon.

Some caution is warranted, however, as *further research* in needed on this issue. One of the reasons is that we need to test whether we can generalise this finding to *other countries*. The sample of countries in which this association was found is, after all, rather limited. In some of the other chapters, we even found opposing evidence. In Chapter 4, Kerkhof et al. report no correlation between insecurity and membership, but this finding could be due to the specific characteristics of their sample. In Chapter 9, van den Berg and Masi report no relationship between worrying about one's job and union membership in Sweden, whereas Sverke et al. (Chapter 8) even report a negative association between insecurity and membership in their case study of a Swedish hospital, with members reporting *less* insecurity than non-members. The latter might be due to the role played by the unions in the restructuring process in that specific organisation, but also to the prominence of unions in Swedish reality. One could therefore argue that the prominence of a union in a given society moderates the association between job insecurity and union membership. In societies where most workers are members of a union, union membership probably decreases insecurity, due to the protection offered by the union. In countries where unions are less dominant, insecure members might join a union, in order to protect themselves against insecurity and (the negative consequences of) dismissals.

Another important methodological problem requires further research. In all chapters, results from cross-sectional studies are reported. The mere correlation between job insecurity and union membership can be interpreted in various ways, and does not allow causal interpretations, as assumed in some of the chapters in this volume. This is illustrated in the study of van den Berg and Masi (Chapter 9), who state that being a member increases job insecurity among workers (e.g. increases worrying about their job), whereas others (e.g. Nätti et al. in Chapter 2 and Steijn in Chapter 3) state that insecurity leads to membership, instead of the other way round. The only way to analyse whether insecurity *causes* one to join a union, is by performing *longitudinal* studies in which the same cohort of workers is followed up in time. These longitudinal designs are lacking at the moment, and this strongly limits our conclusions. One possible way to overcome this problem is by asking *intentions* to join a union among non-members, and perhaps also intentions to leave among members. Little research on the relationship between job insecurity and such intentions has already been published, however.

Even though our findings need replication and more sophisticated designs in the future, the fact that one can observe an association between job insecurity and union membership in most studies is an important finding for *union practice*. This finding could mean that the economic crisis (and massive unemployment) will not necessarily decrease membership figures, but could even lead to an increase. This observation holds a pitfall, however. An increase of membership, because workers try to protect themselves against job insecurity, will probably also lead to increased expectations from unions. As a consequence, unions need to develop new actions and strategies in order to accommodate for these expectations. This might lead to another problem. Expanding demands from unions will increase their workload. The growing expectations of members could also create additional problems for unions, as growing expectations might be more difficult to fulfil.

Another issue relevant for union practice relates to the specific demands of members when they face insecurity. Goslinga (Chapter 5) analyses this issue in a study among union members. He concludes that unions can indeed alleviate the negative consequences of job insecurity by offering information about job opportunities and about the labour market. Additionally, they could provide career guidance and advice. Job insecurity thus calls for an extension of the actual services unions provide for their members, with a package of 'new services', developed to decrease feelings of insecurity among workers. On the one hand, these new services will enable to attract new members and to retain the actual ones. These new tasks, as stated before, will however also increase the pressure of work for union activists and officials.

Job Insecurity and Other Forms of Union Participation

Only two chapters in this volume report research results on the three other forms of union participation: voting in union elections, participation in actions and becoming a union activist. The lack of research on these forms contrasts with their importance to unions, as unions need actions and activists in order to achieve their goals, recruit new members and propagate their views and values.

In Chapter 4, Kerkhof et al. report a study on *voting in union elections* in the Netherlands. Studies on this issue are rather exceptional in Europe, let alone studies which combine this issue with the topic of job insecurity. Interestingly, these authors do not find a direct relationship between insecurity and voting: insecurity does not increase nor decrease the intention to vote for representatives of workers in the works council. They do however report an interaction effect with various attitudes. Using Hirschman's theory (1970) about exit, voice and loyalty, they conceptualised participation in the works council as a voice reaction: an active and constructive response to a dissatisfying situation (e.g. job insecurity). Instead, their results suggest that non-voting should be considered as a kind of neglect: a passive and destructive reaction to dissatisfaction, since they found that the intention to vote was lowest among employees combining job insecurity with either low job satisfaction, low organisational commitment, or low trust in the works council. Their results suggest that we need to take the dominance of a given phenomenon into account, when analyzing the possible effects of job insecurity. In this specific sample (civil servants in municipalities) voting is the norm, and non-voting the exception. In consequence, non-voting could be the phenomenon most likely to be affected by insecurity.

Goslinga in Chapter 5 is the only one in this volume to report on the association between job insecurity and *participation in union activities*. Using a sample of union members, he examines a rather large variety of action modes, ranging from instrumental ones (e.g. receiving legal advice or contacting union activists with a question) to more militant ones (e.g. participation in industrial action, such as strikes). Important is that he focuses on actual behaviours: 'real' participation during the previous six months before the interview. In analyzing his data, he uses a stress approach, by distinguishing between primary control and secondary control. Primary control relates to collective attempts to change the situation, whereas secondary control relates to attempts to deal with the situation individually, by adapting to the situation (e.g. by changing ones expectations; 'cognitive control'). Interestingly, he observes no association between aspects of union participation that can be labelled as primary control (e.g. collective action). Individual action seems a far more common reaction to insecurity than participation in industrial action. Insecure workers contact their union for help or legal advice, and attend union meetings in order to get more information. These (individual) actions are all instrumental for coping with job insecurity at an individual level, since information might reduce insecurity, and might suggest ways of finding more secure employment. Goslinga's results thus suggest that collective unrest and collective outbursts of industrial action as a result of job insecurity are probably rather exceptional.

Both Goslinga (Chapter 5) and Kerkhof et al. (Chapter 4) include *union activism* in their analyses. Kerkhof et al. focus on the intention to become a candidate in works council elections, whereas Goslinga examines holding a representative position at the moment of the interview. Job insecurity turns out to be unrelated to activism in both chapters, suggesting that the individual perception of insecurity does not motivate workers to become union activists.

It is rather difficult to draw definite conclusions from these observations, however. There is an obvious need to analyse these issues in further detail in *future research*. The reported evidence is first of all limited to the Netherlands only, which makes it impossible to generalise the results to other countries. Voting behaviour has only been studied in a sample of civil servants in municipalities, and participation in actions was limited to union members. Clearly, representative and more heterogeneous samples are needed. The analysis of industrial action was limited too, as only a small number of respondents reported that such actions took place at their workplace during the last six months. Additionally, one could argue that the focus in analyzing industrial action was probably too broad. Previous research has shown that workers might be likely to participate in industrial action, if these actions are related to the actual (or perceived) cause of job insecurity (e.g. van Vuuren, 1990). Participation in more general actions is not perceived as effective, since they are not aimed at the source of insecurity. It would be interesting to perform more specific case studies in organisations where job insecurity occurs and industrial action is taking place, in order to find out whether the perception of insecurity is related to participation in actions (or the intention to become a member or an activist), and under what circumstances.

Job Insecurity and Union Attitudes

Three chapters of this volume (Chapters 5, 6 and 7) focus on the relationship between job insecurity and *attitudes towards unions*. In two of these chapters, Isaksson et al. (Chapter 6) and Hellgren et al. (Chapter 7) restrict their analysis to a single organisation undergoing restructuring. Since the union was actively involved in the restructuring process, trying to reduce dismissals and attempting to negotiate favourable agreements, these case studies offer the unique opportunity to assess the consequences of their involvement on the union attitudes of those affected. In these two organisations, no association is found between job insecurity and commitment to the union. In his analysis of a more heterogeneous sample of union members in the Netherlands, Goslinga (Chapter 5) does not find a relationship between both variables either. Hellgren et al. (Chapter 7) explain this absence by stating that commitment probably refers to a deeper level of involvement with the union. To affect such a deeply-routed attitude, a longer exposure to organisational turmoil might be required. Union satisfaction could be regarded as a more immediate affective attitude, able to register more direct responses to downsizing and job insecurity. Surprisingly, however, job insecurity is not correlated with job insecurity either in Chapter 6 or Chapter 7. In the studies reported, job insecurity only seems associated with union justice (Chapter 7) and union support (Chapter 5): workers who feel insecure perceive their union as less just and less supportive. But one could of course also inverse this relationship, by suggesting that support and feelings of justice reduce job insecurity.

The finding that job insecurity is associated with specific union attitudes has important consequences for *union practice*. This finding first of all suggests that job insecurity not only affects (aspects of) union participation in a direct way (as discussed in Chapters 2 until 5), but also in an indirect way, through its impact on union attitudes, as suggested by Hellgren et al. in Chapter 7. Goslinga (Chapter 5) even substantiates this by showing a positive association between union support and participation in union activities. Next, the finding that job insecurity is associated with union justice opens possibilities to reduce the harmful effects of organisational restructuring, because justice concerns are part of global process control. The latter has been found to reduce the harmful effects of uncertainty and stress. This suggests that unions can play a role in mitigating the negative consequences of downsizing, by increasing feelings of justice and control over the restructuring process.

The results in Chapters 6 and 7 however also show that the involvement of unions in the restructuring process is not without risks for the unions themselves. Especially Isaksson et al. (Chapter 6) demonstrate that the union gets blamed for less favourable results, whereas it does not get the credits when the results are positive. This was apparent in the reactions of those who lost their job: they were less satisfied with the involvement of the union and with the assistance the union offered. The attitude of these workers towards their former employer (organisational commitment) was unaltered, however. The opposite seems to happen among those who found a new job. They were more positive about their former employer, but not about their union. Similar observations are reported by Hellgren et al. in Chapter 7. Once more, these results emphasise that unions are subjected to additional pressures due to job insecurity and restructuring. They need to address these issues, in order to reduce strains for workers. One of the ways of dealing with this issue is to get involved in the process itself. This involvement, however, opens the possibility that members will reproach them for being responsible for dismissals, and for not handling the consequences of the downsizing process in an acceptable manner.

One last finding needs to be mentioned, related to the previous topic. In several chapters, the results suggest that the respondents do not perceive an opposition between the union and the employer or the organisation. Isaksson et al. (Chapter 6) report a positive association between organisational commitment and satisfaction with the involvement of the union in the restructuring process. After performing regression analyses, both attitudes seem to contribute to each other. Hellgren et al. (Chapter 7) report a similar finding, by showing that union justice and organisational justice are correlated positively. Again, a regression analysis suggests that organisational justice contributes to the perception of union justice. The positive association of union attitudes with organisational attitudes can lead to various conclusions. One of them could be that employers do not need to fear the involvement of unions, as both unions and employer are perceived as allies by their employees.

Another interpretation is that unions clearly need to state their policies and need to stress the difference between their goals and those of the organisation. Otherwise, workers could perceive them as being responsible for the downsizing operation and its negative consequences.

Can Unions Mitigate the Negative Consequences of Job Insecurity?

The last topic that has been discussed in this volume relates to the question whether *unions* can *mitigate* the negative consequences of job insecurity (and downsizing). This issue is of course also related to the previous discussion, because the involvement of unions in the restructuring process can be perceived as a collective coping strategy, aimed to reduce the harmful effects of insecurity and lay-offs. Sverke et al. address this issue in Chapter 8 by analyzing whether union members use different coping strategies than non-members when confronted with job insecurity. They expect a potential buffering effect of union membership against the negative consequences of downsizing for survivors. No such buffering effect was found, however. Job insecurity leads to similar reactions for members as for non-members: it increases exit (e.g. withdrawal) and voice reactions (e.g. protesting). Yet, their results do suggest a direct effect of union membership on the reactions discussed. On the whole, members showed more positive attitudes towards their organisation than non-members. Members were less inclined to leave the organisation (exit reaction), and expressed less disengagement in the downsizing process (voice reaction). Surprisingly too, members scored higher on organisational commitment, suggesting that they were more loyal to the organisation. These results fit in well with the results discussed in the previous section, emphasizing a positive association between union attitudes and attitudes towards the employer. Sverke et al. argue that the more 'employer friendly' reaction of union members is caused by the fact that they benefit from collective forms of voice by their union. As a consequence, they feel less need to engage in individualised voice activities. This also reduces the negative effects for the organisation, and once again shows that unions can be supportive to the organisation, rather than incompatible.

The results found in Chapter 8 could partly be due to the context in which they are found. After all, Swedish industrial relations are illustrious for being co-operative. Van den Berg and Masi take this assumption one step further in Chapter 9, by comparing the responses to downsizing in two contrasting countries: Sweden and Canada. Their emphasis is on the socio-institutional context, and the differences in reactions it might produce. Canada is chosen as an example of a country with weak job and income protection, and weak but adversarial unions. Sweden constitutes an example of a country with strong job and income protection, an active labour market policy, and strong as well as co-operative unions. Their main finding relates to the association between worrying about one's job and union membership. As discussed before, they find no such relationship in Sweden, and a positive one in Canada. In the latter, membership is associated with worries over loosing one's job in the future. The authors interpret this finding as an indication that the presence of a union in a strongly adversarial system of labour relations exacerbates worrying over job loss. As such, Chapter 9 fits into the discussion on the mitigating effect of unions on job insecurity, even though their results suggest the opposite (e.g. aggravation instead of mitigation) in Canada. Their findings could, however, also be understood in another way. It is equally possible that workers more often join a union in a country where they are more vulnerable. As a consequence, it seems logic that insecure workers choose to join a union when they feel insecure in Canada, whereas job insecurity could be less (or not) related to union membership in a country where job protection is more common. The fact that a large majority of Swedish workers belongs to a union adds to this, because this leaves little variation for an association with variables such as job insecurity.

Some Concluding Suggestions for Future Research

Policy makers sometimes mockingly state that scholars always end their reports with the statement: 'one needs more research on this topic'. In the case of the topic of this volume, however, such a statement rather seems an understatement. Even though the topic discussed is obviously an important one, surprisingly little research has been devoted to the association between job insecurity, union participation and union attitudes. In this final chapter, some hints regarding the future direction of research on this issue have already been given. To conclude, however, some suggestions for a larger future research programme need to be mentioned. In a nutshell, research would benefit by adapting an interdisciplinary, cross-cultural and longitudinal perspective. It also needs to broaden its scope.

The inclusion of psychologists as well as sociologists in this volume proved to be a good start for a more integrative and *interdisciplinary* study of the topic of job insecurity and its relationship with union attitudes and participation. From a *theoretical* point of view, such integration will no doubt enrich our understanding of this issue. Therefore, it was interesting to witness a wealth of different theoretical accounts in the different chapters (especially within the more psychological oriented ones), even though these various views have not been combined that much thus far. Especially the integration of psychological views with sociological ones could prove fruitful in the future. This recommendation of course also fits into the need to broaden the scope of future research.

Next, the inclusion of authors from different countries in this volume obviously emphasised the need to perform more *cross-cultural comparative* research on this issue. The contribution of van den Berg and Masi (Chapter 9) was a good example of the usefulness of such an account. Their results call for an enlargement of the countries involved in a comparative design. Testing the various hypotheses developed in this volume in different countries will enable us to conclude whether we can generalise our findings across cultures and nations. This is rather important, as the institutional context of the countries involved strongly varies (e.g. Ferner and

Hyman, 1998), as do the structures of the unions in these countries (e.g. Sverke, 1997). These structural differences could strongly influence the results reported. Analyzing whether these structural differences do indeed alter our results is not only relevant from a theoretical point of view (since it will enable to identity additional 'causal' variables). It will also enable to develop more country specific policy recommendations, tailored to the specific needs and context of the country involved. Enlarging the amount of countries involved will also enable to test the specific impact of contextual variables in a more rigorous way, by using multi-level analysis (e.g. Snijders and Bosker, 1999).

The need for *longitudinal* designs has already been stressed before in this chapter. This need is rather obvious, as it is the only valid way to analyse whether job insecurity influences specific forms of union participation, or specific union attitudes, rather than the other way round. The difficulty in interpreting the results of cross-sectional research became apparent in the chapters focussing on union membership. Some understood the reported association as an indication that job insecurity motivated workers to join a union, whereas others suggested that it showed the impact of unions on their attitudes (e.g. members become more insecure due to communications from the union). An additional problem is that many workers joined a union in the past. As a consequence, the finding that their actual membership is associated with their actual perception of insecurity cannot prove that they joined a union for this reason in the past.[4] The need for longitudinal studies does also apply to the other forms of union participation, and especially to participation in union activities or becoming involved in unions as a union activist. It could also be interesting to analyse whether feelings of insecurity accumulate over time, culminating in an increased intention to participate (or actual participation) in e.g. union actions. Such accumulated feelings could also add to feelings of unjust treatment, which seem to motivate workers to become active in a union (e.g. by becoming an activist of shop steward, see e.g. De Witte, 1996).

Finally, there is also a need to *broaden* the *scope* of research on the relationship between job insecurity and union participation (or union attitudes). This call has already been made regarding 'traditional' research on job insecurity (e.g. Sverke and Hellgren, 2002). Because of its scarcity, a similar call is all the more warranted regarding union participation and union attitudes. First of all, we simply need more research on this topic, as many aspects of this relationship have not been explored at the moment, and because we do not know whether we can generalise the results found in a given country to another one. Additionally, we need more research on the association of job insecurity with the different aspects of union participation, such as participation in activities and actions, voting in union elections and becoming a union activist, as especially these topics did not receive much research attention in the past. A broadening of the scope could also include the test of the effect of different aspects of job insecurity. In the introduction, the difference between quantitative and qualitative job insecurity was mentioned (e.g. Hellgren, Sverke and Isaksson, 1999). Even though some authors used composite scales (e.g. in Chapters 4 and 5), suggesting that both aspects are correlated, it could be interesting to analyse whether qualitative insecurity has similar consequences for union participation and union attitudes as quantitative insecurity. Finally, it could also be interesting to broaden the scope by adding more qualitative research designs. In this volume, quantitative research designs were dominant, leading to often sophisticated statistical analyses. Only in Chapter 9, quantitative results were supplemented by qualitative ones, thus adding to the richness of the interpretations and conclusions. Future research should try to balance both methods. This could even lead to the interdisciplinary broadening of our research, as called for at the beginning of this section, by including qualitative case studies by sociologists or historians.

References

De Witte, H. (1996), 'Are Trade Union Members (Still) Motivated by Ideology? A Review of the Importance of Ideological Factors as Determinants of Trade Union Participation in (the Flemish Part of) Belgium' in P. Pasture, J. Verberckmoes and H. De Witte (eds), *The Lost Perspective? Trade Unions Between Ideology and Social Action in the New Europe. Volume 2: Significance of Ideology in European Trade Unionism*, Avebury, Aldershot, pp. 275-304.

De Witte, H. (2004), 'Job Insecurity: Is It a Problem and What Should we Do?', *Keynote Speech at the Second South African Work Wellness Conference*, Potchefstroom, South Africa, 24-26 March 2004.

Ferner, A. and Hyman, R. (eds) (1998), *Changing Industrial Relations in Europe*, Blackwell, Oxford.

Hellgren, J., Sverke, M. and Isaksson, K. (1999), 'A Two-dimensional Approach to Job Insecurity: Consequences for Employee Attitudes and Well-being', *European Journal of Work and Organizational Psychology*, Vol. 8, pp. 179-95.

Hirschman, A. (1970), *Exit, Voice and Loyalty: Responses to Decline in Firms, Organizations and States*, Harvard University Press, Cambridge, MA.

Klandermans, B. (1996), 'Ideology and the Social Psychology of Union Participation' in P. Pasture, J. Verberckmoes and H. De Witte (eds), *The Lost Perspective? Trade Unions Between Ideology and Social Action in the New Europe. Volume 2: Significance of Ideology in European Trade Unionism*, Avebury, Aldershot, p. 259-74.

Klandermans, B. and van Vuuren, T. (1999), 'Job Insecurity', Special issue of the *European Journal of Work and Organizational Psychology*, Vol. 8(2), pp. 145-314.

Snijders, T. and Bosker, R. (1999), *Multilevel Analysis. An Introduction to Basic and Advanced Multilevel Modeling*, Sage, London.

Sverke, M. (1997) (ed.), *The Future of Trade Unionism. International Perspectives on Emerging Union Structures*, Ashgate, Aldershot.

Sverke, M. and Hellgren, J. (2002), 'The Nature of Job Insecurity: Understanding Employment Uncertainty on the Brink of a New Millennium', *Applied Psychology: An International Review*, Vol. 51(1), pp. 23-42.

Sverke, M., Hellgren, J. and Näswall, K. (2002), 'No Security: A Meta-analysis and Review of Job Insecurity and its Consequences', *Journal of Occupational Health Psychology*, Vol. 7(3), pp. 242-64.

van Vuuren, T. (1990), *Met ontslag bedreigd. Werknemers in onzekerheid over hun arbeidsplaats bij veranderingen in de organisatie*, VU Uitgeverij, Amsterdam.

van Vuuren, T., Klandermans, B., Jacobson, D. and Hartley, J. (1991), 'Predicting Employees' Perceptions of Job Insecurity' in J. Hartley, D. Jacobson, B. Klandermans and T. van Vuuren (eds), *Job Insecurity. Coping with Jobs at Risk*, Sage Publications, London, pp. 65-78.

Notes

[1] Note, however, that personality traits have not been included in the research reported in this volume. So, no conclusions can be draw regarding the differential impact of personality versus structural characteristics on the perception of job insecurity.

[2] Note, however, that van den Berg and Masi do not present their analysis as such. The specific focus in their contribution allows to fit their study in this topic, however.

[3] Note that the latter was not found in the Netherlands, however (see Chapter 3).

[4] One could even suggest that union membership was unsuccessful in reducing their feelings of job insecurity.

Index

Printed in the United States
by Baker & Taylor Publisher Services